ALPHA LATZKE is Professor Emeritus at Kansas State University. Head of the Department of Clothing and Textiles at that institution for many years, she had taught previously in secondary schools and in the Extension Service of the United States Department of Agriculture. Professor Latzke is co-author of several books in the field of clothing.

HELEN P. HOSTETTER is Professor Emeritus of Journalism at Kansas State University, where she was Director of the Home Economics–Journalism curriculum. Professor Hostetter has also served as Editor of the *Journal of Home Economics.*

THE WIDE WORLD OF
CLOTHING

- *ECONOMICS*
- *SOCIAL SIGNIFICANCE*
- *SELECTION*

ALPHA LATZKE

HELEN P. HOSTETTER

BOTH OF KANSAS STATE UNIVERSITY

THE RONALD PRESS COMPANY • **NEW YORK**

Preface

This textbook is designed for the introductory course in clothing selection. It not only serves as a guide to the fascinating world of clothing but also provides an understanding of its various psychological, historical, sociological, and economic aspects.

In recent years, clothing educators have increasingly stressed the contributions of anthropology, psychology, sociology, and economics to the field of clothing. Faculty and graduate students began to draw on these social science fields as a means of explaining the clothing behavior of both primitive and modern man. Another shift in emphasis has been away from home construction of apparel to selection of ready-to-wear garments, and away from laboratory courses to reading–discussion classes in which enriching material from other disciplines is being used.

The authors produced this book to meet a need on their own campus. Mimeographed versions were used for several years in the basic course at Kansas State University. In addition, various illustrative materials from the University's collections of clothing, textiles, slides, and photographs were used to supplement the course reading. Several hundred students and a number of faculty members were involved in class-testing these materials.

The book which grew out of this experience has five main objectives:

1. To help students understand the influence of clothing and fashion on present-day society, and the psychological and social needs that can be met through clothing.
2. To widen students' cultural horizons by informing them about the clothing and body decoration practices of other peoples.
3. To develop an understanding of how the fashion world operates both in the United States and abroad and of the interrelationship of the producer, the retailer, and the consumer.
4. To acquaint the reader with buying aids available to the public.

5. To help students evaluate their own practices in buying clothing and then to formulate criteria for the wise choice of wardrobe. (Extensive material has been provided to assist in developing these evaluation skills, including a full-page color wheel in Chapter 4.)

The authors sincerely hope that in meeting these objectives, the book will also communicate something of the sense of excitement and fascination they have gained from being involved in the "wide world of clothing."

ALPHA LATZKE
HELEN P. HOSTETTER

Manhattan, Kansas
January, 1968

Acknowledgments

The authors gratefully acknowledge their indebtedness to the many persons who have helped in the preparation of this book:

To the faculty members of the Kansas State University Department of Clothing and Textiles, who taught from the mimeographed material and offered constructive criticism which was most helpful.

To Lucille Blair, head of Hudson–Blair, Inc., a leading merchandising and buying office. She gave valuable assistance with the material on Seventh Avenue, the country's clothing center in New York, and on the way buyers in the New York resident offices service their client stores across the nation.

To two members of the Chambre Syndicale de la Couture Parisienne for their invaluable assistance with the chapter on France's role as leader of the fashion world: M. Daniel Gorin, president of that organization, and Mrs. Marjorie Dunton, Canadian-born press attachée for English-speaking countries— herself once a member of the Paris couture. They not only checked the manuscript for accuracy but also offered comments and contributed much information and several photographs for the chapter.

To Leon Stein, editor of *Justice*—bimonthly publication of the International Ladies' Garment Workers' Union—who gave much appreciated assistance with the history of the garment industry.

To Judith Jeannin, fashion editor of *The Record* of Hackensack, New Jersey, and of *The Morning Call* of Paterson, New Jersey. She helped to gather photographs for the chapter on wardrobe building.

To Evelyn Undorf, who did the fashion sketches in Chapter 4. These sketches were adapted from *McCall's Easy Sewing Book*, copyright 1964.

To Gifford Kendall and Garry Smith, university students who have also had experience in the retailing of men's wear, for drafting the suggested wardrobe for a college man.

To magazines, newspapers, and business firms which generously supplied needed illustrations. Credit lines indicate their contributions.

To students from abroad who graciously served as models of modern dress in their own countries. These were Rosette Tetebo of Ghana, Mrs. Vir Bela Hans of India, and Sarah Tung of the National Republic of China. Also to Kim DeJac, whose maternal grandparents and great-grandparents were from Mexico, and who modeled the Mayan costume; and to Verna Lange, graduate student at the University of Kansas Medical Center, for posing for us in her dietitian's uniform.

And lastly, our thanks to Esther Latzke, widely known business home economist, who served as critic of the book in its final stages.

A. L.
H. P. H.

Contents

CONTENTS

APPENDIXES

I

THE ROLE OF CLOTHING

1

Why Clothes?

Why did early man start to wear clothes? What made him give up the freedom he had enjoyed without them? These questions have long intrigued the social scientists, and also come inevitably to the student of clothing. The anthropologist seeks answers among primitive peoples still to be found in some parts of the earth, and from cave paintings and artifacts of prehistoric times. The psychologist looks for clues partly in studies of infants and young children.

NARCISSISM

Scientists of both areas have concluded that dress developed as a result of man's narcissism, that is, his pleasure in his own body, and his desire to make himself as attractive as possible physically.

Narcissism "finds a natural expression in the showing off of the naked body and in the demonstration of its powers," declared Dr. John Carl Flugel, one of the first psychologists to become seriously interested in clothes. In his book *The Psychology of Clothes,* he commented that narcissism can be observed in many children "in the nude dancings and prancings in which, if allowed, they will indulge. . . . Much the same kinds of satisfaction are doubtless obtainable in later life from the exhibitionistic activities of the dancer and of the athlete, both of them clad as a rule in attire scantier than that which modesty allows for ordinary occasions." [1]

3

Figure 1–1. Piazza Armerina, in central Sicily. Detail of pavement in an imperial villa built around 300 A.D. The bikini bathing suit of the 1960's was a revival of an ancient costume. (Courtesy of Superintendent of Antiquities of Eastern Sicily.)

DECORATION: MOTIVE FOR DRESS

Consciously or unconsciously, people are at first interested in clothes and ornaments as devices for enhancing the attractiveness of the body, but gradually they develop an interest in clothes for their own sake. In the words of the psychologist, people sublimate or transfer their crude exhibitionistic urges to clothes.

According to Flugel, the shift in interest from exhibitionism to clothes is less complete in women than in men, and that is why "there is always a greater readiness in women to combine displaced exhibitionism with actual exposure, as in the décolleté." [2] The popularity of the bikini bathing suit, introduced in the early 1950's by Jacques Heim of the Paris House of Heim, also illustrates the pleasure many women get from self-exposure. The Roman maidens of 300 A.D. pictured in Figure 1–1 appear much less self-conscious than their modern prototypes.

Traditionally, people are more tolerant of narcissism in women than in men, and this difference is revealed in clothes. The Western world especially has idealized the rounded female form

Figure 1–2. Tattooing was a fine art in the Marquesan Islands, where sketches for this engraving were made. (Courtesy of the American Museum of Natural History.)

and has been somewhat critical of the male physique with its greater angularity, hairiness, and muscular development.

Among primitive peoples interest in body decoration seems to be the chief motive for dress. Some tribes paint their bodies or tattoo on themselves an all-over pattern to enhance their own physical attractiveness. Figure 1–2 indicates the skill developed by artists in some areas. Figure 1–3 demonstrates the ingenuity

Figure 1–3. Australian natives ready for a totemic ceremony, their bodies decorated with kapok colored by pipe-clay and blood. (Courtesy of the American Museum of Natural History.)

Figure 1–4. A Mayogo woman of the Congo has used scarification of face and body for decorative effect in lieu of clothing. (Courtesy of the American Museum of Natural History.)

of other primitives in the use of local materials, in this case kapok, clay, and blood for dyeing.

Through this body decoration the primitive can make himself stand out from the crowd and can achieve a feeling of increased dignity and influence. Also, these primitives have found that striking decoration is extremely effective in attracting the opposite sex.

Tattooing and painting have also been used to show tribal connections and rank within the tribe. Another decorative device adopted by some savage tribes is scarring—that is, making cuts on the body, then working clay into the cuts so the flesh will heal in welts.[3]

The Mayogo woman of the Congo in Figure 1–4 must have endured a considerable amount of pain for beauty's sake. With the men, the scarring and tattooing sometimes are grotesque, to

Figure 1–5. For this Mobali woman of Africa scar tattooing, metal armbands, bead necklaces, and a mouth distender are indications of status. (Courtesy of the American Museum of Natural History.)

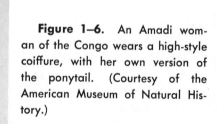

Figure 1–6. An Amadi woman of the Congo wears a high-style coiffure, with her own version of the ponytail. (Courtesy of the American Museum of Natural History.)

strike terror into enemies. Grotesque masks and headdresses also are used as a means of frightening away enemies and evil spirits.

In many primitive societies, especially in hot climates, the only piece of wearing apparel is a hip cord from which can be hung an apron or needed equipment, or weapons or trophies. Even in rigorous climates clothes apparently were not used originally for protection. We all recall stories about the Indian of colonial America who, in response to exclamations of amazement at his scanty attire in snowy weather, shrugged, then pointed to a colonist's bare face and said, "Me all face." Members of the Yahgan tribe of Tierra del Fuego, at the southern tip of South America, have been reported to wear a small fur cape as their sole protection against a bitter climate.[4]

Very early, apparently, men and women began to use shells, bones, and similar ornaments to hang upon themselves. Trophies of the hunt and of tribal wars also provided many decorative ornaments which increased the wearer's prestige. The primitive, both male and female, liked to wear rings on fingers, ankles, neck, waist, and hips.

Some ornaments were used to exaggerate tribal characteristics, such as the earlobes or the lips, beyond their natural size. The Mobali woman of Figure 1–5 wears a lip distender. From primitive times to the present, fashion, it appears, has been interested in the grotesque. The Amadi woman of Figure 1–6 affects a hair style no more bizarre than some styles of our own period in the United States.

In some primitive tribes only the woman wore clothes, and then usually only after she was married to indicate that she was the property of her mate. In other tribes only the harlot was clothed. Today's wedding ring had its origin in metal rings often worn around the legs or neck to indicate such ownership and sometimes to protect the wearer from evil spirits.

PROTECTION: SECONDARY MOTIVE FOR DRESS

As the human race is believed to have originated in tropical parts of the earth, man probably used body coverings for protection somewhat belatedly, and most likely only as he moved into less equable areas. Then he found that coverings made of plant fibers and skins not only were decorative but also protected him from heat and cold, and from insects, thorny underbrush, and stony terrain. Coverings also made it possible for him to be active when most of the lower animals had to withdraw into shelters.

Protection from the evil spirits which primitive man believed were all around him was another, but probably a secondary, reason for his wearing clothes and amulets, or charms. Hiding his sex organs, he believed, would keep demons from making him sterile. Women wore their aprons and hip clothes in part for the same reasons.

Some anthropologists, however, are skeptical about such motivation for covering the sex organs. ". . . Conspicuous coverings made of gleaming shells, gourds, bark, hide, cloth, or grass do not serve to divert attention but rather to attract it," comments E. Adamson Hoebel. Even though there may have been some superstitious motivation for dress, the decoration factor undoubtedly was of primary concern.[5]

CLOTHES TO ATTRACT THE OPPOSITE SEX

Most scholars, then, have concluded that clothing originated in man's desire to play up his own physical charms and make himself more attractive to others, especially to the opposite sex. Among savages body decoration starts at or near the genital organs and often is used in connection with a ceremony celebrating the attainment of some stage in sexual development, as the arrival of puberty or the selection of a mate.

According to Flugel, "The ultimate purpose of clothes, and often indeed their overt and conscious purpose, is to add to the sexual attractiveness of the wearers and to stimulate sexual interest of admirers of the opposite sex and the envy of rivals of the same sex." Sexual life, both among the primitive and among the civilized, supplies the strongest motive for wearing clothes.[6] Complete nudity is not erotic (sexually stimulating), as various psychologists and psychiatrists have long pointed out.[7]

In any one season today's designers of fashion characteristically select one or more of seven "themes" to play up in women's clothes: the neck or the breasts, the waist or the abdomen, the hips, the buttocks, the legs, the arms, or the length or circumference of the body itself. James Laver, the British fashion historian, and some psychiatrists call these "shifting erogenous zones"—that is, shifting areas that have sex appeal. Designers emphasize their selected theme and cover most other parts until men's interest in that theme has waned, then they cover it and emphasize some other part.[8]

In the Edwardian era of the early 1900's the exploited erogenous zone was woman's derrière, to which bustles and back draperies directed attention. Figure 1–7 shows the African prototype of the bustle. In the 1920's legs were fully revealed for the first time in a thousand years, and today they still hold in-

Figure 1–7. Both in primitive and in sophisticated cultures, an article of apparel used to cover a body area, as a gesture of modesty, actually directs attention to that area. Here women of the Congo sport their version of the bustle. (Courtesy of the American Museum of Natural History.)

terest, though skirts have vacillated between the ankle and above
the knee since then. In the 1920's bosoms were flattened and
well covered, but a decade later they again came into their own
along with the small waist. "Falsies" and the "uplift bra" were
used to draw attention to that part of the feminine anatomy.

In earlier periods the tight corset had a similar objective.
Constricting the waist emphasized breasts, abdomen, and buttocks; it also forced women to breathe from the upper part of
the lungs, giving the breasts a respiratory movement, and added
allurement to the opposite sex.[9] Ever since the Renaissance,
however, the bosom has been a favorite theme of the fashion
designer—and the manufacturer.

Designers vary, of course, as to the obviousness or subtlety of
their handling of a theme. Sophie, the designer for Saks Fifth
Avenue and the wife of its president, is known for her emphasis
on the softly feminine, on gentility; however, she admits, "I try
to make a woman as sexy as possible and yet look like a perfect
lady." [10]

The part of the body selected for fashion emphasis is always
either bared or emphasized by drawing the clothes tightly around
it as a "second skin," or by exaggerating it through padding.

"In witnessing female exposure man is often more acutely
conscious than woman herself of its sexual intention," declared
Flugel. "Moreover he cannot consider the exposure to be 'harm-
less' since it seems to him a direct incitement to more definitely
sexual conduct. . . . Men may therefore (rightly from their
viewpoint) accuse women of immodesty, and women (also
rightly from their viewpoint) may reply that sexuality was seen
where none was present (i.e., consciously recognized) or that
they have a more natural and healthy attitude toward the
body." [11]

Manufacturers and retailers, of course, capitalize on these
erotic details for sales promotion. The stretch factor in textiles,
introduced in the 1960's, proved a bonanza for them. It appeared in practically every major category of fabrics for use in
a wide variety of garments—first in ski pants, then in slacks, and
then in wash-and-wear cotton shirts and in blue jeans. Though
the stretch fabric *can* bring added comfort to clothes, its sexiness

was what provided the chief sales motivation, according to the Summer 1964 issue of *American Fabrics*. Many women were buying their stretch pants a size smaller than that which would give comfort.

"It is generally agreed that the sexual aspects of decoration are fundamental and must inevitably remain of primary importance whether we would or no," said Flugel.[12] He made a plea for recognition of this sexual element in dress, for increased "tolerance of the human body in its natural form, and thus an acceptance of reality," and for enjoyment within limits of the satisfactions that clothes can give.[13]

C. Willett Cunnington, the English fashion historian, commented, "There are two propositions which most of us would accept as being true without need of proof: that woman's costume adds to her powers of sex attraction and that she uses it very largely for that purpose, whether consciously or unconsciously."[14]

Lawrence Langner in his stimulating book *The Importance of Wearing Clothes* declared that woman's clothes at their best "supply a discreet invitation to indiscretion. At their worst, they represent a vulgar display of her wares, like an overcrowded shop window. The low-cut gown must not be cut too low, the tight fitting skirt must not fit too tightly, the bosom may protude but not obtrude, and the dividing line is always set by the good taste of the wearer. Thus dress is woman's subtle invention to tempt, but not insist on, masculine admiration."[15]

MEN'S CLOTHES: FROM ORNATE TO DRAB

Men's clothes, once as provocative as those of women, have had no seductive or ornamental frippery since the days of the French Revolution. Few men after the revolution dared to display the elegance and richness of dress which had been characteristic of the court. The breeches and culottes long popular with the aristocracy were displaced by trousers, previously worn only by British sailors, and a jacket or vest, originally the dress of Piedmont workers. Heels, buckles, and rosettes for men's shoes were supplanted by a soft, heelless slipper fastened with plain strings and worn with socks instead of long stockings. All symbolized the dignity of work.

The French Revolution was not the only influence which changed men's clothes from the ornate to the drab. The teachings of Calvin and Martin Luther, and of Protestantism in general, were equally important.[16] Today, in their leisure-time dress, however, men are moving toward more colorful, less severely plain clothing—and even toward sexy attire, if the stretch jeans and stretch trousers of the teen-agers are any indication.

DIFFERENT DRESS FOR THE SEXES

Extreme differences between the dress of the two sexes have no compelling physiological reason. Such differences have evolved because men like to have sexual differences emphasized.[17] Though marked differences have existed in most of recorded history, skirts have been worn by men and trousers by women probably longer than the reverse has been true.[18] Even today, men as well as women in some parts of Hungary and Greece and in South and Central America wear skirts. The Scots cling to their kilts, at least for ceremonial occasions. Figure 1–8 shows two of the royal Greek *evzoni*, both members of the king's guard, in gala dress. An upper-class Egyptian in Figure 1–9 is wearing the fashionable dress of his homeland.

In some countries the two sexes dress alike. In Red China men, women, and children all wear a jacket and trousers of drab blue or gray cotton, padded in winter, with no differentiation for rank or sex. Their austere dress symbolizes the leveling of classes. Women wear their hair cut in a mannish bob, or hanging to their shoulders or in a long braid. Gone are the figure-revealing sheath dress, or *ch'i p'ao,* and the high-heeled shoes and jewelry which gave prewar Shanghai the title of "Paris of the Orient." In 1955–56, however, came a change. Government-sponsored style shows introduced dresses in new designs, with loose, full skirts covering the legs—and no suggestion of the sheath dress! Shanghai's factories began to turn out colorful prints. But today, pants are still the mode and dresses are rarely seen.

Figure 1–8. Two *evzoni,* members of a rifle unit of the Greek army, ready to do a folk dance. Historically, skirts have been worn by men and trousers by women at least as much as the reverse. (Courtesy of the Royal Greek Embassy Information Service.)

In the Western world, for many types of work and for sports and casual living, men and women have adopted almost identical clothing: trousers (shorts or slacks) and shirts. Woman's adoption of masculine dress has become so common that with her laws forbidding the wearing of apparel of the opposite sex are not enforced. But with a man it is a different matter; his appearance in public in a woman's clothes—except, of course, for a masquerade—is punishable as a misdemeanor. He is considered practically indecent and is suspected of homosexuality.

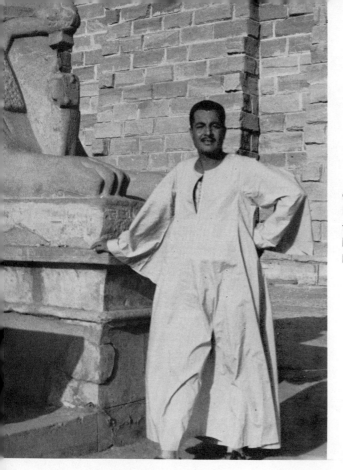

Figure 1–9. An Egyptian guide uses as his uniform the loose flowing dress of the farmers and villagers. The urban class wears conventional European dress.

Laver suggests that women's adoption of men's dress is perhaps inevitable, signaling the complete emancipation of women, the end of the patriarchal system, and the rise of a matriarchy.[19] One factor likely to keep women from completely abandoning feminine dress, however, is the desire for beauty. Trousers cannot hide figure defects or draw attention to a woman's good points as a dress can do so artfully. Even the most skillfully tailored trousers reveal rather than conceal physical shortcomings.

"No woman should run around the streets in pants . . . women look lousy in pants," declared Norman Norell, one of America's top designers, in an interview published in *Women's Wear Daily*. Pauline Trigere, another leader in the design field, added in an interview in the same publication, "We women don't know how to wear pants . . . there is not enough variety of sizes to accommodate all our little derrières." [20]

MODESTY: ANOTHER MOTIVE FOR CLOTHES

Modesty is a definite motive for clothes, but only a secondary one, today's social scientists believe. The urge toward modesty apparently developed after the wearing of clothes had become habitual. Children are not born with this urge. They are naturally bashful, but they have no sense of shame at the exposure of any part of their bodies, no feeling that some parts of the body are "not nice." Savages who wear clothes do so with no apparent idea of modesty. As we have already noted, they are likely instead to shift from nakedness to clothes for sexual stimulation.

"The sense of modesty is merely a habit, not an instinct," insists the anthropologist E. Adamson Hoebel. A person whose sense of modesty is outraged by a behavioral situation contrary to custom gets a terrific shock, both emotionally and physically. Fear and anxiety are aroused by his lifelong feeling that those who do not follow the customary behavior pattern will be punished by social or perhaps even supernatural agencies.[21]

Hoebel tells of one explorer's report of purchasing the big wooden cylinders worn in the earlobes and lower lip by Botocudo women of the Amazon region. The explorer had to offer extremely tempting goods to get one of the women to part with her wooden plugs. After giving them up she fled to the jungle overcome with embarrassment, though she was completely at ease without *clothes*. Such incidents clearly indicate, as Hoebel points out, that the use of clothing does not arise from any innate sense of modesty, but that modesty results from *customary* habits of clothing or ornamentation of the body. Modesty is based on an agglomeration of fears, declared Havelock Ellis in *The Evolution of Modesty*, particularly on the fear of arousing disgust; it is also allied with an acute consciousness of sex.[22]

Tradition or custom determines what part of the body must be hidden to avoid a feeling of embarrassment or shame. In the days of King Henry VIII, exposing the upper arm and shoulder was considered the ultimate in indecency. A scantily clad Moslem woman in some parts of the world will hide her face, not her body. An Arab woman in some areas will be embarrassed if the back of her head is exposed but not if her bosom is bared.[23,24] A woman's legs for almost 2,000 years were considered an unmentionable part of the anatomy and were referred to obliquely as "lower limbs."

The bare foot has only recently been emancipated. For nearly 2,000 years, because of religious taboos, it was regarded as impure. In eighteenth-century Spain, during the time of Philip V, the carriage was equipped with doors which could be lowered to hide the feet of a lady descending from it. Murillo was severely rebuked by officials of the Inquisition for painting the Virgin Mary with her toes showing beneath her robe, though it was perfectly proper for him to show her with bared breast. The modern woman of fashion in the Republic of China wears a snug sheath gown with a high-collared bodice that covers both neck and bosom, but its skirt is slashed so high as to reveal practically the full length of her leg (Figure 1–10). Whenever a fashion uncovers some part of the body that has usually been covered, it is considered immodest by standards of the preceding period.

Any part of the body not normally considered attractive sexually may become so by being habitually concealed from the opposite sex. Furthermore, the garment which conceals it, as well as the garment which conceals an area of more obvious sexual concern, itself comes to have considerable attraction. "Pantie raids," which occur on some campuses, illustrate the point. Modesty is complex, unpredictable, and often irrational. Even in the same social group it differs according to time and place— in church, on the patio, on the street, and on the beach.

The Book of Genesis gives modesty as the primary motive for clothes. Adam and Eve disobeyed God's order not to eat of the fruit of the Tree of Knowledge. Having eaten, they became aware of their nakedness and ashamed of it and made aprons of fig leaves for themselves, primarily to cover the sexual parts of their bodies. God himself made more adequate clothing for them from skins. The story illustrates nicely Ellis' point that modesty is allied with acute consciousness of sex.

To summarize, modesty admittedly is largely a matter of traditional outlook and is notably unstable and unpredictable. Though modesty is viewed somewhat skeptically by some people, our traditional morality, derived from Jewish and early Christian sources, still rates it high. The girl and the woman

Figure 1–10. University student from the National Republic of China wearing high-fashion formal dress, the ch'i p'ao, as interpreted in 1966–1967.

with a conscience will certainly consider the impact of her clothes on masculine viewers and will not wear those which are unduly exciting sexually.

Obviously, sexy clothes are not even fashionable, as Bernard Roshco points out in *The Rag Race*. "The tight, low-cut dress that stuns a roomful of men is intended for Hollywood producers and similar types who insist on seeing everything in wide screen. Since a woman's dress reveals who she is, as well as what she has, the woman who prefers to play the lady makes her stand behind fashion."[25] In studying the pictures of the winners of the Ten Best-Dressed Women Award in any year, you will not find the blatantly sexy or seductive in their dress; you will see instead simplicity and elegance.

CLOTHES TO SHOW PLACE IN SOCIETY

From the time that man first adopted clothes, he has used them in part to show his place in society. This motive, Laver declares, has always figured as importantly as the motive of self-decoration to attract the opposite sex. He labels the two drives hierarchy and seduction and comments, "Fashion breeds on seduction and thrives on snobbery." [26]

Envy and the urge to imitate the envied so as to reach their status make impelling motives for following fashion leaders. The desire to "belong," to be accepted as a part of some social group, also provides a powerful motive for dressing in the mode, especially during adolescence. Most adolescents, throughout their high school and college days, are interested not so much in standing out from the crowd through superiority of dress as in being as much like all the rest as possible. If "everybody" is wearing slacks instead of skirts, parents will have great difficulty getting their daughter into anything except slacks that are identical with those the others are wearing. Later, she may still insist on slacks, but may want a pair that shows some individuality and thus helps her demonstrate her superiority within the group.

For the businessman, most docile of all followers of fashion, conformity to the mode gives a feeling of security within the business world and of superiority to those outside the business world. The business uniform, the charcoal gray suit with its inconspicuous tie, symbolizes his belonging to a "superior" class, that of business.

Social pressures both from equals and from subordinates enforce the businessman's conformity. As Elizabeth Hawes, widely quoted writer on the fashion world, points out in her book, *Men Can Take It*, even the boss dares not break with convention. If he goes to the office in comfortable sports clothes he is aware of the raised eyebrows as his associates comment, "So he's all dressed up today!" She reports on a conversation with a "big operator," whom she asked why he did not wear comfortable clothes for a business conference on a very hot day. "Fine chance I'd have of putting over a deal!" he told her. "This morning I had a meeting with one of the biggest real estate dealers in Palm Beach, one of the largest hotel owners in America, and the best lawyer in New York. What could I have done with them if I hadn't been dressed as they were?" [27]

Clothes help to crystallize and maintain class distinctions in any society. In some parts of the world they distinguish the aristocracy from the peasants, the white-collar from the blue-collar workers. These very terms, which every reader understands, eloquently demonstrate the influence of clothes in indicating and maintaining people's status.[28] Of course, in a democratic society such as the United States, a person can move from one level of society to another, but clothes can still be a powerful factor in the shift to a higher or lower level.

Clothes can also make the poor practically invisible. As Michael Harrington has pointed out, the benefits of mass production are more conspicuous in clothing than in most other areas of American life. "It is much easier in the United States to be decently dressed than it is to be decently housed, fed, or doctored. Even people with terribly depressed incomes can look prosperous. . . . There are tens of thousands of Americans in the big cities who are wearing shoes, perhaps even a stylishly cut suit or dress, and yet are hungry." [29]

Most people dress partly to conform to the pattern of their own social group or to assert leadership within that group. Clothes testify to our being part of a social world, the college campus, the suburban community, high society in the big city or the summer resort—or wherever we live.[30]

COMFORT: A MOTIVE FOR DRESS

Comfort in dress today rates higher with the American woman than it has in the past, especially for recreation and for casual living. In general the American woman wants, sometimes even demands, garments that do not restrict movement, fabrics that feel good next to the skin, warmth in winter, and coolness in summer. Within limits! Much in the clothes picture today still spells discomfort.

For formal and semiformal occasions, when the demands of comfort and of fashion clash, comfort is likely to rate a poor second. Both the college woman and her mother will cheerfully wear a restrictive foundation or a waist cincher if the mode demands it. In bitter winter weather they are likely to wear a smart, light evening wrap even though it provides little warmth. And if the strapless evening dress is in vogue on campus, the college woman will stoically submit to its whalebone-reinforced bodice though it may gouge the flesh.

The most glaring examples of the flouting of demands of comfort are women's shoes. Too many women will endure torture in their eagerness to make their feet appear smaller than they really are. Many a girl and woman will stoutly insist that her three-inch heeled shoes are "really comfortable," even when she kicks them off at every opportunity.

Only rarely does a crusader appear among designers. Most recent among them was Margaret Clark Miller, who won the 1963 Nieman–Marcus Award for designing beautiful, functional, and comfortable shoes. This talented young creator of Margaret Jerrold shoes started out designing for the I. Miller firm. But the average shopper has never heard of, much less seen, a Margaret Jerrold shoe. Once again fashion won over common sense.

As Langner comments, women feel that high-heeled shoes make them more attractive, even though wearing them results in poor body posture, an unsteady and mincing gait, and less than graceful body movements.[31] Rudofsky in his book *Are Clothes Modern?* reserves for high-heeled shoes some of his most scathing comments:

> The American shoe manufacturer's idea is quite consistent with the Oriental tradition of foot perversion. And it seems that women not only fail to deplore such infliction but welcome the absurdity of man's taste to enlarge their stock of coquettishness. The metamorphosis of the successful woman aviator or woman executive from a powerful personality into a cooing odalisque cannot, it seems, be satisfactorily accomplished without recourse to high-heeled shoes.[32]

Low-heeled shoes, nevertheless, have been winning favor both with youth and with the mature. Young women wear them not only for sports and for casual affairs but also informal parties—in pastel kids with decorative touches. The homemaker of today no longer insists, as did her mother, that she must have the same height of heel for housework as for street and church wear. True, the big toe may be forced out of its natural straight line, but at least the foot need no longer be on stilts, even for formal evening wear. No one can predict with certainty, however, what the mass of womankind would do if Dame Fashion should again decree, "Stilts only!"

Comfort in dress, nevertheless, has gained much ground. The eighteen-inch waist of the corseted past is no longer coveted by the modish young woman of today, who is likely to have a waist measure of about twenty-five inches. The layers of clothing that once incased the body have been markedly reduced. When preparing for the day's activities, the fashionable woman of the Gibson Girl period in the early 1900's first put on a chemise, then a wasp-waist corset, next a corset cover perhaps with ruffles on the inside "to build up her figure," then her knickers (panties), next perhaps a bustle, and finally two or sometimes three petticoats. In contrast, today's young woman wears only one or two layers of underclothes: a bra, a pantie-girdle, and perhaps a slip.

Max Lerner in his book *America as a Civilization* points out ". . . the long secular trend in American fashions, which has steadily drawn away from the cumbersome garments to the freer ones and from the concealing to the revealing ones. Again, as part of the long secular trend, each of the 'vamp' or 'glamour' phases is a step further toward the cult of legs and breasts that expresses American sensuality." [33]

CLOTHES AS A WEAPON

One aspect of clothes, however, has not been touched upon by fashion writers: clothes as a weapon used for defiance of authority. For the American beatnik and the English Mod, clothes are a symbol of revolt, of refusal to conform to patterns of behavior set up by society. Figure 1–11 shows a group of Mods at a dance. The clothes rebel is still a conformist, but he apes the wearing apparel and the behavior of a clique of his peers. His clothes give him a sense of belonging, of social security

Figure 1–11. English Mods at a dance. They spend a considerable amount of time and money on clothes, which tend toward the foppish. (Courtesy of Odhams Press Ltd.)

which he probably has been unable to get from parents and teachers and from more conventional schoolmates and older associates. Deviation from the generally accepted way of dressing is often accompanied by deviation from socially accepted behavior.

OTHER MOTIVES

The reader may think of other reasons why people wear clothes, but most of them will come under one or another of the motives already discussed. For example, people dress to improve their appearance or to hide physical defects so far as possible. They also get aesthetic pleasure from their clothes—from color, texture of materials, and line. People find in clothes a way to project their own personalities and to use their creative abilities. In dressing herself a girl is really like the painter who puts a portrait on canvas: neither knows whether the results will be pleasing or disturbing to the beholder.

To quote Max Lerner again: "Being smart means for the American woman staying within the frame of fashion but adding her own individual touches. . . . The editors of the fashion magazines have become female Napoleons ruling their domains. Yet even they can rule only by giving their subjects room for individual creativeness." [34]

NOTES

1. John Carl Flugel, *The Psychology of Clothes* (London: Hogarth Press and The Institute of Psycho-Analysis, 1930), p. 86.

2. *Ibid.*, p. 108.

3. E. Adamson Hoebel, *Man in the Primitive World: An Introduction to Anthropology* (2d ed.; New York: McGraw-Hill Book Co., 1958), pp. 248–49.

4. *Ibid.*, p. 241.

5. *Ibid.*, p. 241.

6. Flugel, p. 26.

7. Edmund Bergler, *Fashion and the Unconscious* (New York: Robert Brunner, 1953), p. 26.

8. James Laver, "Laver's Law" interview, *Women's Wear Daily*, July 13, 1964, pp. 4–5.

9. Havelock Ellis, *Studies in the Psychology of Sex IV: The Evolution of Modesty*, Vol. I (New York: Random House, Inc., 1942), p. 172.

10. Bernard Roshco, *The Rag Race* (New York: Funk and Wagnalls, Inc., 1963), p. 138.

11. Flugel, pp. 108–09.

12. *Ibid.*, p. 185.

13. *Ibid.*, p. 188.

14. C. Willett Cunnington, *Why Women Wear Clothes* (London: Faber & Faber Ltd., 1941), p. 42.

15. Lawrence Langner, *The Importance of Wearing Clothes* (New York: Hastings House, 1959), p. 146.

16. *Ibid.*, p. 188.

17. Bernard Rudofsky, *Are Clothes Modern?* (Chicago: Paul Theobald, 1947), pp. 128 and 164.

18. *Ibid.,* p. 129.

19. Laver, p. 5.

20. *Women's Wear Daily,* July 13, 1964, p. 5.

21. Hoebel, p. 240.

22. Ellis, p. 134.

23. Rudofsky, pp. 19 and 24.

24. Laver, pp. 2 and 3.

25. Roshco, p. 4.

26. Laver, p. 33.

27. Elizabeth Hawes, *Men Can Take It* (New York: Random House, Inc., 1939), pp. 161–63.

28. Langner, p. 102.

29. Michael Harrington, *The Other America* (New York: The Macmillan Co., 1962), p. 5.

30. Rudofsky, p. 232.

31. Langner, p. 205.

32. Rudofsky, p. 172.

33. Max Lerner, *America as a Civilization* (New York: Simon and Schuster, Inc., 1957), p. 648.

34. *Ibid.,* p. 602.

FURTHER READING

HOEBEL, E. ADAMSON. *Anthropology: The Study of Man.* 3d ed. New York: McGraw-Hill Book Co., 1966. Sections on race and cultural capacity and on clothing and ornament. An interesting presentation of the current thinking of leading anthropologists.

LAVER, JAMES. "What Will Fashion Uncover Next?" *Reader's Digest,* LXXXVII (September, 1965), pp. 142–45. An article summarizing the basic thinking of one of England's foremost authorities on historical costume.

LANGNER, LAWRENCE. *The Importance of Wearing Clothes.* New York: Hastings House, 1959. A sound and entertainingly written discussion of clothes by a man who is closely connected with the theater and the fashion industry, and who studied under the psychologist Alfred Adler of Vienna and the sociologist Thorsten Veblen. Of his twenty chapters, you might read six: 3, Clothes and Sexual Stimulation; 5, Clothes and Modesty; 8, Clothes, Religions, and Cultures; 9, Clothes and Government; 10, Clothes and Behavior; and 13, Clothes and Conformity.

ROACH, MARY ELLEN, and EICHER, JOANNE BUBOLZ. *Dress, Ornament and the Social Order.* New York: John Wiley & Sons, Inc., 1965. Part 2 on origins and functions of dress and adornment and Part 3 on the diversity of cultural patterns in dress make especially good reading.

RUDOFSKY, BERNARD. *Are Clothes Modern?* Chicago: Paul Theobald, 1947. A provocative criticism of clothes by an internationalist who achieved fame as an architect in Italy and Brazil and then turned to industrial designing—including apparel, stage sets, and furniture. Three chapters to start with (all unnumbered) might be these: Typography of Modesty, Clothes in Our Time, and Sartoriasis or the Enjoyment of Discomfort.

STUDY SUGGESTIONS

1. Which of the seven "shifting erogenous zones" are designers playing up in the current fashion books? What means do they use?
2. Do you find any examples of fashion's interest in the grotesque in hair treatment, accessories, or dress designs?
3. How important do you consider the "hierarchy drive" on your campus? Illustrate. Do you know anyone who seems to use clothes as a means of becoming a leader?
4. Do you know anyone who does not conform to the mode? What seems to be his or her status? Can you recall examples of clothes worn as a symbol of revolt?
5. Do the public schools in your community have any dress code for pupils? What do the school administrators say of the effects of dress on behavior?
6. Do cliques in these schools adopt any special dress or dress accessory which would indicate to outsiders that they "belong"?
7. Can you recall any fashion which you at first considered immodest or in bad taste but later took for granted?
8. Striking decoration attracts the opposite sex, according to some writers. Does this seem true to you as you think of eye makeup, painted toenails and fingernails, and lipstick? Do you feel that the young women who use striking makeup get generally favorable attention?
9. Make a fashion check at some busy place on campus or in a business area to determine what percentage of women in the community wear pants, trousers, or shorts, and how many really look good in them. Tally the number you find wearing dresses, those wearing pants well, and those wearing pants that are unbecoming.
10. Do you see any signs of the weakening of businessmen's conservatism in dress? Check at some restaurant frequented by businessmen during their lunch hour, or at the meeting place of men's service clubs or the local chamber of commerce.
11. Find out what several of the business firms of the community require as to dress for their women employees. Are there requirements as to hose, heels, color, style, or dress? Do any firms have dress requirements for their men employees?
12. Can you find in this season's fashions any examples of uncomfortable clothes which men or women are wearing apparently with enjoyment?

2

Clothing and Culture

Dress is the key to an understanding of any people's culture, way of life, and socioeconomic progress. Archeologists digging in the ruins of ancient civilizations eagerly examine any vestiges of cloth, costumes, and personal ornaments for clues to the culture of that period and area.

It is not easy to define culture as it relates to this chapter. We might say that it is the complex of distinctive attainments, beliefs, and traditions which make up the background of a racial, religious, or social group. Culture also involves that group's accumulation of knowledge and the system of values by which it measures people and events.

"If I should be allowed to choose one out of all the books published a hundred years after my death, I would take a fashion magazine to see how women were dressing," once declared Anatole France. "Their fripperies would tell me more about the society of that future day than all the philosophers and preachers." By society France did not mean the party life of the well-to-do, of course. He meant the daily life of the people, their ideals and interests, and their concern for industry, the arts, and religion.

We shall test this idea of dress as the key to a people's culture by analyzing the textiles and costumes of the people of five different nations around the world: the Chinese of the Han dynasty, the East Indians, the Maya of Central America, the Ghanaians of West Africa, and the Yapese of the West Pacific.

28

CHINA: DRESS AND CULTURE

The surviving textiles and costumes of the Han period in China (206 B.C. to 220 A.D.) include fragments of polychrome-figured silks, some woolens, and a few cottons. One complete costume of the period was discovered in Mongolia and is now in a museum in Leningrad, Russia. A few of the fragments are of woven silk gauze, with an open effect like that of marquisette, a fabric popular in old China for dress on hot summer days, worn over contrasting colors to give a delicate and shimmery effect. No one has yet found brocade dating to the Han period, but archeologists believe that the Chinese were weaving it at this time.[1]

All the textile pieces reveal almost incredible skill and varied techniques of weaving and embroidering. Colors are rich and harmonious; weaves are of exquisite texture, with all-over patterns of rolling clouds, scrolls, and wild beasts. Embroideries are mostly of naturalistic floral designs done with painstaking care, chiefly.in the chain or loop stitch.

Silks and Ornaments

Silk had come into general use in China in the Chou dynasty (1122 to 256 B.C.), but it was not until around 550 A.D. that Europeans learned the carefully guarded secrets of the breeding of the silkworm, the methods of unreeling the silk from the cocoons, and the weaving of silk as an industry. Two Nestorian Christian monks discovered these secrets while carrying on missionary work in China and revealed them on their return to Europe. In the eighth century silk was still so rare in Europe that it was sold for its weight in gold—yet it was a routine fabric for dress for half the people in the larger cities of China. The poet Tu-Fu wrote of one village near Chang-an, the capital city of the period, that had silk factories employing 100,000 men.[2]

The textile fragments of the Han period are not the only clues to the dress of that day. Buckles and ornaments for clothing have also been found, many with incrustations of turquoise and precious metals which reveal great artistry in the people. Their weaving showed great technological advancement.

For state ceremonies, courtiers and their ladies wore beautiful court robes which contributed much to the pomp and pageantry of their life, enabling them to assume elegant manners and to conform to the exacting rules of court procedure. These rules and manners had been codified by K'ung-fu-tze (Confucius) and his students more than two centuries before the Han period and covered practically every human relationship. They were written down in the "Record of Rites," which not only covered etiquette but also set up quite puritanical rules of conduct aimed at forming character and maintaining a stable social order. Unfortunately, Confucianism had faults as well as virtues, and eventually froze the nation into a conservatism that was hostile to progress.[3]

The Han emperors were the first to make Confucianism the official philosophy of government. Confucianism considered the ruler to have a divine mission; it approved of a hierarchical form of imperial government and of society as a whole, but it vested much power in the emperor's counselors and ministers—the bureaucrats who helped to govern the nation. These bureaucrats were expected to criticize the emperor if he acted in a manner contrary to what was wise and virtuous by Confucian standards. They were Confucian scholars, graduates of an imperial university founded in 124 B.C., open to bright young men from all over the nation regardless of family rank.[4] Three thousand students were enrolled in this state university by the end of the first century B.C.; toward the end of the Han dynasty (220 A.D.) there were 30,000.[5]

Clothes: Clues to Rank

In no other nation were clothes so definitely an indication of social rank as in China. Dress was prescribed by law and custom not only for the emperor and the princes of all ranks and the Mandarins (top Chinese officials), but also for the husbands of the emperor's daughters (by the empress and by his concubines), nobles, servants and eunuchs, merchants, coolies, actors, and prostitutes.

In the Sui dynasty (589 to 618 A.D.) the Emperor Wen selected yellow, symbolic of the earth, as the color reserved for the emperor alone, both for dress and for the tiled roofs of his palaces.[6] In general the reds, oranges, and purples were also reserved for the imperial household, but there were exceptions. For weddings, all classes of people could wear red, the symbol of joy. Today, red is still used for weddings in the bridal dress and in candles and banners embroidered or painted with good luck characters. Small children and Buddhist and Taoist priests could also wear red.

The dragon became the special symbol of the emperor in the T'ang dynasty (618 to 908 A.D.), during which China became the greatest and most civilized power in the world. Europe was

Figure 2–1. Emperor's sacrificial robe of the late 1700's, with five-clawed dragons, symbols of the royal family, writhing among clouds. The emperor wore this robe when he conducted the annual sacrifices to heaven. (Courtesy of the Metropolitan Museum of Art, bequest of William Christian Paul, 1930.)

sunk in poverty, intellectual darkness, and theological strife.[7] Later, the dragon was widely used on coins and in a great variety of art work, so that for the Western world the dragon came to symbolize China.

A beautiful example of the emperor's sacrificial robe in the Ch'ien Lung period (1736 to 1795) is shown in Figure 2–1 and in details of another court robe in Figure 2–2. Both are in *k'o ssu* (cut silk) weave. At the bottom of the sacrificial robe are undulating stripes symbolizing waves, with spray breaking at the top. At intervals in the waves appear upjutting mountains representing the earth. Bats, which symbolize happiness, fly among the clouds. The two dragons facing each other as they writhe among the clouds are grasping in their claws the pearl which grants every wish.

Ceremonial robes for a woman were almost identical with those of her husband or father, except that they were slit down the sides instead of the middle of the front and back.

In the reign of the Manchu emperor, Ch'ien Lung, when the American colonies were struggling for their freedom, court costumes were if anything more elegant than in preceding periods. A different type of costume was specified for each of the twenty-four periods of the Chinese calendar, with a special weight of silk and satin for each and with fur lining in winter.

Costumes of the Mandarins throughout Chinese history make a fascinating study. Each of the nine grades of civil officials and the nine grades of the military—all Confucian scholars—had a distinctive costume, with a special color and stone or metal used for the buttons and a special symbol for the decorative square appliquéd to the front and back of the robe.

For example, the military official of the second rank had red for his color, coral for the button material, and the leopard of India as his symbol. The animal was pictured at the center of a beautifully designed and executed piece of needlework. One example in the New York Metropolitan Museum of Art is shown in Figure 2–3. It is done in satin stitchery with the Peking knot, later outlawed by royal edict as "the forbidden stitch" because it caused so many people to lose their eyesight. The stitch is really

Figure 2–2. Detail of an imperial court robe of the Sun Chih period (1644 to 1661) done in *k'o ssu* weave. (Courtesy of the Metropolitan Museum of Art, bequest of William Christian Paul, 1930.)

Figure 2–3. Mandarin square with the leopard insignia of military officials of the third rank. Background and design are all in the "forbidden stitch." (Courtesy of the Metropolitan Museum of Art, bequest of William Christian Paul, 1930.)

a French knot but is so small and done with such a fine thread and needle that it must indeed have been hard on the eyes.

Few museums today have a complete set of the eighteen Mandarin squares. Since practically every embroidery stitch known to the Chinese was used in these squares, they make a rewarding study. The world will never again see their equal, for no one today has the patience and the skill required to produce them.

What do these textiles and clothes of the Chinese throughout their history reveal about the people? Among other things, they certainly show that the Chinese were sensitive to beauty and had a remarkable degree of skill and artistry in their handicrafts.

They also show that society was stratified and that among the upper classes formality ruled in social contacts.

With such a high degree of skill and beauty attained in clothing and textiles it is not surprising to learn that China, as Will Durant declares, had one of the oldest and richest of living civilizations. It also had:

> . . . a tradition of poetry reaching as far back as 1700 B.C.; a long record of philosophy, idealistic yet practical . . . a mastery of ceramics and painting unequalled in their kind; an easy perfection, rivaled only by the Japanese, in all the minor arts; the most effective morality to be found among the peoples of any time . . . a society that was civilized when Greece was inhabited by barbarians, that saw the rise and fall of Babylonia and Assyria, Persia and Judea, Athens and Rome, Venice and Spain.[8]

INDIA: THE SARI, SYMBOL OF A CIVILIZATION

The Indian sari provides a good means by which to test our thesis that clothes offer a clue to a people's culture. This strip of material about forty-five inches wide and five to nine yards long dates back to early in the Vedaic period (2000 to 1000 B.C.). The way it is draped and fastened about the body has changed, as have the garments worn beneath it, but the beauty and versatility of the sari have given it a permanent place in the wardrobe of Indian women of all classes.[9]

Invasions by the Aryans, the Mongols, and the Huns, and later the British, brought little change in women's wear. Today the sari is still important in the trousseaux of rich and poor, in religious ceremonials, and in state functions, as well as for everyday wear. And no wonder. Whether handspun and handwoven or made in a factory, whether made of cotton or of silk with threads of gold or silver, the sari is an example of the craftsman's artistry, his feeling for color and design. Properly handled, it is flattering to all figures.

Undoubtedly, saris were among the textiles carried by Indian ships to Arabia and Egypt around 860 B.C. along with other characteristic Indian products: cotton and silk materials, shawls and muslins, brocades of silver and gold, perfumes and spices, pearls and rubies.[10]

The Antiquity of Cotton

No one knows where cotton originated, but one of the oldest known specimens of spun cotton yarn was found in the ruins of Mohenjo-Daro, a city of northern India deserted around 3000 B.C. A Hindu hymn in the *Rig Veda* of 1500 B.C. speaks of cotton; and long before Christ was born the ancient city of Dacca was producing muslins so fine that a pound of cotton was said to make more than 250 miles of yarn. The fabric made from this yarn was so gossamer that when spread on the grass it was almost invisible. Around 450 B.C. Herodotus wrote that in India people made cloth from "a sort of wool that grows on wild trees" and that the women plucked lint from the seed, carded it, and spun yarn for weaving on their hand looms. Their sheer cotton fabrics were used for saris.

The word muslin was first used to designate a fine cotton cloth made in Mosul, and the name calico was given to a fabric first made in Calicut, on the southwestern shore of India. The Hindus were long considered experts in bleaching and dyeing and are believed to have been the first to do textile printing from blocks.[11]

India's Fabulous Textiles

Rome at the height of its power paid tremendous prices for Indian silks, brocades, muslins, and cloths of gold. "Textiles were woven with an artistry never since excelled," declared Will Durant in *Our Oriental Heritage*. "From the days of Caesar to our own, the fabrics of India have been prized by all the world. From homespun *khaddar* to complex brocades flaming with gold, from picturesque pyjamas to the invisibly seamed shawls of Kashmir, every garment in India has a beauty that comes only of a very ancient, and now almost instinctive, art." [12]

The Indian sari undoubtedly had its share of responsibility for inspiring the European of the Middle Ages to seek a new and better route to India. He could logically have reasoned: A people who could produce silk and cotton threads of such fineness, dye them to get such beautiful colors, and weave them into magnificent textiles must have reached a high level of civilization.

It is not surprising to find that those same Indians had developed the Arabic numerals, the decimal system, and algebra; that they had worked out a system of mathematics superior to that of the Greeks in everything but geometry; and that they had developed a method of tempering steel superior to any known in the Western world until modern times.[13]

The Sari's Testimonial

The sari, through the centuries, has told us much about Indian life and Indian culture. First, it shows us that the Indians have considered dress to be important.[14] The literature of the people reinforces this deduction by references to dress as "an adjunct of personality" and as a valuable factor in insuring acceptable social behavior. One writer five centuries before Christ reported that the people of Vaisali had a great liking for beautiful clothes and that, in going to meet The Buddha, they dressed in clothes which contrasted with their complexion—the fair ones in dark clothes, the dark ones in lighter and brighter colors.

Second, the sari shows that the Indian people have long had a lively sense of beauty allied with sensuousness and with highly developed artistry and craftsmanship. The antiquity of India's skill in creating beautiful fabrics is further indicated by the legend that when The Buddha died or "attained Nirvana" around 500 B.C., at the age of eighty, his body was wrapped in a Banaras fabric shot with rays of dazzling blue, yellow, and red.

Jewelry, another apparel art, achieved a similar excellence. Excavations in India in 1924 brought to light beautiful gold and silver bangles, ear ornaments, and necklaces created 5,000 years ago. The pieces are so beautifully designed and executed that they might well have come from Tiffany's.

Third, the sari indicates that the people were traditionalists; they respected the contributions of the past. It also suggests resistance to change and perhaps to progress. As Max Lerner comments in his book *America as a Civilization,* changing fashions are an index of the pace of social change within the society, and stability of dress expresses the stability of status.[15]

In India the sari is still omnipresent. The efficient secretary in a modern office building, the saleswoman in the store, the wife of a high government official, and the mother in her home all wear the sari. How many times a day, one wonders, must each of them pause to toss over her shoulder the end of the sari which has fallen off as she bent over to open a file drawer, pull out a bolt of cloth, or lift a baby from the floor. The end could be held in place with a brooch or a row of snap fasteners—but it is not.

Fourth, the sari mutely testifies to the status of women through the way it has been worn. In Vedaic times (2000 to 1000 B.C.) the head and neck were uncovered. During this period, a woman had considerable freedom. She mingled freely with the men at feasts and in dances and religious sacrifices; she could study and engage in debate. She was at least consulted when the time came to select a mate and could remarry after her husband's death.[16]

Then came long centuries in which the sari completely covered the woman, except for her eyes. In those periods a woman was to be seen by no man except her husband and her sons; her husband was her lord and master, to be obeyed and served without question. Few widows remarried. *Suttee*, the cremation of the widow through leaping onto her husband's funeral pyre, became common, especially in families of high rank. Though some groups, among them the Sikhs, forbade *suttee*, it did not disappear until 1829, when the British made it a statutory offense.[17]

Today the sari bears witness to the increasing freedom of India women. As in Vedaic times, it reveals the lines of the feminine figure, often with a bare midriff.

Figure 2–4 shows the Nive or national style of draping the sari over a snug-fitting blouse and a separate skirt. One end is thrown over the left shoulder and allowed to hang gracefully down the back. Another method of draping is the Sakacha style, for which the wearer uses a nine-yard-long sari in such a way as to make a separate skirt unnecessary. She draws the sari between her legs at one point in the draping. For the woman engaged in manual labor it gives considerable freedom of action.

The *burka*, pictured in Figure 2–5, is worn by Moslems in India and in surrounding countries, sometimes over the sari and sometimes over a *shalwar* (long trousers) and *kameez* (blouse). In orthodox Moslem families girls don this all-enveloping cos-

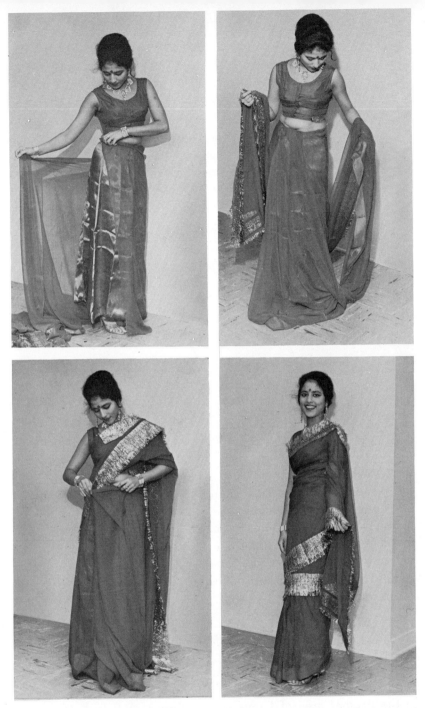

Figure 2–4. A young Indian woman demonstrates how to drape a sari in today's national style. Foundation of the costume is a snug-fitting bodice and straight skirt, with bare midriff. Six wide pleats in the center front of the sari allow for plenty of movement in a dress of much beauty and charm. (Photo by Larry Towns.)

Figure 2–5. The *burka,* worn by Moslem girls in Asia after they reach puberty. The strip of punchwork in the front of the headpiece permits the wearer to see without being seen.

tume when they reach puberty. Today, among the educated and the well-to-do, the *burka* is being abandoned. In rural Moslem areas women wear it chiefly when they go to town or to the city. A university man in Lahore, Pakistan, told an American visitor in 1965 that not more than one in twenty girls enrolled in the university reverts to this costume after graduation, and that among the well-to-do and educated perhaps one in five is still "in purdah."

THE ANCIENT MAYA

Centuries before the Spanish conquerors came to the New World, the Maya developed a remarkable, complex civilization in the present area of Guatemala and part of British Honduras and Mexico. In its most brilliant period, 300 to about 900 A.D., the Maya nation comprised about 100,000 square miles, a little less than the area of the state of New Mexico. Its formative period dates back to 1500 B.C. Signs of cultural regression began to appear late in the classical period, 300 to 600 A.D., and the Spanish conquest hastened its final disintegration.

Mayan Astronomer–Priests and Their Records

In the fourth or third century B.C., Mayan astronomer–priests devised a simple numerical system which archeologists declare "even today stands as one of the brilliant achievements of the human mind." It involved the mathematical quantity zero, "a notable intellectual accomplishment." [18] This mathematical concept is now known to have been developed earlier by Hindu scholars, but news of it did not reach Western Europe until the early Middle Ages, several centuries after the Maya had developed their flexible system.

The Mayan religion, focal point for much of the culture, was complex. Priests formalized the religion, elaborated the rituals, and held a dominant place in society by claiming to interpret the wishes of an ever-increasing number of gods. The priests' knowledge of astronomy and mathematics, which enabled them to predict eclipses accurately, was undoubtedly the key to their hold on the people. Temples, especially those with astronomical observatories, became important centers of learning.[19]

Much of their learning and accounts of historical events were recorded in hieroglyphic manuscripts. Unfortunately, fanatic Spanish priests burned all the manuscripts they could get their hands on, declaring them to "contain nothing in which there was not to be seen superstition and lies of the devil." Only three manuscripts have survived but none of them deals with the history of the Maya.

Tales Told by Dress and Textiles

No costumes or textiles of preconquest periods survive to help us determine the level of Mayan culture. Only a few charred pieces of cloth have been found in the sacrificial well at Chichén Itzá. But these charred textiles, along with the carvings on wood and stone, the paintings of human figures on plastered walls and pottery, and the figurines molded in clay and stucco, offer eloquent testimony.[20]

The Maya apparently discovered cotton, before the Christian era, and cultivated it as their second-largest crop after maize. They spun cotton thread and wove it into cloth on their looms, often in intricate patterns.

For a skirt the women wore a straight piece 'of woven cotton cloth held in at the waist by a band or thong; with it they wore a rectangular piece of cloth resembling a short cowl, which was placed over the head to hang down in front as a covering for the breasts. Long before the Spaniards arrived the Mayan women had added the *huipil* (pronounced we-peel'), a long, straight piece of cloth woven with a square opening in the middle for the head. They usually sewed up the sides of the *huipil* at least to the hips, leaving openings for their arms, and wore it over the skirt but not completely covering it. Embroidery, feather work, or carved stones sometimes decorated the neckline and hem. Some of the women tattooed themselves from the waist up, except for their breasts; all anointed themselves with a sweet-smelling red ointment.

The men, whatever their social rank, wore a breech cloth, sandals with straps, and sometimes a draped rectangle of cloth as a cape. The breech cloth was a strip of cotton about "five fingers wide" and long enough to go around the waist several times, to be pulled between the legs, and to hang down in front and in back.[21] The garb of the commoners was strictly functional; that of the rulers, the nobles, and the priests was magnificent.

For the elite the ends of the cloth were embroidered and decorated with cut stones or brilliant feathers from tropical birds. Costume accessories included necklaces, wristlets, breast plates, collars, big ear plugs, nose and lip ornaments, and ornaments for the waist, legs, or arms made of bones, wood, shell, stone, feathers, or animal teeth. Their deerskin sandals, too, were ornate. The back part, cupped around the heel, was beautifully ornamented, as were the thongs holding them to the feet. The cape might be a highly decorated jaguar skin instead of cloth. Large parasols and decorated litters added color to processionals.

Most impressive of all masculine attire was the headdress worn by the priests and nobles—a tremendous, plume-bedecked affair created on a wicker or wooden scaffolding, often as tall as

Figure 2–6. Yucatán fiesta costume of today, a direct copy of ancient Mayan dress. It is made from a straight piece of cloth the same width throughout, with a hole cut for the head and embroidery at neck and on skirt. Modeled by Kim De-Jac, whose maternal grandparents and great grandparents were Mexican.

the man himself.[22] The centerpiece might be a carved head of a jaguar or a serpent or a bird.

Mayan dress had not changed appreciably for 550 years before the Spaniards arrived, a fact which indicated a stable and sometimes static society. The national costume of the Maya of today is a faithful copy of the *huipil:* it is made from a single length of material, the same width at the shoulders as at the hem, with openings for the head and arms and embroidery around the neck and hem. It is still worn over a straight skirt, which also has embroidery around the hem. Figure 2–6 shows a child wearing the fiesta costume of today in Yucatán.

Reports on Dress and Customs

Bishop Diego de Landa, who went to Central America in 1549, remains our most valuable source of information about the Maya. He was a keen observer, but in his book *Relación de la cosas de Yucatán* he undoubtedly exaggerated some negative aspects of Mayan life, especially their religion, to justify his treatment of the Maya.

In early times, children of both sexes could go naked until they were four or five years old; later, girls wore the *huipil* practically from birth, while boys were free of clothes until they were five or six years old. When boy met girl on a walk, the girl would lower her eyes and might even step aside until he had passed.

Mayan women could not hold public office or enter a temple, but murals show them taking part in some important affairs. Their status was somewhat like that of women in early Greek civilization; no woman could vote, own property, or hold public office, and each was the ward of her nearest male relative. The father of the Mayan family was definitely the head of the house, but the mother was treated with deference. Children were reared to respect all their elders.

As a symbol of chastity Mayan girls wore a red shell hanging from a string that was tied around the waist, and Mayan boys wore a white bead fastened to the hair on top of the head. When children reached puberty the Mayan priest, assisted by some of the elders (both men and women), conducted a special ceremony removing the shells and beads to indicate readiness for marriage. The Maya were monogamous, but divorce was easily obtained, and subsequent marriages required no formalities of any kind.[23]

The father was responsible for selecting a good wife for his son. With the help of a professional matchmaker, usually a woman or a friend, the father investigated eligible girls and decided how much he could afford for a dowry. After the final selection had been made and the priest had pronounced the couple man and wife, they went to live with the wife's parents for five or six years.[24]

Mayan Achievements

Though the Mayan civilization can be credited with many brilliant achievements, some of its aspects were primitive. Metal did not exist in that part of the New World; thus metal tools were unknown. Stone tools were used for everything from the quarrying of limestone slabs for monuments and temples to the execution of the most delicate carving. The wheel was unknown for throwing pottery, spinning thread, or transporting people and materials. Invention of wheeled vehicles seems to be closely related to the availability of large animals for transportation, and the Mayas' only domestic animal was the dog.

As George W. Brainerd, the eminent archeologist, concluded:

The most notable Mayan achievements . . . were in abstract intellectual fields, and here they surpassed all other New World civilizations and equaled or surpassed many in the Old World. . . . The Peten jungle seems an unfavorable setting for the development of a civilization, but the Maya transcended its limitations. The simple agricultural system which it enforced was made not only to fill subsistence needs but also to produce food surpluses. The relative poverty of natural resources prevented a great deal of technological advancement, but the existing technology was employed skillfully enough to fill the needs of a people whose emphasis was largely upon the esthetic refinements of their products rather than upon quantity or mass.[25]

GHANA: ITS TRADITIONAL TEXTILES

The Kente cloth of Ghana makes another fascinating study. A green, yellow, and maroon example of this traditional handwoven textile now has a permanent place outside the eastern entrance to the General Assembly Hall of the United Nations. The cloth is of native silk, about twenty by thirteen feet in size, and represents three and a half months of work for ten skilled weavers. Designs and techniques of the Ashanti weavers who produced it have been famous since ancient times.[26]

Kente cloth is woven in four-inch strips in complicated patterns and bright colors, sometimes raw. The strips are then sewn together in an infinite variety of patterns, usually in staggered formation so that the repeats are never together. A strip of this Kente cloth six to ten feet long is worn by men today for official occasions, draped in toga fashion, with one arm and shoulder left uncovered. Figure 2–7 shows how it is used for feminine dress, and Figure 2–8 gives a close view of the fabric.

The origin of this unique textile is lost in antiquity. Originally, the Ashanti weavers were attached to the court. Any chieftain who wanted a robe made had to get royal approval not only for the weaving but also for the particular design to be followed. Made first in cotton, these robes later were often of silk—from yarns stripped out of European textiles. Later, weavers learned how to utilize spider silk. Tree bark was the source of dyes.

As with the clans of Scotland, each tribe in Ghana has long had its own special pattern. Each fabric is rich in symbolism, indicating the social status and the sex of the wearer. It may also illustrate a well-known proverb to the initiate or have ritualistic functions.

Another traditional textile from Ghana is the Adinkera cloth, consisting of an off-white ground printed with bold, sophisticated designs usually in dark brown. These designs are rich in symbolism that reflects Ghana's life and culture.

Women of Ghana sometimes wear a length of the Kente or the Adinkera material or some other textile draped in toga fashion. Occasionally, they wear a Mother Hubbard type of dress, especially for maternity periods. The typical national dress of the women today, however, is the three-piece costume already referred to in Figure 2–7. The wearer first draws a straight length of fabric about two and a half yards long about her hips, with the overlay ending at one side. To hold it in place, she ties a cord around her waist. Then she pulls it up under the cord so that the material will end above her ankles. The wearer takes care of any extra length by folding it down over the cord to create a peplum effect. Then she dons the bodice, which is form fitting and low necked and usually has cap sleeves. It also has a peplum, about ten inches wide, with inverted pleats at the French dart line back and front. The third part of the costume is a long scarf of matching material.

What clues to culture do these Ghanaian fabrics and costumes provide? The intricacy of the designs and the skill achieved by

Figure 2–7. Rosette Tetebo, a home economics student in the United States, is wearing the three-piece costume of present-day Ghana, made from the traditional handwoven Kente cloth.

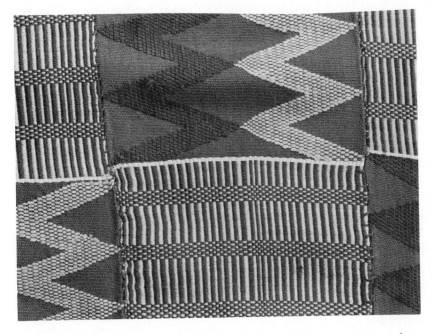

Figure 2–8. Kente cloth detail showing how designs are staggered.

the Ashanti weavers bear testimony to a fairly advanced stage of civilization, though it apparently developed long after those of China and India. It is not surprising then to find that Ghanaians also made beautiful miniature brass carvings and wood sculpture, pieces which have had tremendous influence on Western art of the last century.

YAP ISLAND: THE GRASS SKIRT

Dress worn by the natives of the tiny island of Yap in the West Pacific offers sharp contrast to that of China, India, the Maya, and Ghana. Of Malay origin, the Yapese apparently are of relatively pure stock and still cling to many of their age-old customs. They have unique racial and language characteristics quite distinct from those of the other Pacific islands. Only since the United States took over administration of the island under United Nations mandate in 1947 has there been an attempt to work up a written Yapese language with a grammar.

Though Yap has been governed successively by Spain, Germany, and Japan, and is now under the trusteeship of the United States, the women still wear their homemade grass skirts, which hang from the hips to the ankles and leave the navel uncovered, as pictured in Figure 2–9. The multiple layers of the narrow grass fronds are plaited into a hip band. A girl may wear as many as three or four grass skirts to be sure that she is well covered, especially from hip to mid-thigh. Grass layers below the thigh are less dense than above, though the girl will be much embarrassed if she thinks her legs can be seen, even dimly, as she walks.

The total weight of these skirts may be from fifteen to twenty pounds, and if they get wet they may weigh as much as thirty pounds. When the girl sits down she carefully arranges her skirts so as to cover her legs to the ankles. Everyday skirts are the natural soft tan of dried grass. For dress occasions, they are dyed in a few raw colors—yellow, red, blue, and green. Today, this is generally done with commercial dyes. The colored grass may be arranged in contrasting panels, with no set pattern for the colors.

Figure 2–9. Yap Island girl getting a refreshing drink from the coconut. Her grass skirt of six layers is very heavy when it gets wet. (Photo by Roy Goss, administrative assistant in the Yap district of the U. S. trust territory of the Pacific.)

The Yapese woman wears nothing above the hips, being completely unself-conscious about the upper part of her body. Occasionally, however, she will don a Western type of blouse if she is going into the part of the island inhabited by Americans. As a matter of courtesy, most of the American women on the island wear shorts only in their homes, and change to dresses which cover at least part of their legs when they go into native quarters.

Babies of both sexes among the Yapese go naked until they are thoroughly toilet trained, partly because water for washing is scarce. Again, as a gesture of courtesy, the mother who is taking her baby where Westerners will see it, usually covers it. Heads of girls are shaved from birth, usually until puberty.

Men wear a breech clout originally of shredded coconut fiber, now usually of cheap, imported Japanese cotton and often dyed red. This garment, called a *thu*, is a three-by-six-foot strip of material. The wearer wraps it around his waist, pulls it between his legs, and finishes with a short end hanging down in front and a long one behind. In "the old days" only the Yapese were permitted to wear a long "tail" behind; tributary islanders had to wear a short one both fore and aft.

What level of culture does Yapese dress indicate? Obviously a primitive one. The fact that the Yapese did not reach an advanced level of civilization does not necessarily indicate any inherent inferiority, of course. Physical environment is important in the development of any culture, as anthropologists point out. No one knows for sure where the Yapese came from originally, but their South Pacific homeland was probably warm and not invigorating. Furthermore, that homeland may well have been a cluster of isolated islands. As Hoebel comments, "Isolated peoples always stagnate, be they Mongoloid, Negroid, or Caucasoid. . . . Culture, not race, is the great molder of human society." [27]

The Yapese have long done basketweaving but have constructed no looms for the weaving of cloth. They have never needed anything warmer than grass or shredded coconut fibers for their clothes. In ancient times they made pottery for their own household needs, but they never developed ceramics into a fine art as did the Chinese.

This brief study of the clothing and textiles of five peoples provides only a glimpse of the insights to be gained from the study of dress through the centuries.

NOTES

1. Alan Priest and Pauline Simmons, *Chinese Textiles: An Introduction to the Study of Their History, Sources, Technique, Symbolism, and Use* (New York: The Metropolitan Museum of Art, 1931), pp. 4–11, 49–52.

2. Will Durant, *The Story of Civilization*, Part 1, *Our Oriental Heritage* (New York: Simon and Schuster, Inc., 1954), p. 703.

3. *Ibid.*, pp. 658–77.

4. W. Theodore DeBary, Wing-Tsit Chan, and Burton Watson, *Introduction to Oriental Civilizations*, LV, *Sources of Chinese Tradition* (New York: Columbia University Press, 1960), p. 264.

5. *Ibid.*, pp. 257–58.

6. Priest–Simmons, pp. 41–49.

7. *Ibid.*, pp. 48–52.

8. Durant, p. 640.

9. Kamala S. Dongerkey, *The Indian Sari* (New Delhi: All India Handicrafts Board, 1959), p. 9 ff.

10. Durant, p. 400.

11. *Ibid.*, p. 478.

12. *Ibid.*, pp. 479 and 585.

13. *Ibid.*, pp. 527–28.

14. Dongerkey, p. 11.

15. Max Lerner, *America as a Civilization* (New York: Simon and Schuster, Inc., 1957), p. 647.

16. Durant, p. 401.

17. *Ibid.*, p. 493.

18. Sylvanus Griswold Morley, rev. by George W. Brainerd, *The Ancient Maya* (3d ed.; Stanford, Cal.: Stanford University Press, 1956), p. 237.

19. *Ibid.*, p. 428.

20. *Ibid.*, p. 380.

21. Victor W. von Hagen, *The Ancient Sun Kingdoms of the Americas: Maya* (New York: Harcourt, Brace & World, Inc., 1961), p. 224; and George W. Brainerd, *The Maya Civilization* (Los Angeles: Southwest Museum, 1954), pp. 66–68.

22. Morley–Brainerd, p. 174.

23. *Ibid.*, pp. 165–66.

24. *Ibid.*, pp. 167–68.

25. *Ibid.*, pp. 424–41.

26. "The Textiles of Ghana," *American Fabrics*, No. 51 (Fall–Winter 1960), pp. 51–61.

27. E. Adamson Hoebel, *Man in the Primitive World: An Introduction to Anthropology* (2d ed.; New York: McGraw-Hill Book Co., 1958), p. 147.

FURTHER READING

Boucher, François. *20,000 Years of Fashion: The History of Costume and Personal Adornment.* New York: Harry N. Abrams, Inc., 1967. As the book's jacket comments, this book is a "picture album tracing mankind's efforts through the ages to alter or improve the appearance of the human body, to make the self a work of art and to adapt it to the necessities of climate and daily life." M. Boucher is the director of the French Center for Costume Studies and is honorary curator of the Musée Carnavalet, a museum of modes and manners.

Boyer, David S. "Micronesia—The Americanization of Eden," *National Geographic*, CXXXI, No. 5 (May, 1967), p. 702 ff.

DeBary, W. Theodore, Chan, Wing-Tsit, and Watson, Burton. *Introduction to Oriental Civilizations: Sources of Chinese Tradition.* New York: Columbia University Press, 1960. Chapter II, Confucius, pp. 17–35. Students will be interested in reading some of the sayings of Confucius listed here and in discussing his definition of a gentleman.

Durant, Will. *Story of Civilization,* Vol. I, Part 2, *Our Oriental Heritage,* New York: Simon and Schuster, Inc., 1935. Book II: India and Her Neighbors; Book III: The Far East. An extremely enlightening and interesting book. If time is limited you will find that the most rewarding sections are: Chapter 17, The Life of the People (India); Chapter 23, The Age of the Philosophers (of China); and Chapter 24, The Age of the Poets (of China).

Hurtado, Eusebio Davalos. "Into the Well of Sacrifice: I. Return to the Sacred Cenote; II. Hunt in the Deep Past," *National Geographic,* CXX, No. 4 (October, 1961), p. 540 ff.

Morley, Sylvanus Griswold, rev. by George W. Brainerd. *The Ancient Maya.* Stanford, Cal.: Stanford University Press, 1956. "An Appraisal of the Maya Civilization" by Betty Bell, pp. 424–41. You may find this summary of Dr. Brainerd's conclusions so arresting that you will want to skim other chapters in the book, perhaps Chapter 2 on the people and Chapter 13 on architecture.

Priest, Alan, and Simmons, Pauline. *Chinese Textiles.* New York: The Metropolitan Museum of Art, 1931. Since the book has fewer than a hundred pages of reading and illustrations, it will not take you long to read it through.

von Hagen, Victor W. *The Ancient Sun Kingdoms of the Americas: Maya.* New York: Harcourt, Brace & World, Inc., 1961. Chapter II, The People, pp. 221–46. Easy, interesting reading. After you have read these pages, you may want to read all 198 pages on the Maya.

STUDY SUGGESTIONS

1. Imagine yourself a sophisticated visitor from outer space dropped down onto your campus. List details of the dress of faculty and students which could supply you with clues to the culture of the day.
2. Visit the nearest art museum to see its collection, if any, of Chinese costumes or costumes of today's underdeveloped countries.
3. Is dress in the United States today an "adjunct of personality" as The Buddha's contemporaries believed? Discuss and illustrate your points.
4. Is dress today used as a means of "insuring acceptable social behavior"?
5. If any woman who wears a sari lives in your community, ask her to visit your class and to demonstrate how the women of her homeland drape a sari. Kandyans of Ceylon, for example, drape it quite differently from the ways in India.

3

Clothing and the Individual

The clothing of the American girl reveals as much about the customs of her country and the social forces that influence her as the dress of the woman of India or the costume of a Yapese woman. This composite known as the American girl is derived from the image of hundreds of thousands of individuals, reflecting the diversity in the cultural pattern of our time—differences arising from occupational and social needs, from limitations set by the financial conditions of the family, and from the physical characteristics of individuals. The individual, her attitudes and goals, must be examined if one is to understand what clothing means to the American girl.

BASIC DESIRES

For most people interest in dress goes far beyond the need for protection. Custom has established certain articles of clothing as essential for decency; our ideals of health and cleanliness have brought about the inclusion of other essentials. In addition, clothing contributes to the attainment of certain desires: physical comfort, social participation, conformity, prestige, self-expression, attracting the opposite sex, and aesthetic expression. The need to satisfy these desires varies from one person to another, but each affects to some degree the individual's attitudes toward dress.

Comfort

When asked, "What satisfactions do you expect from your clothing?" most people will promptly say, "First of all, comfort." Physical comfort, a relatively simple satisfaction, means protection from heat, cold, rain, and sharp objects. Today's concept of comfort also requires that body movement be unhampered, that clothing be lightweight and pliable, that it feel smooth to the skin, and that it permit sufficient passage of air to allow evaporation of moisture from the skin.

Yet the skeptic may well question the importance of physical comfort to the individual when he considers how often fashion leads to discomfort: the cinched-in waist, skin-tight jeans, spike heels. When skirts are well above the knees, sheer hose and lightweight shoes offer little protection on a cold, rainy day. Only when fashion turns away from the pointed toe and the spike heel does the feminine population accept low heels and a more natural shoe outline. Though everyone fully enjoys such a change, desire for comfort does not bring it about.

Social Participation

The desire for companionship and for participation in the activities of some social group is strong in most people. No one wants to feel alone. He wants to belong, sometimes to an exclusive social group, sometimes to a more loosely knit group in which his participation may be more or less casual.

To be accepted by the group the individual must first be approved, and that means he must meet set standards of dress and behavior. His apparel must be appropriate. An outfit that is too dressy, a color that expresses poor taste, may delay or prevent admission into the group. Often, small details determine success or failure in human relationships.

In one community a newcomer was being coached by a boy of his own age as to clothes to wear to school: "If you want to belong to the right group, wear your pants low down on your hips and a dark plaid shirt with the long pointed collar buttoned down at the back as well as at the front." Somewhat older boys and girls will not demand such strict conformity, but even mature people tend to be suspicious of a newcomer who shows marked individuality. Usually, only a strong leader will venture to introduce something radically new in dress.

Conformity

Conformity to the ways of the group provides enormous protection for its members. No one is criticized for customary activities; each member finds his confidence strengthened through following group practices. Whether the conformity is voluntary or involuntary, the effect is much the same.

Slaves to fads and fashions enjoy the advantages of conformity. They have surmounted an important hurdle between themselves and social approval by dressing like others; they have identified themselves with the customary.

The effect created by the short-short skirts of the mid-1960's was anything but flattering, but the girl who wore one was following a fashion that had the stamp of approval of her peers. She could feel confident, even well dressed, because she was wearing what "everyone else" was wearing.

Not everyone has this desire for conformity in dress. It varies from one age group to another. Adolescents are probably more influenced by "what everyone else does" than are mature people. The mature are more likely to experiment with variations from a well-defined way of dressing, introducing some of their own ideas. Those who feel the least secure in their social group inevitably place the greatest importance on conformity.

The uniform worn by the armed forces is a good example of involuntary conformity in dress. Every branch of the military service stresses grooming and a "starchy" appearance. When the young recruit is required to meet certain rigid standards of dress, he often finds that he has gained a great deal of confidence as he is identified with one of these groups, even though formerly he may have been careless in his dress. This effect of increased confidence is also found in other career areas in which uniforms are required. Figure 3-1 illustrates a student of hospital dietetics in the uniform of her profession. A uniform such as this

Figure 3–1. Verna Lange, a young graduate student of hospital dietetics at the University of Kansas Medical Center, gains prestige through wearing her uniform.

lends an element of prestige to the wearer and therefore helps to instill confidence in her.

Similarly, members of religious orders and sects gain a certain confidence and sense of protection, and a considerable degree of respect, from conforming to a fixed type of dress symbolic of principles on which their way of life is based.

Clothes: A Prestige Factor

The desire to command admiration from a group may overshadow other desires. It is particularly strong among those who are moving up in the social scale. Different social levels do exist in the United States, though some think of it as a classless society.

Clothing is but one of the areas of consumption that show the extent of this desire for prestige. Expensive homes, automobiles, boats, and other sports equipment are conspicuous and become a means of gaining favorable attention. Clothing, however, can be observed quite apart from the place where one lives, and it is therefore useful to the ambitious who are not able to acquire some of the more expensive luxuries. People sometimes neglect the necessities of life for clothes that will attract attention.

Some people gain prestige by wearing "correct dress," by faithfully following fashion, by owning an extensive wardrobe, or by displaying beautiful and expensive clothing. Present-day wardrobes often contain many more garments than are needed. The girl who owns fifteen sweater and skirt outfits is using them for their prestige value. Many girls have found that half this number provides enough variety for their wardrobe.

The business or professional man gains prestige through his choice of clothing. His ultraconservative dress has come to be a virtual uniform. He often does not permit himself even a hint of color in his necktie, in spite of his dark suit, white shirt, and black shoes. Any deviation from this conservative pattern might lead customers and clients to question the wearer's sound judgment, and therefore might stand in the way of business success. In a few business organizations executives have identified themselves by wearing some insignia of their position. In one, they have voluntarily adopted dark red jackets with the firm's crest worn on the pocket. In another, each young person in training for a junior executive position wears a white carnation in his buttonhole during business hours.

Self-Expression

The identification of self with clothing is inevitable. Clothing virtually becomes one's body surface, so that any criticism of one's dress is likely to be construed as criticism of the wearer. After all, clothing reflects the taste and judgment of the wearer. Anyone who has tried to help others improve their appearance through dress knows how much tact is required. The person being helped feels that he, rather than his wardrobe, is being criticized, and as a result his feeling of security is shaken.

The clothes that a person chooses are to a great extent an expression of the concept he has of himself. They reflect his personality. *Personality* is that composite of traits which determines the way a person reacts to his environment. It is measured in terms of such characteristics as sincerity, forthrightness, gentleness, gaiety, submissiveness, eagerness, and their opposites —a list of qualities not all-inclusive. Each person possesses a unique combination of traits. Personality then is not merely a measure of the attractiveness of an individual as is implied when a girl says of an acquaintance, "He has loads of personality." It is his characteristic behavior which reveals his personality.

Those who seek to present themselves in a favorable light attempt to reflect the personality traits that they admire most. The young woman who sees herself as a forthright, even aggressive, businesswoman will tend to choose simple lines with dark and strong colors, and to avoid the dainty, frilly sort of garment that the more demure, retiring person finds pleasing. A close relationship exists between the clothing chosen and personality.

A girl often assumes more than one role in the course of a day or a week. And each role influences her choice of dress. For the college campus, for example, she may readily accept the pattern of college life and go to classes looking like dozens of other girls, in an easy-fitting sweater and tailored skirt, loafers, and a pea jacket. When she leaves the campus for a weekend in a nearby city she may present herself as a sophisticated young woman dressed in a smart street outfit that will cause heads to turn as she passes. For a picnic she may assume a tomboy role. For an important social function or when her date is the "favorite man on campus," she may present her most alluring, feminine self. In each case the clothing she chooses, consciously or unconsciously, reflects the concept she has of herself—or the person she would like to be.

A girl's dress also shows what she thinks of herself physically. If she feels that she lacks the lovely proportions of the current ideal for the American girl—tall, slender, and youthful—she makes use of various devices in dress design to remedy what she sees as her physical faults and to create an illusion of the proportions she so much admires. She adds to her apparent height by her choice of line; she suggests extra width to her shoulders either by padding or by using effective design; she slenderizes her hips by the skillful placing of lines in the skirt and the elimination of undesirable fullness. She uses these and many other devices to improve her physical appearance.

Similarly, the overweight young man will avoid suits with unflattering lines. He will be concerned about lines suggesting height. He will avoid an appearance of bulkiness in his clothes, both in fabric and in cut, and will select a topcoat of a solid dark color rather than a conspicuous plaid with strong oppositional lines.

Attracting the Opposite Sex

Few young people are aware of the basic instinct that motivates them to groom themselves and to don attractive clothing. Whether it be a girl of the South Sea islands with her garland of flowers and grass skirt, or a young Igorot tribesman with his gaily decorated G string and jaunty cap, or a young American dressed in the current fashion, each in his or her own way is announcing interest in gaining favorable attention from the opposite sex. They want to be recognized by their peers as individuals, and to express their interest in others.

Although there are various means of attracting the opposite sex, clothing is perhaps one of the most important. Undoubtedly, clothing that distinguishes one sex from the other offers greater possibilities than does dress that is alike for both men and women. In fact, dress serves as a secondary sex characteristic. When women wear women's clothing and men wear typically masculine attire, each can be promptly identified as to sex.

In this country young people spend more for clothing between the ages of sixteen and twenty-four than at any other time in their lives. During these years they are most likely to be seeking a mate. Families, recognizing the importance of social contacts for sons and daughters, are usually ready to make financial concessions so that their children will be able to appear as well, if not better, dressed than others in their social group.

The girl who gains favorable recognition is usually the one who avoids flamboyant dress. Too much individuality might even frighten off the boy whose attention she covets. Therefore, she usually chooses clothing that enhances her appearance rather than dress that shocks the observer into giving her attention.

Aesthetic Expression

The need for aesthetic expression is an age-old requirement of man. Primitive people as well as those of highly advanced cultures have sought ways of expressing beauty and change of mood, or ways of increasing self-esteem. As was pointed out in Chapter 1, adorning the human body is one of the earliest forms of aesthetic expression. Before clothing was worn, primitives decorated their bodies with elaborate designs, sometimes painted, sometimes tattooed or created from scars in the flesh. Havelock Ellis, a social psychologist, declared that the adornment of the human body—along with music, poetry, and dancing—marks the beginning of the most exquisite arts in civilization.

Dress offers many opportunities for aesthetic expression. Whether it is derived from the assembling of a dress and its appropriate accessories by the college girl, or the creating of a beautiful costume that calls for all the imagination and skill of a famed designer, dress can be a satisfying means of expressing the self. Many books have been written on the subject.

American women are known for their good looks, partly because they choose clothes that satisfy their need for artistic expression. Max Lerner, a keen observer of America as a civilization, has said, "America's greatest work of art may well turn out to be the American woman, from sixteen to fifty, whether stenographer or society belle, shop girl or movie queen. She is known the world over for her pertness, her spirit, and her looks, for the contours of her figure, the smartness of her clothes, and the vitality of her person." [1]

VALUES

Clothing is an aid toward understanding a person. It expresses the values that are important to him. To some, material things are of primary importance; to others, less tangible matters are desirable, as friendships, respect from associates, and the good will of others.

The values that the individual holds important are the ruling forces in his life. Values are defined as the fundamental beliefs and feelings for which a person or a group has affective regard; that is, toward which he has an emotional response.

Concern with beauty, self-improvement, economy, or gaining distinction and individuality from dress suggests that worthy values are directing one's behavior. All too often, however, attitudes such as insincerity, selfishness, or ostentation are evident, suggesting that unworthy values govern expenditures for dress.

A thoughtful person may well question his attitudes toward dress. He may ask himself: Do I want to create a striking appearance or would I prefer to be inconspicuous? Do I want my dress to express my real self or to flatter me? Do I want my clothing to give me self-confidence or merely to meet the requirements for decency? Do I want my clothing to be more important than the self expressed in my face?

The individual's responses to these questions will express his values. For most people the answers will not be clear-cut. For some occasions the most utilitarian dress will be his choice; for others more distinctive or glamorous apparel will seem desirable.

The girl who places undue emphasis on dress submerges her own self. If she takes the middle road, however, recognizing the importance of fashion without being a slave to it and expressing taste in her choices, she will be admired by her acquaintances.

Taste, the ability to discern and appreciate that which is beautiful and appropriate, can be developed. People who display taste usually avoid extremes but are sensitive to changes in customs and fashions and wish to remain in step with prevailing modes. The finest dress designers tend toward understated, almost timeless, interpretations of fashion. They seek beauty and appropriateness in dress. For any woman, the supreme compliment concerning her clothes is to say that she has taste.

PHILOSOPHY OF CLOTHING

The values and goals held by an individual provide clear insight into his philosophy of dress. Philosophy in this context means a consistent personal attitude toward reality expressed in beliefs and principles of conduct.

A young girl tends to reflect her family's values, many of which color her behavior through life. But as she grows up, has new experiences, meets people whose values are different, she may discard some of her values and modify others, so that by the time she has reached maturity she may hold quite a different set of values from those of her parents.

Each person has a unique set of values. Certainly the value placed on clothing varies from one person to another. How can value given to dress be the same for a family that must hold to the strictest economy and for one that can indulge in many luxuries!

Social change upsets many traditional values and modifies standards of clothing. Let us consider a few of these. Today, clothes are generally produced outside the home, placing emphasis on selection and bringing about acceptance of standards of construction set by the manufacturer—often lower than those once held in the home. Women gainfully employed have more money to buy clothes today than in the past, but little time to spend in making clothes. The adolescent girl is often allowed to choose her own clothing, thus gaining experience before she has had a chance to develop standards. The relaxing of puritanical ideas of proper dress has greatly influenced what is acceptable in apparel. There are many more changes that could be mentioned, but each has had its effect on the values that are important to individuals. Certainly these influence how money is spent for dress. Everyone should give thought to the clothing values important to himself and understand his own philosophy of dress.

NOTES

1. Max Lerner, *America as a Civilization* (New York: Simon and Schuster, Inc., 1957), pp. 639–50.

FURTHER READING

KOHLMAN, ELEANORE L. "Personal Values, What Are They?" *Journal of Home Economics*, LIV, No. 10 (1962), pp. 819–22.
ROACH, MARY ELLEN, and EICHER, JOANNE BUBOLZ. *Dress, Adornment, and the Social Order*. New York: John Wiley & Sons, Inc., 1965. Part

5: A Social Self, pp. 214–51. Selected readings related to dress and the individual.

RYAN, MARY SHAW. *Clothing: A Study in Human Behavior.* New York: Holt, Rinehart and Winston, Inc., 1966. Chapters 4 and 5, pp. 81–107. The relationship between clothing and the personality and attitudes of the wearer.

STOUT, DOROTHY RUNBECK, and LATZKE, ALPHA. "Values College Women Consider in Clothing Selection," *Journal of Home Economics,* L, No. 1 (1958), pp. 43–44. A study made of Stephens College students.

ZIMMERMAN, C. C. *Consumption and Standards of Living.* New York: D. Van Nostrand Co., Inc., 1936. Chapter 1. A discussion of systems of living and dominant values describing manner of living.

STUDY SUGGESTIONS

1. What do your clothes say about your attitude toward fashion: that you are a conformist or that you show individuality in following the mode?
2. What do today's fashions tell us about the social roles of the sexes?
3. What do today's fashions say about the values motivating people?
4. Are grooming and good manners frills? Or do they make a contribution to the individual? To the group? To society in general?
5. How is clothing used as a social tool?
6. Why do some women resist following fashion?
7. Do the frequent changes dictated by fashion make any contribution to human welfare?
8. Describe some types of dress that you see worn today and discuss the personal attitudes that they reveal.
9. Write a statement of your own philosophy of dress.

4

Design Applied to Dress

To achieve success in the creation of apparel, every designer must know and understand the four elements of design and the four principles which determine their use. These have been the guidelines for creative work in textiles and costume for centuries; they can be traced back to ancient civilizations. The student of clothing, then, needs to study these elements and principles to understand how they can be used and to appreciate the meaning that each conveys.

ELEMENTS OF DESIGN

The art elements—*line, form, color,* and *texture*—are the building blocks used in creating any design. Whether it be arranging the furnishings for a room, setting up food and table accessories for a color photograph, painting a picture, or designing a costume, all of these elements come into play.

The significance attached to any one of these elements arises partly from a physical law and partly from its emotional connotation, which is derived from the viewer's previous experience with that element. For example, a given texture may arouse pleasure in one person, revulsion in another. One child may draw away from a furry texture; another may bury his face in it in pure delight. The involuntary response of a person to straight vertical lines is to sit or stand straight. They suggest strength, dignity, no nonsense. The meaning attached to the various elements of a design is often said to be a part of our social heritage.

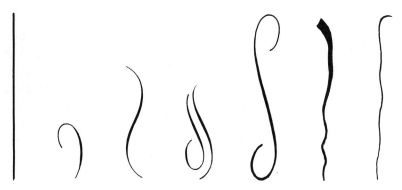

Figure 4–1. Curved lines are graceful. Small curves suggest buoyancy. Wavering curves suggest weakness.

Line: Boundary of an Area

Lines are the boundaries of areas. They determine the shape of an article or break an area into smaller areas. *Line has character* according to whether it is straight, curved, continuous, or broken. As has already been pointed out, straight lines, because they are direct and unwavering, suggest purposefulness and strength. Curved lines, because they are flexible, convey a feeling of grace and movement, as Figure 4–1 illustrates. Curved lines vary from the bouncy and buoyant to compound or S-curves, which may be rhythmic and graceful or weak and purposeless— reminiscent of the curves of a limp string.

In direction a line may be vertical, horizontal, or oblique. Vertical lines are associated with ideas of steadiness and vigor; horizontal lines, with rest or calm; oblique or diagonal lines, with movement and transition. Figure 4–2 illustrates line direction.

Figure 4–2. The direction taken by a line imparts meaning to a design. The vertical movement implies strength; the horizontal movement suggests repose; the oblique movement indicates force or animation.

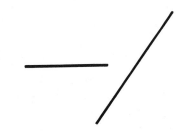

Both the character of a line and its direction influence the impression conveyed when it becomes part of a design. A long evening gown of cream-colored moire with a bell-shaped skirt suggests formality, dignity, and elegance. The predominantly vertical lines of the skirt, softened in character by restrained curves, are carried into the lines of the smoothly fitted bodice. Texture, color, and line all contribute to the feeling of formality: the nature of the fabric, its shimmering surface, its stiffness, and its color; the vertical lines of the dress modified into slight curves; the simplicity of the design as a whole.

In contrast, a sleeveless chiffon evening dress may suggest youth and gaiety: its neckline slightly scooped, its waistline dropped to the hips, and its knee-length skirt made in three circular tiers. Horizontal lines dominate the dress, but these are not straight and continuous. The ruffles form small round curves to give the feeling of playfulness and vivacity. Thus, the undulating line modifies the restful feeling of straight horizontal lines.

The most striking example of the influence of the direction and the character of line on the impression conveyed in a dress design is the Mondrian-inspired, short-skirted shift popularized in the mid-1960's, with its strong oppositional lines crisscrossing the surface in a windowpane effect. Vertical lines meet horizontals with an impact that suggests opposition, as is evident in the dress design shown in Figure 4–3.

Form: Shape of an Object

Form, or the shape of an object, is determined by the lines enclosing it. Line bears an important relationship to shape, but shape connotes more than the outline of an area. It deals with the dimension of depth as well as height and width.

When the lines of a form are straight and of equal length, width, and thickness, the result is a cube. When the length is greater than the width for a given depth, an oblong shape results.

But when curved lines occur in a form, imagination can call up an infinite variety of shapes depending upon the curvature of the lines and their lengths. A sphere appears round no matter how it is viewed. The enclosing lines, smooth and evenly curved, suggest completeness. An ovoid object such as an egg, for example, gives a more complex appearance than the sphere because

Figure 4–3. In this shift, strong oppositional lines suggest strength and sturdiness. A St. Laurent design, showing the Mondrian influence. (Photograph courtesy of *Harper's Bazaar*.)

the degree of curvature varies. One end is more bulbous than the other, and the length can be distinguished from the width or depth. This greater complexity makes the ovoid more interesting than the sphere.

No better example of beautiful form or shape can be found than that of the well-proportioned human figure. The contours that flow smoothly from one area to the next, the pleasing relationship of the larger areas to the smaller, result in beauty recognized by artists of every period.

A dress, too, has form or shape. Not only does the observer take note of the silhouette, but he immediately establishes depth in the design. Unconsciously, he carries the waistline and the hemline around the figure, although at first glance he sees only a portion of each. A dress design naturally must take into account the same dimensions that relate to form—height, width, and depth.

The outline of a garment, its silhouette, is the first thing noticed. The silhouette indicates skirt length, the placing or omission of the waistline, and the presence or absence of fullness or flare in the skirt. It also indicates the snugness or looseness of the blouse through the torso, and the style of sleeves or their omission. A change in the mode is at once reflected in the silhouette of a garment.

A study of fashions between 1760 and 1937 shows that only three skirt silhouettes existed in those more than 175 years and that each, with modifications, recurred in the same order once in a 100-year period. These silhouettes were the straight or tubular skirt, the bell-shaped or bouffant skirt, and the bustle skirt with considerable fullness swept to the back (Figure 4–4).

Today, the tubular and the A-line silhouette are seen most often, but bouffant and bustle effects are found in designs for

Figure 4–4. Skirt silhouettes that recur in Western fashions: *left*, the bustle back; *center*, the tubular; and *right*, the bouffant. (Sketches by Evelyn Undorf.)

evening costumes and bridal gowns along with gowns whose skirts are as straight as an architectural column.

The details within the silhouette may be so varied as to make their classification impossible. The lines and the spaces which they establish give variety and individuality to the design. Whereas fashion once approved great elaboration in a dress design, today it apparently prefers the virtual absence of detail. The beauty in today's costume often depends upon skillful placement of line and excellent fit. The sleek and simple dress may require one or two accents of jewelry to add interest and avoid too severe an effect.

A good dress design is always related to body structure. It emphasizes good points and minimizes poor ones in the wearer. It generally follows the body's contours, but does not exaggerate those contours in any way. The design provides interesting variety, yet seems unified. It reflects the purpose for which the garment was intended as well as a currently accepted style.

Color: Visual Sensation from Light Waves

Color is a quality of visual sensation called forth when the eye is stimulated by radiant energy, that is, by light waves of certain lengths and intensities.

For many people, young and old, color is the design element to which they react first and most strongly. Children at an early age enjoy color and learn to distinguish hues. The dynamic quality of color is unmistakable: it has a powerful effect on the emotions; it expresses feelings or moods and meets a need inherent in human nature.

In choosing a wardrobe or planning the decoration of a room, perhaps the first decision anyone makes concerns color. The way in which color is used is an important measure of taste.

What causes the difference in hues? Children learn that light passed through a prism is broken into various colors: red, orange, yellow, green, blue, and violet. Scientists have shown that each of these colors, component parts of sunlight, is produced by a light wave of a specific length, different from that of all others. Red is produced by the longest visible ray, yellow by the shortest.

The human eye can distinguish one hue from another because of the reflection of light of a particular wavelength from the surface of an object. Although white light is made up of all colors, a surface is selective in its affinity for light rays and absorbs practically all of the visible rays except the wavelength producing the color. A fabric appears blue because its surface reflects only the blue ray and absorbs all other wavelengths.

More than one system has been devised to designate color. An important one is the Munsell system, recognized for its contribution toward standardizing colors. When accuracy in the measurement of hue, value, and intensity of a color is essential, the Munsell system of color analysis is employed. Manufacturers and scientists value this system because they can use it to describe and duplicate any color precisely.

Another color system is the Prang system, suggested by Sir Isaac Newton; it is often taught in public schools and widely used by artists who work with pigments. As fabrics are for the most part pigment dyed, our discussion of color will be in terms of this system.

The Prang system divides colors into three *primaries*—yellow, red, and blue—and three *secondaries*—orange (a mixture of yellow and red), green (yellow mixed with blue), and purple (red mixed with blue). The *complementary* color of any given color is its opposite in the color wheel, as shown in Figure 4–5 (page 73). When complementary colors such as red and green are mixed in paint, the result is gray; when they are woven tightly together in fabric, the result is a fabric that is almost gray in effect. But two complementary colors used side by side in a larger area will give emphasis to each other. Think of what orange and blue do to each other when the two colors are used together.

Three attributes make it possible to describe or duplicate a color accurately. They are *hue, value,* and *intensity. Hue* is the name of a color, as yellow, green, or violet. *Value* is the lightness or darkness of a color. Values range from the lightest tints to the darkest shades that can be distinguished from black. *Intensity* refers to the purity or the grayness of the color. A color is of high intensity when it has the quality of that color in the rainbow. The medium and low intensities of a color are more subdued, approaching gray, and are therefore easier to use, especially in dress. Pure colors are often trying to the wearer and difficult to use successfully in a color harmony.

Color has an emotional impact on people, a fact which should be considered in wardrobe planning. Much of our feeling about colors has been transmitted to us through our environment and is part of our cultural heritage. Primitives associate yellow, orange, and red with light, warmth, and life-giving blood; hence they think of these colors as cheerful and lively. Green, the color of growing things, came to symbolize youth, vigor, and hope. Blue was associated with the sky, where heaven, the dwelling place of the Deity, was thought to be, and so came to symbolize love, peace, and fidelity. In our culture white represents chastity and purity, and is usually chosen by brides for a first wedding. In some parts of the world, however, as among the Chinese, white has been used traditionally for mourning and red, symbol of joy, is the favorite for weddings. In some cultures yellow symbolizes jealousy; in others, treachery or cowardice. The idiom "he has a yellow streak in him" is one surviving trace of this unpleasant association. Purple has been much used through the centuries for royalty and the judiciary; thus it connotes dignity, justice.

Although color symbolism influences personal reactions to the various colors, people tend to attach their own meaning to a color, depending upon their past experience and associations. One person may dislike lavender, another green, because those colors suggest something unpleasant. "Lavender looks old and musty," the one may say, while the other may declare, "Green looks like poison."

Preference for a color and aversion to it are often highly subjective reactions. If a person considers a certain color unbecoming to him, he is likely to feel that it is an ugly color. Actually, no color is ugly. Prejudice against a given color is often built up through trivial incidents. A person can increase his appreciation and enjoyment of color by observing how color is used in rare old textiles and fine modern fabrics, in paintings and good color prints. The artist or the skilled designer of textiles works with every color, combining them in such a way as to achieve a beautiful whole—using the dull colors as shadows in the pattern, the bright ones as accents.

When considering colors for dress, let your taste be guided at first by the taste of those with wide experience. Continued experiments to express your own personality through color develop the ability to create beautiful effects that are becoming and at the same time distinctive.

The color wheel, shown in Figure 4–5, is the basis for the Prang color system. On it appear twelve normal colors, that is, colors of full intensity as found in the rainbow: yellow at the top and red and blue at the points of an equilateral triangle placed within the circle. The secondary colors—orange, green, and violet—are placed at the points of another equilateral triangle, with violet at the bottom midway between blue and red, green midway between blue and yellow, and orange between red and yellow. Between each primary and its nearest secondary color is an intermediate or tertiary color. For example, between yellow and green is yellow-green; between green and blue, blue-green; and so on around the circle.

Each of these twelve colors has a range of values from light to dark: white, high light, light, low light, middle value, high dark, dark, low dark, and black. Each color has a wide range of intensity: full intensity, half intensity, gray, and many steps between these intervals.

White is said to be the presence of all colors. For light rays visible in the spectrum, this is true. But when all colors *in pigments* are combined, a neutral gray results, rather than white. Black is said to be the absence of color.

Often, the colors on the wheel are divided into warm and cool colors. Those colors between yellow and violet are classified as warm—including the oranges, reds, and red-violets; those found on the opposite side of the wheel are considered cool—the yellow-greens, greens, blues, and blue-violets.

The art of combining colors to produce a pleasing effect is one that can be learned only by careful study of the effects of varying hues, values, and intensities, one with the other. A few precepts can serve as guides, however:

1. In combining two colors that differ in value or intensity, use the stronger one for a smaller area, and in such a way as to emphasize some good feature, as a pretty face or a trim waist. Using different colors in equal amounts has a monotonous effect.

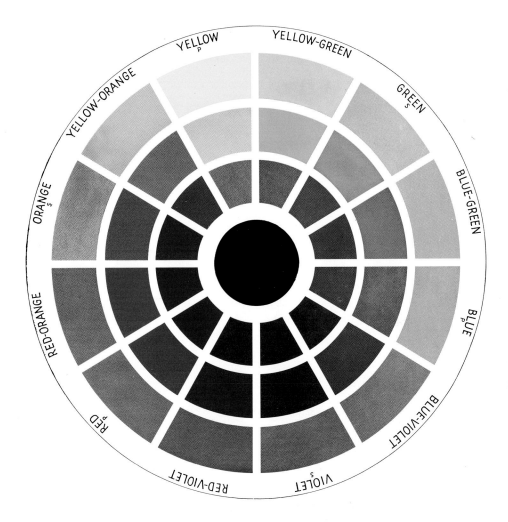

Figure 4–5. The color wheel, made up of twelve colors, basis of the Prang color system.

2. To make a light color seem still lighter, or brighter, combine it with a dark color. The light color also makes dark colors seem still darker by contrast. No contrast is so sharp as black and white; the black looks blacker and the white, whiter for their association.
3. If a bright color is paired with one that is much grayed, the grayed color will be further neutralized.
4. Bring together different values of the same color from light to dark or from a high to a grayed intensity. This results in a pleasing color harmony, especially if the components are used in different-sized areas as well as in different values.

The first three of the precepts concern achieving effects through contrast, one of the important ways of combining colors effectively.

Some writers on color schemes prefer to discuss them in terms of the various kinds of colors used:

1. Complementary colors, those opposite each other on the color wheel
2. Analogous colors, those next to each other on the wheel, taking care not to cross over a primary color
3. Monochromatic colors, different values and intensities of the the same color
4. Triad colors, those at the points of an equilateral triangle on the wheel: the primaries—red, blue, yellow; the secondaries—green, orange, violet; and the tertiaries—red-violet, yellow-orange, blue-green, yellow-green, blue-violet, red-orange

Combining two strongly contrasting colors requires skill if harmony is to be achieved. Success depends upon the use of varying intensities and values.

Texture: Appearance and Feel of a Material

Texture, another element of design, refers to the appearance and feel of the surface of a material. Its interpretation depends upon the senses of sight and touch. Like color, line, and form, texture inspires some degree of emotional response.

Although the qualities of a texture are most readily recognized through touch, we know at once how a given material feels without touching it because of previous experience with it. Texture may be rough or smooth, pliable or stiff, lustrous or dull, soft or harsh, coarse or fine—to list but a few of the words used in describing this element.

Texture is perhaps one of the most significant factors in a design. In a fabric it can be used appropriately or inappropriately for a given purpose. A firm, closely woven fabric made of strong cotton yarns promises satisfactory wear in sport skirt. Its surface is smooth and firm, one that insures a well-tailored appearance. A fabric of the same fiber made with loosely woven, nubby, and lightly twisted yarns, may have a beautiful surface quality but will not suggest utility. Its irregular surface gives it drapability, depth of color, and richness. Such a fabric will be reserved for use in a design with soft lines and perhaps deep folds, and one that will not be subjected to rugged wear.

Because of the great variety of textile construction processes developed by modern technology, no specific texture can be associated with any fiber. Wool can be made into a sheer crepe that has the draping qualities of a fabric made of silk; or it can be manipulated so as to produce a broadcloth that is glossy and supple. It also can be made into a rough-textured tweed suitable for a man's tailored jacket.

Similarly, a fiber such as cotton appears in fabrics that differ widely as to texture. Such differences in the final product result both from the quality inherent in the fiber and from the way it is handled. Variations in weave, new finishes, and methods of bonding two layers of fabric together have altered the appearance of cloth until it is difficult to identify the fiber from which any given fabric has been made. The blending of several kinds of fibers into a yarn can produce a texture that makes the fabric appear to be wool when actually little or no wool is in it.

The appearance of a fabric is largely determined by what its surface does to the light that plays on it. A fabric with a deep nap, such as fleece coating or a velvet with its raised pile, appears darker and much more luxurious than a piece of satin dyed the same color. Little light is reflected from a pile surface. In fact, the multiple reflections within the fabric deepen the color and give it added richness. Satin reflects light because of the unbroken length of its surface yarns, which dilutes its color. The fabric appears less soft than the velvet even though it is made of the same quality of silk fiber.

The texture of a fabric determines the quality known as "hand," that is, its characteristic body as felt in the hand. The terms used to describe hand relate to the feel of the fabric, its resilience, flexibility, crispness, compressibility, stretchiness, and compactness—whether it is of a dense or an open structure. As shown in Figure 4–6, a stiff fabric like taffeta results in a silhouette different from that achieved with a sheer fabric like chiffon.

Certainly, the hand of a a fabric influences its use. A beautiful effect is created when the fabric has body that is consistent with the idea of the design. For a bouffant effect, where the fullness starts at the waist and is controlled by gathers or soft

Figure 4–6. *Left,* a stiff fabric like taffeta increases the apparent size of the wearer. *Right,* a soft fabric like chiffon adds little or no bulk to the figure, but because it clings it may reveal figure faults. (Sketches by Evelyn Undorf.)

pleats, a stiff, crisp fabric is required: taffeta, organza, organdie, moire, or slipper satin. For a draped effect, a heavy crepe will lend itself to manipulation on the bias, as well as on the straight of the fabric, because of its great flexibility. Only when the lengthwise and the crosswise yarns in the fabric are well balanced will the deep curves formed by the drapery be smooth and graceful.

For the design that depends upon soft, straight-hanging folds for its interest, many fabrics would be effective: a soft, sheer crepe of wool or silk, chiffon, voile, or tissue gingham. Textures that are rough and heavy are suitable for sports or utility wear. Smooth, lightweight fabrics are appropriate for dressier occasions.

Fabrics that have an inherent coarse or rough texture, such as tweeds, give a bulkier appearance to the wearer. They are well suited to the person who has an athletic figure and whose movements suggest vitality and strength. Smooth-textured fabrics are better suited to the small-boned petite figure.

The designer can use contrast in textures with good effect if he is careful to avoid inconsistencies. So long as the combination seems unified, he can use variety to create interest. Leather or wooden buttons make a pleasing trim for a brown tweed coat. The polished surface of the buttons complements the coarse texture of the woolen cloth, and their color blends with that of the fabric; a feeling of sturdiness carries through from fabric to trim. If the buttons were of glass or mother-of-pearl, their inconsistency with the tweed would be most evident. Such buttons seem to belong on a finer, smoother, and more delicate fabric.

Occasionally, a designer will use jeweled buttons on a tweed suit or coat. In doing so he flouts the principle of unity, hoping through variety and contrast to gain approval for his creation. Such violations of design principles rarely enjoy much success.

DESIGN PRINCIPLES

The choice of beautiful and becoming dress depends upon an understanding of the principles of composition that govern the creation of any design. Whether it be the painting of a picture, the choosing of harmonious furnishings for a room, or the clothing of the body with a dress and its costume accessories—jewelry, gloves, hat, and shoes—the principles of composition must be employed if the effect is to be pleasing.

These principles are universal. Testing the dress of any culture by them reveals the extent to which the people of that culture have organized their ideas concerning design. Spontaneous, instinctive use of strong color and line may produce a fresh design even when it flouts the principles employed by the sophisticated designer. In this chapter principles long followed by the designers of Europe and of the United States are discussed.

To have unity, all the parts of a design must seem to belong together. When the designer fails to establish oneness in his creation, both he and the viewer are left with a feeling of dissatisfaction. But when he gives the principles of composition due consideration, he satisfies an important law of aesthetics and creates unity. The wearer and his clothes then seem to belong together, and neither his physical self nor his dress nor his personality traits dominate the picture. Harmony exists between the wearer and his clothes.

These principles upon which unity in a design are based are *dominance, proportion, balance,* and *rhythm.*

Dominance: Emphasis on One Feature

The principle of dominance calls for emphasizing the important feature of a design and subordinating all other features. Henry Poore points up the need for unifying a design through the use of dominance: "All major arts insist on having a captain and on rating his forces in a descending scale from this supremacy." [1]

Often, a costume will present so many points of emphasis as to violate the principle of dominance. One example is a dress that is trimmed with a band of contrasting color around the collar and down the center front to the hem, on the cuffs, and on patch pockets on each side of the blouse front and skirt front. Such a design leaves the observer with a feeling of confusion. No one feature dominates.

A similar dress having as its only trim a contrasting band around the neck that continues in a line from neck to hip pleases

Figure 4–7. A dominant line placed so as to center attention on an attractive feature, such as the face, helps to unify the wearer and her costume. (Sketches by Evelyn Undorf.)

the eye by its very directness and simplicity (Figure 4–7). The wearer may well add either earrings or a bracelet in the color of the binding and yet not seem overdressed.

Another example of emphasis used in a subtle way may be seen in an ensemble for party wear. A dress of sheer white, cut on flattering lines and worn with a pair of sparkling or colorful earrings, will draw attention to the wearer's eyes and make them the dominant note. Any other accessories should be subordinated in size and brilliance of color.

When a girl wears a costume so striking that she herself appears insignificant, she has failed to realize that she should be the center of interest and that her costume should play a minor role. She can be overshadowed by color that is too strong, design lines that run counter to those of her figure, or bold stripes or plaids. As a result, those who observe the total effect will fail to find unity between her and her dress.

Monotony results when too many accents compete for attention and when accents are too often repeated. To hold the observer's attention, and to give him a sense of satisfaction in what he sees, the significant feature must be evident and must be supported by features of less importance. Individual parts of a design are less important than the whole.

Many women make the mistake of having too many points of emphasis in one costume: a bright scarf at the throat, a conspicuous pin at the shoulder, decorative buttons marching in a double row down the front to the hemline, a tricky touch at the cuffs. The result is that nothing is emphasized. It is a good idea to

Figure 4–8. Dominant lines focus attention on some part of the costume. The broad collar widens the shoulders. Large pockets accent the hips. A hemline trim draws attention to the knees. Not everyone can afford to emphasize these areas. (Sketches by Evelyn Undorf.)

decide on one center of interest and then subordinate the rest. For example, use the double row of buttons for its slenderizing effect and skip the rest—or perhaps have just one other point of secondary interest, as the scarf in a muted color. The eye will follow a dominant line, as is evident in Figure 4–8.

The successful designer of a costume creates one main center of interest supported by minor points of interest. Unusual shapes and details serve as accents to attract attention and lead the eye on to the point of major emphasis.

Table 4–1

Device for Rating a Costume for Overuse of Accessories

Articles of Apparel	*Point Value*
Shoes	
Plain	1
With sling back	1 additional
With buckle, bow, or strap	1 each
Hose	
Plain	1
Clocked, colored, textured, figured, or dimensionalized	1 additional
Dress	
Solid color	1
Figured	1 additional
Buttons, not of self-fabric	1 additional
Belt or buckle, not of self-fabric	1 additional
Collar and/or cuffs of contrasting color	1 additional
Suit	2
Buttons, not of self-fabric	1 additional
Belt, not of self-fabric	1 additional
Piping or other trim of different color	1 additional
Blouse of different color	1 additional
Necklace	1
Broach or pin	1
Earrings	1
Glasses	1
With dark or decorative rims	1 additional
Gloves	
Plain	1
With decorative stitching	1 additional
Hat	
Trimmed with self-material	1
Other trim as ribbon, veiling, flowers	1 for each
Wristwatch	1
Bracelets	1 for each
Rings	1 for each
Scarf	1
Purse	
Plain	1
Clasp, trim, or frame different	1 additional

Many women tend to overdress, failing to realize that deciding what *not* to wear is as important as deciding *what* to wear.

Whenever the student dresses for class, for the street, or for a party, he should put together items of an ensemble which fulfill the aesthetic requirements of emphasis as well as those of other principles of good design. No matter how lovely the individual items in the ensemble, the total effect will be confusing and lacking in good taste if too many details are bidding for attention.

The Rule of Fourteen devised by Eleanor King is helpful in checking an ensemble for overuse of accessories.[2] Any costume totaling more than fourteen of the points listed in Table 4–1 is almost sure to violate the standards of good taste. The shorter the skirt of the costume, the fewer the accessories allowed. For a costume with the skirt above the knees, the permissible limit would be ten. Actually many good ensembles with skirts of conservative length score as low as eight or ten points. The final Study Suggestion at the end of the chapter shows the table's use.

Proportion: Relation of One Part to Another

In a unified design the relationship between the major and the minor parts of the design and between each of these parts and the whole is governed by the principle of proportion. Proportion is the relation of one part to another, in magnitude or degree. When this relation is satisfying, good proportion exists. The proportions of the Venus de Milo have long been recognized as an expression of a satisfying relationship: the arms and the legs to the torso; the arms to the legs; the hands to the arms; the feet to the legs; the head to the total height and width of the figure.

A pleasing costume has good proportions as illustrated in Figure 4–9. The art world has followed the teaching of the Greeks in this as in most other aspects of design. The Greeks taught that proportions of two to three or three to five are more pleasing than are two to two (equal areas) or two to four (one twice the size of the other). They also considered the relation of parts to be pleasing if the smaller area was to the larger as the larger was to the whole—such as three is to five as five is to the whole —in this case, eight. Greek architecture and sculpture show how these laws of proportion were applied.

Figure 4–10. Note the relative proportions of head and hair, of jacket, of miniskirt, and of legs. The effect of this ensemble is less than pleasing. (Sketch by Evelyn Undorf.)

Figure 4–9. Two well-proportioned dress designs. *Left,* the lines have a pleasing effect as they break up the smooth-fitting shift. *Right,* skillful placing of the yoke and the width of the peplum and collar result in a well-proportioned suit. (Sketches by Evelyn Undorf.)

The discriminating person is disturbed by the sight of a woman dressed in a suit whose jacket length from neck to lower edge is the same as the length of the skirt that shows below. A two-to-three or a three-to-five relationship would be much more pleasing.

When skirts are extremely short, a trend popular in the 1920's and the mid-1960's, the waistline too often bisects the dress. Designers sensitive to good proportion usually try to avoid this disturbing effect either by eliminating the belt or by shifting the waistline to the hipbone or to a point above the natural waist for an empire effect. The half-belt is another device used to avoid the two-to-two relationship. In Figure 4–10 the designer has failed to achieve good proportions.

Scale is another aspect of proportion. It is concerned with the relationship of the sizes of the various parts of a design to each other, and the relationship of the entire ensemble to the wearer. To be pleasing there cannot be too great a difference in scale.

The small, feminine woman who chooses an oversized handbag or who wears bold jewelry as part of her ensemble has failed to keep size relations consistent with her own proportions. Equally inconsistent is the use of small, insignificant pieces of jewelry or a tiny handbag or hat by the large woman, particularly one who is overweight. The smallness of these accessories, by contrast, emphasizes the wearer's size.

Within a dress design the various parts may contribute to a pleasing effect or may distract from it because they are out of scale. Only when the size of collar, cuffs, or other trimming areas bears the right relationship to the dress as a whole can the principle of proportion be satisfied.

The coiffure is inevitably a part of a woman's ensemble, one of the most important factors in her general appearance. Since it is part of the ensemble it must be in harmony with the dress and the occasion—simple and conservative for general wear, more elaborate if desired for special occasions. Sometimes, however, it violates one of the design principles, that of proportion.

Hairstyles too often are adopted without consideration of the face which they will frame, the body build and contours, or the costume with which they will be worn. The bouffant hairdress of the early 1960's, for example, looked grotesque on small, delicately featured girls and women because it was out of proportion with their bodies.

In the mid-1960's shoulder-length or longer straight locks were worn hanging free, a hairdress equally trying but posing a different design problem. Long straight lines, which contradict the curves of the youthful face, predominated, with the result that the wearer lost all appearance of animation; she looked wan and tired.

"Concern with the coiffure is one of the most intense interests of mankind," declares the anthropologist E. Adamson Hoebel.

"We know not when the earliest prehistoric men and women first began to play with cranial hair. All recent primitives from those of the lowest cultures to the highest treat the hair. All civilized people do likewise. . . . In culture after culture, it serves to symbolize social position and to differentiate sex." [3] Cave paintings of European nomads more than 20,000 years ago indicate that the peoples of that distant past placed great emphasis upon the feminine hairdo.

Since concern about hair treatment is universal, it deserves the attention of students of costume.

Balance: Satisfying the Need for Equilibrium

Balance is the principle of design which satisfies the need for a sense of equilibrium. As in every other art form, a costume should have balance so that the elements in one area make no stronger demand for the attention of the observer than do the elements of the opposite area. The elements of the two areas need not be exact duplicates. A small breast pocket on the left side of a center closing can balance a large pocket on the right side of a skirt front if the blouse pocket is given a decorative touch, as an appliquéd shield or a pin.

The two attention-getting features need not be equal in size and quality, but they should be made to seem of equal importance, as in the example of the pockets. The pin or appliqué gave enough importance to the little pocket to make it seem equal to the big one.

If the right half of a design is practically a mirror reflection of the left half, that is, if it repeats the left half in reverse order, the design is said to have *formal balance*. If there is no duplication of details in the two halves yet the two exert an equal pull on the attention, the design is said to have *informal balance*. The dress designs in Figure 4–11 illustrate balance.

A designer might trim the bodice of a soft crepe evening dress with a band of self-colored beading, running it from the right shoulder to a point at armscye level on the left. The iridescence of the beads would provide the only note of contrast. To balance this trim, the designer might drape the fabric at the left side of the skirt front in soft, diagonal folds. The beaded left side closing of the bodice would be the most important accent of the dress,

Figure 4–11. *Left,* dress design illustrating formal balance. *Right,* design showing informal balance. (Sketches by Evelyn Undorf.)

yet the skirt drapery would balance it because of its larger area. The dress would have informal balance.

A feeling of balance is also achieved in a design if the base of a costume suggests stability sufficient to carry the weight of the upper parts. Most designers consider that the lower part of a costume should be darker than the top, rather than lighter, if there is to be any difference in value. Then it will seem to be stable, to have balance. In general, the skirt is darker than the blouse and shoes are darker than the suit or dress. But designers sometimes experiment successfully with flouting this rule, achieving new and interesting effects.

Rhythm: Related Movement

Rhythm is related movement. In costume design, as in music, rhythm is essential for a pleasing result. Lack of rhythm leaves the beholder with a vaguely dissatisfied feeling, even when he cannot quite put his finger on the cause. There is rhythm in poetry—at least in the conventional metered poetry of the classics, if not in some modern poetry. Rhythm can be seen in the spirals of a seashell and in the waves breaking on the shore.

A dress, too, has rhythm if the designer has arranged details so that the eye is led smoothly from one to the next throughout the garment. Rhythm is felt in the flow of line, in the drapery of a soft evening dress, in the rows of buttons or bows used to fasten a garment, in vertical or horizontal pin tucks repeated in the design, in the succession of different values of a color in a chiffon scarf, in the alternation of colors or lines in a striped fabric, in the radiation of lines in a sunburst-pleated skirt.

Figure 4–12. Rhythm has been achieved in both blouse designs: *left,* by repetition of horizontal tucks; *right,* by the use of curved lines in the collar and in the front closing. (Sketches by Evelyn Undorf.)

Rhythm is evident in any orderly design whether it is achieved by repetition of line, gradation of color or sizes, alternation, progressive change, or radiation. The blouse designs in Figure 4–12 are examples of related movement, as is the bustle skirt of Figure 4–4, with its deep folds in the back.

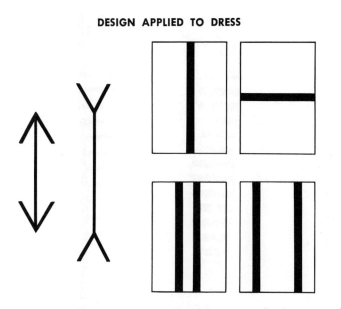

Figure 4–13. The length of a line may appear to be longer or shorter than it actually is depending on its association with other lines. *Left,* the two vertical lines are the same length but the one with arrowheads appears much shorter. *Top right,* the rectangle containing a horizontal bar appears shorter than its duplicate containing a vertical bar. *Lower right,* placing the two vertical bars close together adds to apparent length.

APPLICATION OF DESIGN PRINCIPLES

Most women know that self-improvement can be achieved through dress. But not every woman is able to select a costume that is flattering, one that will hide or minimize details in her face or figure that are less than perfect. Experiments with fads and with the frequent changes of fashion often bring no improvement in her personal appearance.

Only through adhering to design principles can a woman find the dress that really does something for her. According to George Dearborn, a psychologist who has made a study of clothes, "The way we clothe ourselves is one of the surest indices of substantial intelligence." [4]

Designs can create illusions in the mind of an observer—impressions that are quite different from reality. For example, a designer can make a line seem shorter or longer than it is by the way he arranges nearby lines. The two lines in Figure 4–13 are

Figure 4–14. The width of the stripe and the spaces between can create an illusion either of height or of breadth. Generally, vertical stripes suggest greater height, but not always. (Sketches by Evelyn Undorf.)

actually the same length, but one seems shorter than the other. A designer can use stripes, either horizontal or vertical, to produce an effect of plumpness or height. This is accomplished through variations in their width—as indicated in Figure 4–14.

Vertical stripes usually give an illusion of height, but not always. If the vertical stripes of a dress are of equal width and of alternately light and dark colors, they make the wearer seem more plump than she really is. Horizontal stripes usually give an illusion of breadth. If light and dark stripes of a dress are of equal width, they make the wearer appear rounder. But if the dark stripes are much narrower than the light ones, as in the second figure from the right in Figure 4–14, the stripes suggest height.

Let us consider some of the ways to avoid the pitfalls of wardrobe assembling.

Prescriptions for Figure Faults

Before a girl starts shopping for the garments needed to fill the gaps in her wardrobe, it is a good idea for her to don a bathing suit and to face herself in the mirror to determine her physical type, what figure assets to play up, and what defects to hide so far as possible.

The chubby girl, for example, needs to steer clear of clothes that increase her apparent size. A professional woman of our acquaintance still recalls her first purchase as a college freshman without parental guidance. That purchase was a beautiful plaid sport coat of an imported fabric, but it made her seem even more plump than she was. The material was nubby in texture and of light, bright colors, and the back flared from the shoulders. It was much too sporty for even semiformal occasions. A dark plaid in a smooth fabric would have been less trying. But a coat of classic lines, perhaps in a muted heather color, would have taken her many more places and would have been flattering, even if it did not satisfy her desire for something gay.

The chubby girl should wear inconspicuous clothes, simple, semifitted coats and dresses with lengthwise or diagonal lines, perhaps buttoned down the center front. A slight flare in the skirt will make her hips and bust seem less broad. Taboo for her are yokes, flounces, dropped shoulders and bouffant sleeves, contrasting cuffs, full-gathered skirts, and skirts and blouses in contrasting colors. The designs in Figure 4–15 have lines that create a feeling of added height.

As for fabrics, shiny and stiff materials increase the chubby girl's apparent size, whereas dull-surfaced fabrics that drape nicely make her seem smaller. Lightweight, smooth-textured materials tend to have a slimming effect. A bright print will prove most successful if the background is dark or neutral or keyed to one of the colors of the printed design, and if the lines in the print lead the eyes up and down. For colors, cool hues and dark values, somewhat grayed, are most flattering. Garments worn by the chubby girl should have an easy, never a snug, fit.

The tall, thin girl needs lines that lead the eyes in a horizontal movement. The bell and the bustle skirt silhouettes are flatter-

Figure 4–15. For a taller, thinner look, keep the eye moving upward to create a feeling of height. (Sketches by Evelyn Undorf.)

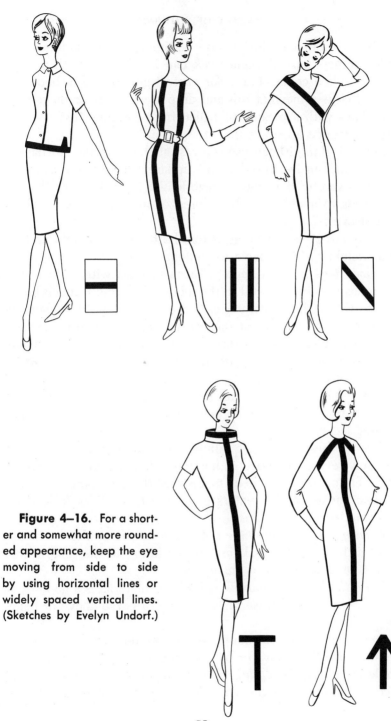

Figure 4–16. For a shorter and somewhat more rounded appearance, keep the eye moving from side to side by using horizontal lines or widely spaced vertical lines. (Sketches by Evelyn Undorf.)

ing, but a tubular outline is also becoming when modified with tunics or peplums. *A bony neck* can be covered with a scarf, cowl, or rolled collar, and *a flat bust* disguised with a bodice or blouse that is somewhat full and draped vertically or diagonally, or perhaps with a pleated or frilled front. Figure 4–16 suggests ways to reduce apparent height.

The tall, thin girl can use contrast at the waistline, perhaps in a wide-crush girdle, to reduce her apparent height, and can wear her skirts shorter than the average length if her legs are shapely. She needs to avoid severely tailored or mannish suits and long, tight sleeves.

There are other figure faults that both the overweight and the underweight girl may have to contend with.

Bowed legs need to be kept inconspicuous with a skirt worn as long as possible but still in the mode. Wearing it much longer than current fashion tolerates only draws attention to the hemline —and the legs. Accents at the waist or the face can make them the center of interest and distract attention from the lower part of the costume. Any kind of trim at the bottom of the skirt or coat obviously is taboo.

A prominent abdomen can be minimized by center panels in the skirt, by boleros that dip below the belt, or by long, straight-hanging jackets.

A large bust needs soft fullness and draping over it. Tightness only reveals the size. A horizontal line across the shoulders and a flaring hem can help to distract the attention elsewhere; cardigan jackets and sweaters give transitional lines to lead the eyes from shoulder to hip.

A sway back and prominent derrière can be hidden by having the waistline dip in the back and by filling in the hollow with fullness or a peplum or a bustle effect.

For a thick waist a narrow belt of self-material is a good treatment. So, too, are blouse lines that dip or curve above or below the waistline.

Heavy upper arms should not be emphasized by a sleeve length above the elbow, or by a sleeveless dress that exposes the whole arm. And *heavy legs* should not invite extra attention by decoration at or near the skirt hem, or by an overly short skirt.

Prescriptions for Facial Types

Anyone whose features are less than perfect and who is unhappy over that fact can apply some of the art principles just discussed to minimize them. The neckline, the coiffure, and the hat can do much to alter pleasantly the picture one presents to the world.

For a short neck and a heavy jaw choose a rather wide V-neck to add apparent length through leading the eye on down the dress. If the V is too narrow, though, the jaw will appear even wider because of the contrast. Bateau, Peter Pan, and turtle necks would be poor choices. In hats, an upswept brim that is broader than the chin-line will reduce the chin's apparent size. The pill box and flat little hat perched on top of the head would be unbecoming.

For a long, thin face wear a scoop neckline, one that is U-shaped, to add width to both throat and face. Fluff the hair out at the cheeks, and wear a hat with a brim that tilts somewhat to distract the eyes from that long forehead-to-chin line, not a brimless hat or one with a táll crown!

For a large nose try a hat with a brim that extends beyond the nose in profile, and bangs that curve out from the face. Avoid center hair parts, hair pulled back from the brows, and flat crowned hat styles.

For a round face avoid repetition of that same curved line in collar and neckline. Instead, use a rather wide V-line to minimize it. Or wear a hat with a tall crown. Pancake hats and round halo hats are definitely off limits.

For a double chin provide interesting details in hair treatment above the ears and wear a hat with an irregular crown or brim. To distract attention from *a receding chin* draw attention to the eyes, if they are attractive, perhaps through earrings, or through a hat with an upturned brim. Wear the hair in a soft arrangement low on the neck, but not down onto the shoulders or short and fluffy.

Reduce the apparent height of *a high forehead* through bangs or a low, swooping wave or a hat that partly covers the forehead. Hair pulled tightly back from the brows would, of course, emphasize forehead height. *A low forehead* is not as easy to handle. Try a center part for the hair or an upswept pompadour. A smallish hat set back off the face will be most successful. Off-the-face hats and flat, pancake styles will emphasize *a piquant uptilted nose.* Big hats would tend to dwarf such features.

Dress Your Type!

Dress your type, both in personality and in coloring, designers urge. If you are outgoing and vivacious, bright colors and splashy prints would be in character. If you are shy and hate crowds, subdued colors and modest patterns would be more appropriate.

Coloring and physique have to be considered, too. Even if a girl is the life of the party, she cannot afford to wear vivid colors if her hair and skin are a neutral blonde color. The vivid color could make her look washed out and her skin take on the tone of putty. She would find intermediate hues more flattering than raw primary colors—say a grayed green-blue or blue-green. She still has a wide range of colors to select from—turquoise to bottle green to midnight blue, as well as off-whites and some pastels. The darker values seem to clear her skin through contrast.

If a girl is buxom, splashy prints and vivid hues only make her look larger. She can dramatize herself in some other way—for example, by using the color she likes best in a somewhat grayed value and in a slenderizing design, perhaps combined with a handsome piece of jewelry. Dark, dull, cool colors are the best slenderizers, of course. Warm colors are more conspicuous than cool ones, especially those that are near full intensity and are of middle value. The large girl looks larger than ever in vivid colors, especially in the warm range of colors. She uses them most successfully just for accents.

Making the Most of Color

In general, the designer urges: When you select a color for your clothes, consider first your hair and skin. They are more important in your color scheme than are your eyes, chiefly because they make up a much larger area. Even if a girl's eyes are her best feature, she can select a dress and coat color to suit her hair, then put near her face a hat, headband, scarf, or pin that is the color of her eyes but a bit lighter or duller to intensify their color.

For practically every type of blonde, becoming color choices include green-blues and blue-greens; but *the ash blonde* needs to keep to the darker values, which will clear her skin and provide some contrast. She cannot use many vivid colors successfully since they offer too much competition with her blonde hair, and may make her look washed out.

The blue-violet to red-violet range is good for blondes but needs to be grayed for the flaxen haired, and darkened for the ash blonde. Obviously beige is not a color for a blonde whose coloring is already a monotone.

The girl who is suntanned or has a sallow skin needs to avoid intense or luminous blues and violets, as they bring out unattractive yellow and orange tones in the skin. The blonde *with a florid skin* should shun the bright green-blues and greens, since they intensify the red-violet skin tones.

For the girl with light hair, fair skin, and blue eyes, cool browns—that is, browns grayed with blue or purple—are good choices, especially if they are accented with violet or rose or blue-violet of a light value. The so-called *Irish blonde,* with fair skin and blue-black hair, has a wide range to select from, right around the color wheel from blue-green to red-violet, so long as she is careful to use values darker than her skin. Her best reds have a tinge of blue in them, and colors she can wear nicely are mauve, orchid, and periwinkle pastels, as well as clear grays, black, and white.

For red-haired girls, as for the wide range of blondes, the color prescription varies according to the hue of the hair— whether it is brick red, one of the red-gold colors, or dark auburn. Here, too, raw vivid colors in clothes compete with the brightness of the hair and make it appear dull; thus the darker hues are most successful for bright red hair and lighter hues for the rich, dark auburns. Browns, either darker or lighter than the hair, yellows, and yellow-greens are pleasing with red hair as are green-blues, but the cold blues and purples are not so pleasing.

The vivid brunette with a rich, creamy skin can wear practically any bright color as well as soft colors and of course black, white, and warm gray. She can wear successfully vivid prints on strongly contrasting backgrounds. If her hair is a somewhat lighter brown and her eyes are hazel, she cannot wear quite such vivid, warm colors; but bright, cool colors in the darker values are becoming, as are off-white and warm pastels that are darker than the skin.

The light-skinned brunette with brown eyes wears beautifully dark yellow-browns with gold or cream, red-browns with rose, and chocolate browns with violet-blues or turquoise.

For the olive-skinned brunette becoming colors are dull tones of yellow-green, mustard, yellow, ocher, copper, dull rust, and reds with accents of turquoise or lapis lazuli. She can also wear bright blue, wine, practically any green or blue-green, and turquoise. In general, it is a good idea to wear colors of a darker value than one's skin, though fashion currently likes to emphasize a suntanned skin with cool pastels.

The brunette whose skin is cool colored, pale with blue or green lights, will find the dark, cool colors or the light values in warm hues most becoming.

For a ruddy skin grayed colors, either light or dark, will be the best choices. If the skin is suntanned, the cool pastels and white will emphasize the tan, as pointed out in the discussion of the olive-skinned brunette. A girl with a sallow skin will be wise to steer clear of gray, yellow, yellow-green, tan, and purple, and to choose instead a red-brown or a dull blue or a cool green.

Cosmetics: Extenders of Color Choice

A girl who is unhappy with the color of her hair or skin can always change it, of course. With the wide variety of hair tints, bleaches, and wigs, and rouge, powder, and lipsticks, no woman is limited to the colors nature gave her—*if she is willing to work at the transformation and spend money for it!*

Expenditures in the United States for cosmetics mounted to $1.5 billion a year by 1960 [5]—a sum which may seem shocking to some observers of the American scene, but not to the psychologist or the anthropologist. "It is not the primitive but the uni-

versal man in us that accounts for this seeming extravagance,"
says one anthropologist. It can be traced to the human need for
favorable response from one's associates. "Cosmetics intensify
personality . . . [and] heighten the stimulus intensity of the
physical presence of one person upon the touch, smell, sight
and perhaps taste of others . . . usually of the opposite sex, but
not exclusively so." [6]

But color metamorphosis is both time consuming and expensive. Bleached or tinted hair looks most unattractive if it reveals
next to the scalp even an eighth of an inch of natural-colored
hair. Nature keys hair and skin together. Anyone who changes
the hair color but not the skin tone may get two colors that do
not harmonize, and thereby intensify her color problem. Makeup
has to extend to all the visible skin area, not just the face.

One final bit of advice: Before deciding on a tint or dye adventure, think through your present color problem carefully—
and how much your current wardrobe is tied to it. You may
decide that it makes better sense to get someone with good color
judgment to help you work out intriguing color schemes for the
hair and skin nature gave you.

The Basic Color for the Wardrobe

One of the most important steps to take in assembling a good
wardrobe is to decide on a basic color—the color background for
coats and suits—to which subsequent purchases can be keyed.
The girl who has a limited sum to spend may have to select one
basic color for year-round use, such as black, dark brown, navy
blue or gray—whichever is most becoming and pleasing. If she
has a little more to spend she can have two basic colors, say dark
brown for fall and winter, and navy for spring and summer. The
neutral colors—beige, light gray, tan, and taupe—combine well
with all these basic colors.

Having selected the background color for her wardrobe, a
girl's next problem is to decide on colors for the rest of her
clothes—the most flattering for her hair, her skin, and her eyes,
and at the same time in harmony with her personality type.

It is important to realize how colors affect mood. Certain
colors give a real lift, while others depress or even repel. Some

people may not be aware of how much color influences morale, but most of them undoubtedly have an emotional reaction to at least a few colors. The same color may have a different impact on different people, of course.

Sometimes, the color a person likes best is not the color which is most becoming to her. If so, she can use it for room accessories, perhaps for pillows or a wall hanging or a picture—or for nightwear or lounging garb.

Problem Figures

Women with figure defects can do much to disguise them by shrewd use of color and line, as shown in Table 4–2. This list is far from a complete catalog of figure defects. Actually, it summarizes some points scattered throughout this chapter. Study of the "Off Limits" list and the "Prescription" for treatment should suggest what you can do to handle your own specific problem.

Table 4–2

Figure Problems and Their Treatment

Figure Problem	Off Limits	Prescription
Stocky figure	Snug fit. Full skirt with bunchy gathers. Yokes and peplums. Wide sleeves and contrasting cuffs. Fussy trim, puff sleeves, bright colors. Fleecy coats, slacks.	Cool colors of muted intensity or grayed values of warm colors. Lengthwise and diagonal lines. Skirts flared or with gores. Coat-style dresses. Buttons down front. Self-material belts. Normal armholes. Cardigans. Heavy, large accessories.
Tall, thin figure	Lengthwise lines. Princess dress. Tight bodice and sleeves.	Short skirts, low heels. Brimmed hats. Long torso designs. Horizontal lines. Separates. Full, flounced skirts. Frilly collars. Capes. Wide belts. Deep armholes.
Wide hips	Tight, fitted skirt. Tube dress. Full skirt. Wide sleeves. Wide contrasting cuffs. Small hat.	Gored skirt or one flared toward hem. Lengthwise pleats and panels at or near center of skirt. Shallow skirt yoke. Short loose jacket. Shoulder emphasis.
Flat bust	Snug blouse.	Full blouse, bolero, or cape. Gathered, frilled, or pleated blouse front. Pockets. Deep yokes.

NOTES

1. Henry R. Poor, *Art Principles in Practice* (New York: G. P. Putnam's Sons, 1930), p. 36.
2. Eleanor King, *Glorify Yourself* (Englewood Cliffs, N. J.: Prentice-Hall, Inc., 1948), p. 85.
3. E. Adamson Hoebel, *Man in the Primitive World* (2d ed.; New York: McGraw-Hill Book Co., 1958), p. 245.
4. George Dearborn, "Psychology of Clothes," *Psychological Monographs*, XXVI, No. 1 (1918), p. 29.
5. Eve Merriam, *Figleaf: the Business of Being in Fashion* (Philadelphia: J. B. Lippincott Co., 1960), p. 96.
6. Hoebel, p. 247.

FURTHER READING

BURRIS-MEYER, ELIZABETH. *Color and Design in the Decorative Arts.* Englewood Cliffs, N. J.: Prentice-Hall, Inc., 1935. Chapters 2, 3, 4, and 5. Good presentation of the science of color.

CHAMBERS, BERNICE. *Color and Design.* Englewood Cliffs, N. J.: Prentice-Hall, Inc., 1951. Chapters 7, 8, and 10. Presentation of a comprehensive color vocabulary.

GOLDSTEIN, HARRIET, and GOLDSTEIN, VETTA. *Art in Everyday Life.* New York: The Macmillan Co., 1954. Excellent treatment of the design elements and of the principles governing their use.

HILLHOUSE, MARION S. *Dress Selection and Design.* New York: The Macmillan Co., 1963. Chapters 9, 10, and 11. Excellent guidance for students of costume on color harmony and choice of becoming colors.

McJIMSEY, HARRIET T. *Art in Clothing Selection.* New York: Harper & Row, 1963. Chapters 7, 8, and 9. Simple, clear presentation of the art elements and of the principles for their use.

STUDY SUGGESTIONS

1. From fashion advertising in a newspaper or magazine cut out sketches or photographs of costumes to illustrate balance, rhythm, emphasis, and line. What means are used to achieve each of these principles of design?
2. From swatches of plaid materials select two or three that seem to you to show good proportion of spaces and lines, and some that you consider poor.
3. Select several photographs in this book and discuss their handling of the four principles of design.

4. From swatches of textiles select two or three textures that you think would be good for a person with coarse, rough skin, and several for a fine, delicate skin.

5. For several different types of dress or coat buttons find a swatch of harmonizing material. Show the class your selections and defend your pairings.

6. Choose materials for a winter coat, a spring church dress, and a summer party dress for (a) a slightly overweight, athletic brunette with brown eyes and fair skin; and (b) a petite ash blonde, quiet and ladylike, with gray-blue eyes. Describe the design in which you would suggest each of these garments could be made.

7. Bring to class a fashion picture which you feel violates the law of emphasis.

8. Analyze the division of space and selection of colors in some modern abstract painting. How pleasing are they? Invite an art teacher to discuss with the class the abstractionist's handling of line, rhythm, color, and balance, and compare it with the work of an artist of a century ago in handling a full-length portrait.

9. Select a body fault, your own or someone else's, and plan in detail a dress that would minimize or camouflage it—through color, design, and fabric.

10. Bring before the class an obviously overdressed young woman. Evaluate her costume according to Table 4–1, taking into account the skirt length. How many points does the costume total? By stripping off some accessories or substituting others improve the effect of the costume.

5

Blueprint for Wardrobe Building

THE FAMILY'S CLOTHING

Providing apparel for all the family so that the basic needs of each member are satisfied and each has a chance for self-expression requires a considerable amount of wisdom. The mother, who has the chief responsibility for clothing the family, is usually keenly aware of her limitations in this area even when the income is ample. Social and economic forces are bringing about changes in the spending patterns for apparel, both for families whose standard of living sets such purchases at little above the subsistence level and for those who use clothing to gain prestige.

Increases in Income

Increases in family income probably exert the greatest influence. The U. S. Bureau of the Census reported that, in 1965, $6,900 was the midpoint in the range of incomes. Almost half the nation's families had annual incomes of $7,000 or more, while fewer than a fifth had incomes under $3,000. Income for one-fourth of all families was $10,000 or more that year. In 1929, by comparison, fewer than one-fifth had incomes of more than $4,000.

The average family income is now higher than ever before and permits increased freedom of choice in clothing: for following fashion, for upgrading the quality of apparel, and for purchasing luxury items that were formerly out of reach. To be sure, inflation has reduced somewhat the actual buying power of this income; the consumer's dollar of a generation ago bought more than it does today.

The price of apparel, however, has increased less than any of the other major categories of family expenditure. The cost of women's and girl's manufactured clothing increased approximately 2.5 per cent between 1957 and 1964; for men's and boys' clothing, 5.8 per cent. These figures do not include shoes. Shoe prices rose about 25 per cent in that period.

In families at the lower end of the economic scale, any increase in income usually brings a rise in the husband's clothing expenditures before it does his wife's. Studies of family expenditures show that husbands tend to buy more clothing items when money becomes available, whereas their wives tend to purchase relatively the same number of items but of better quality. An increase in income usually affects children's clothing less than it does that of adults. Young children are normally satisfied if only basic clothing needs are met. Teen-age children, however, are much concerned about dress and exert the greatest strain on the low-income family.

Among families in the ample-income group, particularly those that are advancing in professional or business circles, the percentage of income spent for clothing is often high. Quality and quantity of clothing worn often indicate the degree of financial success attained and may indeed be an important factor in advancing the status of the family, both financially and socially.

Decrease in Percentage Spent for Clothing

While most families have higher incomes than a generation ago, they are spending a smaller percentage for clothing. In the first quarter of the twentieth century, clothing often represented 15 per cent or more of the consumer dollar. By 1929 the average expenditure in current dollars was 12.1 per cent; in the decade 1930–1940 it dropped to 10.7 per cent, then rose to 12.9 per cent in the war years, 1941–1946. In the years following, clothing held an even less important place in the budget: 9.4 per cent in 1947–1961, 8.3 per cent in 1962, 8.2 per cent in 1963, 8.4 per cent in 1964, and 8.3 per cent in 1965. The slight rise in 1964 over 1963 may have signaled a reversal of the downward trend.[1]

Some families, of course, allot smaller portions of the family dollar to dress; some greater. Family composition, age, and goals influence the size of allotments to dress, so that no figure can be considered a recommended average for any particular family. It can serve as a guide, however.

Why does clothing represent a decreasing proportion of the family's cost of living today? Competing interests are largely responsible. Home ownership is desired today more than ever before. Purchases of furnishings and equipment for the modern home have increased accordingly: labor-saving devices, television, stereophonic equipment. The automobile, often more than one to the family, and sports equipment are important items in the budget, as is the financing of more education for the children. The popular mix-and-match outfits and the substitution of synthetic fibers for the more expensive natural fibers in clothing have also reduced the portion of the family's living dollar spent for clothing.

The Influence of Casual Living

Casual living has been responsible for important changes in family wardrobes. There has been a shift from dignity and formality, once characteristic of the wardrobe for the family that was moving upward in the social scale, to increased informality. Informality in dress is admirably suited to simple, outdoor entertaining and to vacation travel in the family car. Besides, it is not so expensive.

Production of blouses, skirts, and sweaters has skyrocketed at the expense of dresses, suits, and coats, as is evident from Figure 5–1. In 1964 skirt volume was eight and a half times that of prewar years, blouse volume over five and a half times, and sweater volume about three times.[2] By contrast, suit volume was a little more than two and a half times prewar volume, while coat volume was less than one and a half times that of prewar years.

Apparel for all members of the family has become simpler in style, more comfortable to wear, and easier to care for. Even in men's wear there is less formality today than was once consid-

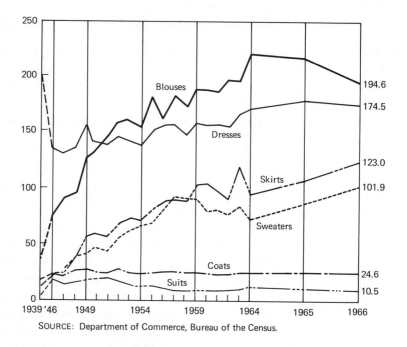

SOURCE: Department of Commerce, Bureau of the Census.

Figure 5–1. Production of women's, misses', and juniors' apparel.

ered proper. Slacks and a sport jacket have taken the place of a suit, not only for off-business hours but also for certain types of business. The short-sleeved dress shirt is another indication of waning formality for men.

Increased leisure has called for more variety in clothing than was found in families a generation ago. Sport and casual clothes are important in many wardrobes that once might have contained only work clothes and "Sunday best." Today, a variety of occasions must be provided for: formal, informal, sports, casual, and work. Although families have been spending a lower percentage of their income for what they wear, most make a better appearance than ever before.

Changing Status of Women

One of the important social changes that is influencing the family's clothing purchases is the position held by women. Today, women comprise about a third of the total labor force, and of these about half are married. Thus, many family incomes are materially increased.

A greater number of women than ever before have finished high school and college. These women are sought after for clerical and managerial positions rather than for unskilled jobs. Their work requires attractive and easily cared for clothing. Also, many women are making a career for themselves in the professions, some of them earning salaries commensurate with those earned by professional men. With the pressure toward "equal pay for equal work," their earnings will doubtless increase still more.

It is estimated that at least nine of every ten women work outside the home some time in their lives and continue to work for a much longer time than formerly—women with college degrees may work for twenty-five years or more. More than one-fifth of the nation's income is estimated to be earned by women.

In families in which the married woman works, the combined income of husband and wife creates a much higher standard of living than would otherwise be possible. Women in the business and professional world obviously need clothing of higher quality and greater quantity and variety than do women whose world is the home. Small economies in dress are not necessary for these women, whereas they are for women who must dress their families on a small part of a moderate income.

Age as Related to Clothing Expenditures

A family's clothing expenditures reflect the stage of its development. In the early years of marriage, particularly while the wife is devoting herself almost wholly to babies and young children, the family's expenditures will probably be low. Social activities are usually restricted, and the wife's clothing probably consists chiefly of easy-care, comfortable outfits that are relatively inexpensive.

The family's need for clothing increases with the years. When the children reach adolescence their need for increased quality and variety of clothing grows, and the cost of their apparel for the last year or two of high school and for entering college may equal or exceed that of their parents.

Yet clothing needs for the parents at this stage of the family cycle are usually also at their peak. The husband has gained a place of some importance in his line of work, and the wife has time for social and civic interests. As the children grow up and leave home, parents are able to spend more and to acquire clothes of better quality than they have had in the past. From this period on, until advancing years restrict their activities, the clothing needs of the parents often claim an important share of the family budget.

People are living longer today. One of every twelve persons is sixty-five or older, and it is predicted that the proportion of older people will increase still more in the years ahead. As a result, the overall average for family clothing expenditures will undoubtedly be affected, probably in a downward direction.

Importance of Appropriate Dress

Appropriate dress is important to every member of the family. For parents as well as children it builds self-respect and contributes to the prestige of everyone in the family. A family member should share according to his or her needs in the total clothing allowance.

There is no better way of arriving at an equitable allotment than to hold a family conference to discuss the problems involved, and to reach an understanding of relative needs. If in such a conference the daughter entering college presents a list of "musts" that she discovers would cost more than half the allotment for the entire family's clothing, she should alter her list so that younger brothers and sisters will not be handicapped. Or she should volunteer to pay for some of the items from her own earnings. Similarly, if the son's proposed wardrobe for the first year in college would cost two or three times what his father would have to spend, he should be willing to scale down his plans or else get a job to pay for the wardrobe.

Young people between the ages of sixteen and twenty-five are making the most important social contacts of their lives; yet they cannot expect other family members to waive all needs and interests for them. Parents who sacrifice their wardrobe to self-centered teen-agers may find later that these children are ashamed of them.

Clothing is less subject to sudden changes in fashion for the father than for the mother, but the average man is aware of current trends and is concerned about dressing correctly for all occasions. Today, the casual way of living has supplanted more formal ways, and a man often purchases casual clothing in colors and patterns once reserved for women's dress. Because he has increased leisure for sports, he often acquires a quite varied wardrobe. For work and business, however, he remains conservative and looks chiefly for comfort and a good fit.

The mother is concerned with satisfying the needs of all family members. Fashion-conscious though she may have been in earlier years, she is mindful of the realities of managing family expenditures and no longer feels so intensely the urge to buy the new or unusual for herself. If she is making no financial contribution to the family income, she is the one most likely to sacrifice her wants in favor of those of her children.

In order to insure socially acceptable dress for their children, parents may have to postpone family goals, especially if some of the children are in high school and college. But clothing costs can be kept in reasonable bounds with careful planning and understanding of problems on the part of each member of the group.

For the mother, planning a basic wardrobe is the most effective way to achieve satisfactory dress on a small allotment. After she has analyzed herself for size, body type, and coloring, she should evaluate current fashions in relation to her own proportions and social activities. She should be honest with herself, so as not to buy clothes that are unbecoming or too unusual for her own living pattern.

Then she can decide on a basic color and select a coat or suit or basic dress to harmonize with it, and start assembling a wardrobe that will be relatively timeless. She should look for quality in material and workmanship in each garment, knowing that she will need to get several years' wear from it. Carefully chosen accessories will bring sparkle to her conservative outfits. When tastefully accessorized, one good basic dress in black or a becoming color that harmonizes with her basic color can take her to many social affairs. Evaluation of her current wardrobe may reveal several garments that can fit into this basic wardrobe after a change of hemline and a trip to the cleaner's.

Interest in Home Sewing

Home sewing helps to relieve the economic pressure for some women, especially those who do not work outside their homes. In the years 1956 to 1965, The Singer Company, the world's largest producer of sewing machines, reported that 3 million women in the United States took its sewing courses. Singer's sale of home sewing machines in that period rose from 567,000 in 1956 to 636,000 in 1965, in spite of keen competition from household sewing machines made in Japan.[3]

Sale of patterns zoomed between 1952 and 1962: McCall's volume increased more than 10 per cent every year for the latter five years, and Simplicity's sales rose from around $12 million in 1952 to about $24 million in 1962.[4] The population during those years was also rising; it increased 19 per cent between 1950 and 1960. Thus, even if each woman had bought only one or two patterns, sales would have shown an impressive increase.

The motive for home sewing is chiefly economy, although some women sew because they have found in that activity opportunity for creative expression. A 1964 customer survey conducted for The Singer Company revealed two additional reasons: the desire to get better-fitting clothes, and the desire to have a larger, more fashionable wardrobe than would otherwise be financially possible.[5] In a December, 1964, report *Barron's* declared, "The single most important reason for the current surge in demand for dress patterns is the fashion trend toward casual and simple clothes, which can be produced readily at home."[6]

Dress patterns have had by far the largest sale, indicating that home seamstresses make dresses more often than they do any other garment. Though all companies promoting commercial patterns have stressed easy-to-make designs, an increasing number of women have been intrigued by the couturier designs offered by most pattern companies and have used them with surprising success.

DRESS FOR THE COLLEGE YEARS

The college wardrobe can help students to achieve their objectives during that four-year stretch between high school and career or homemaking, or it can set up roadblocks that will impede progress. Dress and ornament protect students psycho-logically as well as physically, helping them to gain control over social situations and to feel at ease. Students who cannot "dress the part" in a given situation are likely to feel deprived, inade-quate, frustrated. In *Parnassus,* Ralph Waldo Emerson quoted with obvious interest the comment of a woman friend that, "The sense of being perfectly well dressed gives a feeling of inward tranquillity which religion is powerless to bestow." [7]

Few college students can be completely oblivious of their clothes, but they can come close to it if they know that they are appropriately and attractively dressed. Then they can dismiss clothes from their thoughts and throw themselves wholeheartedly into the activity of the moment. Poise is more easily achieved with a well-chosen wardrobe to provide a feeling of security. Students are also more likely to be friendly and outgoing in con-tacts with others—unless they are snobs and look down on those who have not yet developed clothes sense or who lack the money to spend on clothes!

Amount To Spend

How much should students spend for a college wardrobe? Some would say, "As much as they can afford." But people differ as to their interpretation of what can be "afforded." Polonius, the worldly old man in *Hamlet,* advised his son, Laertes, thus: "Costly thy habit as thy purse can buy;/But not expressed in fancy; rich not gaudy;/For the apparel oft proclaims the man." Laertes, of course, was headed for court life in Paris, the Euro-pean center of fashion. Most universities and colleges do not rate fashion so high, or approve lavish expenditure for dress. But they would approve Polonius' advice to buy quality clothes that are in good taste.

Most people would probably agree that college students are spending more for their clothes than they can "afford" in these four situations:

1. If the clothes budget means depriving other members of the family of their clothing needs
2. If those students have little or no money left to buy tickets for cultural events on the campus and in the community—for theater, ballet, opera, and other music events

3. If wardrobe expenses will mean cutting college life short
4. If the wardrobe is conspicuously better than those of fellow students, arousing in them envy or dislike

With wise planning the average student can acquire the type of wardrobe needed without being guilty of any of these four "ifs." After all, students want their clothes to reflect more than money. If their clothes are becoming, appropriate, coordinated, and reasonably varied, they are on their way toward the taste and sophistication which doubtless are their goals.

Tips for Wardrobe Selection

Listed below are tips for building a moderately priced, coordinated wardrobe. Most of the points have already been discussed at some length; the few new ones need no discussion.

1. Consider your various roles in life before making a purchase. These roles will determine your wardrobe needs.
2. Decide on a basic color for the season, preferably a dark or a neutral color.
3. Plan major purchases first and then build your wardrobe around them.
4. Rotate major expenses, as a winter coat one year, a dressy suit the next, a lightweight coat the third year.
5. Before making any purchase consider whether the garment is becoming in line, color, and style, and whether it fits in with your wardrobe plan.
6. Decide on the sum you can afford to pay for a garment before you start shopping for it, and do not exceed that figure without thoughtful consideration of the consequences of your purchase on your budget.
7. Avoid impulse buying. Discipline yourself.
8. Do not buy any garment, however appealing, if you are well stocked in that type of apparel.
9. Buy separates that can be coordinated to make several costumes: skirts, short jackets, blouses, sweaters, and accessories for women; slacks, shirts, jackets, and sweaters for men.
10. Try things together before you buy them.
11. Buy clothes of sufficiently high quality that they will look new for a long time—will not fade, shrink, or wrinkle easily.
12. Avoid startling colors except for sports and evening wear; they are for those who can afford an unlimited wardrobe.
13. Be your age.

14. Waste no money on faddish items.
15. Do not buy a style that is near the end of the fashion cycle and on the way out—a warning that is less important for men than for women.
16. Think twice before buying a high-style garment, one that is so new or costly or subtle that it appeals only to the few. It *may* catch on and become popular, but it may not.

The College Girl's Wardrobe

Entrance into college marks the beginning of a new phase of living for a girl. Each period throughout her life usually has called for special attire: first a baptismal dress, then clothes for her first day in school, later her graduation dress, and now a wardrobe for the first year in college. Eventually, she will need a trousseau. Dress that conveys to others the importance of the change taking place in a person's life has come to be expected in our pattern of living. In college even the most practical girl has dreams of social as well as academic success and she depends upon her appearance to help her achieve her goals. Time spent in planning that all-important college wardrobe pays off handsomely.

THE WARDROBE INVENTORY: WHAT IS ON HAND? How does your current wardrobe rate? The best way to find out is to take an inventory of what is on hand and to record your findings on a chart such as that given in Appendix A. Then study the inventory using Appendix B.

Chances are, there will be nothing to list in some categories. The listings will vary from college to college. For example, in some colleges few girls will have a floor-length formal evening dress or levis.

One freshman recently found that she had fifteen sweater outfits, certainly more than she needed. "After all, you can wear only one outfit at a time," pointed out a more sophisticated upperclassman. "Most college students have no time at noon to change their clothes; so if you wear a different sweater–skirt combination to classes every day of a six-day college week it will take two and a half weeks of the thirty-six in the college year to go through the lot once. Then if some of the fifteen outfits are mix-and-match, the college year would be over before you could wear all the possible combinations. And there are surely other types of campus clothes you'd want to wear part of the time!"

Finding adequate storage space for a big wardrobe is a problem at most residence halls, where rooms must be shared and closets never seem big enough.

RELATION OF WARDROBE TO ACTIVITIES.   After taking the wardrobe inventory, the student can set down in writing the activities she has and hopes to have in the next year or two: class attendance and life in the residence hall, formal and informal dances, church youth group picnics, conferences, "retreats," movie dates, theater and music programs, and perhaps a field trip for majors in the curriculum, weekend trips with a college organization, or a ski trip to the mountains. She may need to consider also what she will be doing next summer, such as serving as a camp counselor or as a salesgirl in a ready-to-wear shop.

The student should then evaluate her wardrobe in relation to these activities, both current and potential. Can she assemble from this inventory a complete outfit for each of her activities, one she could wear cheerfully? Campus clothes are naturally the most important, and she will want a variety to carry her through the year, through fair weather and foul, through hot days and perhaps bitter cold. To take the hard wear she will give them, her clothes should be well tailored and hold a press, and should be of sturdy, easy-care material.

Glamour magazine reported at the end of one of its "ten best-dressed college girls" contests that the winners, brought to New York for interviews, showed almost infallibly good judgment in their evaluation and selection of campus wear and evening gowns. They showed the poorest judgment in city or street wear, particularly in hats. They had undoubtedly had the least experience in shopping for street wear.

AN ADEQUATE WARDROBE.   Every college and university has its own standards for dress. These may differ somewhat from standards of other institutions, even in the same area. The following wardrobe for the college girl was suggested by students of clothing and textiles at one midwestern state university.

An Adequate Wardrobe for the College Girl

For general campus wear: classes, sports events, casual dates
  Coats: 1 all-weather or trench and 1 car coat
  Skirts: 7 for winter, 7 for spring
  Blouses: 7 coordinated with skirts
  Sweaters: 7
  Shoes: 2 pairs of loafers, flats, or stacked heels
  Snow boots: 1 pair
  Rain boots: 1 pair
For casual wear: picnics, residence hall living, and sports
  Pants: 1 wool stretch for winter, 1 cotton twill for spring
  Jeans: 1 pair
  Shorts: 2 pairs—Bermudas, Jamaicas, or cut-offs
  Sport shirts: 2
  Shoes: 2 pairs—sandals, tennis
  Beach robe: 1 (optional)
For informal wear: church, dates, teas, campus activities
  Coats: 1 warm dress for winter, 1 lightweight dress coat
  Dresses: 3 for winter, 2 for spring
  Suits: 2 for fall and winter, 2 for spring
  Shoes: 3 pairs—medium, stacked, or high heels
For formal wear: homecoming dance, parties, Christmas and spring
  events
    Cocktail type or short party dresses: 2
    Evening wrap: 1 (optional)
    Evening slippers: 1 or 2 pairs
Accessories, lounging wear, underwear: as desired

This is not a minimum wardrobe. College students in every part of the nation each year get along on fewer articles of apparel. Neither is it what many would consider a generous supply of clothes. Rather, it is what most would probably consider adequate.

CLASSICS AND FADS. "Have at least three or four classics in your wardrobe," is the advice given by many clothes consultants. The shirtwaist dress is one example of a classic. In its many versions it is a perennial favorite: sometimes with an A-line skirt, sometimes with pleats or gathers, occasionally sleeveless, often with a notched collar, and sometimes with no collar at all. It is always tailored or at least semitailored, and always opens down the front—sometimes full length, sometimes just to the waist. Designers manage to give the shirtwaist dress a smart new twist each year, so that it is a rare wardrobe that lacks at least one. Other classics are the Chesterfield coat, the trench coat, the sweater and skirt ensemble, and the Chanel type of cardigan suit.

Faddish purchases need not be completely ruled out of one's wardrobe. The average college girl has fun wearing something faddish occasionally, such as Courrèges boots, the miniskirt, or the baby dress of the mid-1960's. But she should consider how the fad will look on *her*. Girls are not all proportioned alike, and the girl with a well-developed figure should ask herself whether the baby dress, for example, is really her type of apparel. Fads give a certain zip to a wardrobe. They also make it possible to experiment a bit, and often identify the student as one of the gang. But they are here today, gone tomorrow, and hence not a good investment. Some girls satisfy their craving through buying relatively inexpensive faddish accessories.

SEVENTEEN'S "COLLEGE FRESHMAN STORY." *Seventeen's* 1965 college freshman wardrobe survey, like its predecessors, revealed what the American girl takes to college and what she spends for this wardrobe. The survey involved interviews of 1,911 girls from all fifty states and thirty-six different colleges. The average amount of money spent on clothing that year was $397.61. These girls of course took to college some garments they had bought during their high school days, and often made no new purchases of such items. The average cost of some of the garments was: casual coat, $36.19; dress coat, $46.21; car coat, $16.07; raincoat, $21.63; suit, $29.64; date dress, $26.54; daytime dress, $23.64; evening dress, $26.55; skirt, $9.57; blouse, $4.19; bulky-knit synthetic sweater, $12.40; fine-gauge wool sweater, $12.26; long pants, $11.19; school flats, $9.61; heels for dates, $11.55; heels for formal evenings, $14.98.

Expenditures for clothes vary widely on every campus. One midwestern university, in the fall of 1964, found that the range for 125 students in clothing-selection classes was from $78 to $1,075 for the year. The median figure was $345 and the average was $360.

Whatever the sum of money available to the freshman for her first year's wardrobe, she would be wise not to spend all of it before she arrives on campus because it is practically impossible to anticipate all needs for a whole year. Even the advice of those who have studied at that college may not be an infallible guide, especially if their activities and interests differ from those of the prospective student. Thus, it is smart to set aside part of the year's clothing allotment.

Figures 5–2 through 5–13 show a range of good choices for the college girl's wardrobe. Even a student from a well-to-do family is unlikely to have such a wide variety, of course. A few costumes by well-known designers are included primarily to show the type of clothes currently in vogue. Shoppers can find similar designs in lower-priced lines and can achieve much the same effect perhaps at half the cost. Also, a skilled home dressmaker can arrive at amazingly good results with a smartly styled pattern and materials of good quality.

The Hat in Relation to the Ensemble.   The hat has been sadly neglected during the last decade or so. In many parts of the United States it was displaced first by the "whimsy," a flower- or ribbon-trimmed bit of stiffened veiling, or by a soft flat bow worn on top of the head. Then hairdressers dealt the *coup de grâce* to both hat and whimsy by conceiving coiffure arrangements so bouffant and elaborate that nothing could be set on top of them. However, a hat is required on certain occasions according to the rules of etiquette which still prevail in the "best social circles." In some churches, too, hats are traditional. The girl who bars hats from her life is failing to utilize an accessory which can do much to improve her appearance. In fact, sometimes the hat gives the final touch that she needs.

Since the hat frames the face it is an attention getter. No other item in the wardrobe needs more careful consideration: it must harmonize with the rest of the ensemble, be in scale with the wearer, and compliment her skin, eyes, and nose. We have already discussed how a hat can minimize facial defects. Of course, one should always *stand* in front of a mirror to study the total impression made by a hat with the rest of the costume one is wearing.

Figure 5–2. A basic coat which can be dressed either up or down to suit the occasion.

Figure 5–3. A tailored coat that would be undaunted by any weather. There is a zip-in pile lining of orlon acrylic. (Courtesy of DuPont Company.)

Figure 5–4. A basic coat for springtime, in powder blue with matching felt hat. (Courtesy of American Wool Council.)

Figure 5–5. The college girl's constant companion, a coat that is warm and sturdy. (Photograph courtesy of *Harper's Bazaar*.)

Figure 5–6. A light tweed suit such as this one with appropriate accessories can be worn for almost any daytime occasion. (Courtesy of American Wool Council.)

Figure 5–7. Warm days demand fresh-looking, simply cut dresses such as this A-line shift for informal occasions.

Figure 5-8. A sophisticated white formal dress cut high in front and low in back. (Courtesy of American Wool Council.)

Figure 5-9. A red slubbed-silk dress that breathes elegance for after-five affairs. (Courtesy of Helga.)

Figure 5–10. A flannel jumper dress teamed with a turtleneck, back-zippered pullover sweater. (Courtesy of Country Cousins, division of the Manhattan Shirt Company.)

Figure 5–11. A nicely coordinated wool sweater and skirt with cotton blouse. A traditional Country Set design.

Figure 5–12. This tunic shift would be perfect for many dormitory or campus activities, popped over pants or tights or skirts. (Courtesy of Bobbie Brooks.)

Figure 5–13. The outdoors girl would dote on this trouser suit of acrilan and wool with its reefer jacket and double flap pockets.

Luckily, a hat need not be expensive, though it *can* cost a sizable amount. Some of the best hat designers are now doing some of their designing for manufacturers of low-cost hats. These hats may be machine-made and have inexpensive trimming but their lines and color may well be quite as smart as those of the handmade, high-priced chapeaux. And they can do quite as much in giving the final fillip to a smart outfit. It is a good idea to get acquainted with a department store's hat bar and the little low-priced millinery shop.

SHOES. Shoes rate special emphasis. No other wardrobe item is quite so important for a person's comfort. The average college girl walks a lot, often more than she has ever walked before—especially if the family car is no longer accessible. Going from her room in the residence hall, up and down stairs to classes in different buildings often scattered over a big campus, and then to the student center for a chat with a friend can total miles of walking in a day.

The price of shoes has risen more than that of any other single article of apparel in recent years. For no other item on the student's shopping list is careful selection so essential. She must take time to be sure that the shoe fits and has high-quality construction and material that will stand up under hard wear. Too often, the student will pay $8 for her school shoes and $18 for her party pumps; actually the reverse would show much better judgment, and probably be more economical in the end. "Tennies" and ballet type shoes are poor choices for day-long wear; they leave the wearer more tired than necessary at the end of the day.

Some of the shoes in the student's inventory may need nothing more than a trip to the repair shop for new lifts and a good cleaning or shine to make them acceptable for the wardrobe. Good care assures maximum service from shoes as well as adding immeasurably to their appearance.

HOSIERY. On some campuses girls wear anklets rather than full-fashioned hose for daytime, "tights" or woolen knee-length socks for winter, and nylons only for dress. In such places twelve pairs of nylons may carry a student through the year, and her outlay for hosiery may be under $15. This economy can be achieved easily if she purchases chiefly "irregulars" and "seconds," and gets expensive hose only if the color she wants is not available in the economy categories. Buying at least three pairs at a time is a thrifty practice, as the wearer then can match up the odd stocking with others of the same color when one develops a run.

LOUNGING WEAR, NIGHTWEAR, AND UNDERWEAR. Students spend a great deal of time in the dormitory—studying, chatting with others, and attending to the various chores of college life. Comfort will be the chief characteristic desired in the clothes for these hours of the day. In some parts of the nation, comfort in the winter will mean warmth, especially for late hours of cramming for a final examination or polishing up a term paper after the heat in the hall has been turned down. Students need a warm robe, nightclothes, and slippers.

When buying *lounging and nightwear* college girls can indulge their craving for the ridiculous, for something whimsical with which to amuse roommates and students down the hall.

For underwear practically every experienced college student would advise the following. Buy good quality garments which can go through a washing machine and then be hung up to drip dry. Check to see if elastic parts can take machine laundering without damage. Few elastic garments can withstand the heat of the drying cycle of laundry room equipment, so drip drying is recommended. Most garments can be pulled into shape well enough to be wearable without need of ironing.

For the economy-minded girl, tailored garments with no filmy lace trim are naturally the best buys. As to how many slips, bras, and panties to purchase, a good rule of thumb is: about a ten-day supply. A week's supply would be enough if a girl could be sure of having time over the weekend to wash the accumulation of soiled garments, but some weekends will be too filled with other activities. Some students, of course, hand wash a bra, hose, and panties every night. Gone are the days of sending soiled clothes home to get them into the family laundry, probably because most residence halls have installed coin-operated laundry equipment.

As for slips the student needs a sufficient variety of both dark and light colors, mostly tailored: one or two of narrow cut to wear with tube skirts, one or two of flaring lines, and probably a half-slip or two. Two roll-on or pantie type *spandex girdles* will usually be sufficient since most girls are slender and firm fleshed enough to need only a bit of smoothing down. The plump girls will look for foundation garments with reinforcements, perhaps a zipper closing, and longer lines that can mold their figures into trimness.

Since girls vary as to figure proportions, the choice of a bra is a highly individual matter. Have it fitted to insure comfort and adequate support. The bandeau type is the usual choice for everyday wear, but a long-line bra, often strapless, is needed for more formal wear.

The College Man's Wardrobe

Like the college girl, the prospective college man would find it helpful to take an inventory of his current wardrobe and to set down in writing the activities he expects to have in the next year or two. He can then evaluate his wardrobe in relation to those activities. Luckily for the college man, the classic and the traditional dominate in men's wear. Styles change relatively slowly, though the rate has been accelerating in recent years. Luckily, too, he can rent seldom-used garments, such as a tuxedo.

Campus and casual wear will figure most prominently in his wardrobe, of course. Like the college girl, he can get added variety into his dress through mix-matching items. He can wear his smart bulky sweater with denims or with a pair of dacron and cotton wash trousers, or his plaid chambray work shirt with his loden green hopsacking slacks or with his "wheats," as light-colored denims are picturesquely called in the Midwest. His navy blazer can be teamed with gray slacks, white shirt, and solid tie for informal parties, or with a turtleneck sweater-shirt, white slacks, and shoes. He can also pair it with a colored shirt, patterned tie, classic crushable hat, and suede shoes for a field trip to a nearby city—or with a classic sport shirt, sandals, and flannel or gabardine shorts. Figures 5–14 through 5–21 present current fashions in men's wear as seen on campuses across the nation.

An Adequate Wardrobe. The wardrobe presented below was drafted for the book by two university men with considerable experience as salesmen in a men's wear shop. In their words, "We planned it for a person from a middle-income family. Many students manage on fewer items, but this list makes what we consider an adequate wardrobe."

An Adequate Wardrobe for the College Man

For campus and casual wear:
  Coats: 1 nylon blast jacket, 1 all-weather or car coat, 1 jacket-length heavy coat, 1 golf jacket (optional)
  Slacks: 4 pairs—2 of cotton-polyester, 1 of dressy worsted, 1 of casual hopsacking
  Shirts: 4 to 6 sport shirts, including plaids, polka dots, and paisleys as fashion dictates; T-shirts as desired
  Sweaters: 7—3 pullovers, some matched with sport jackets.
  Jeans: 4 pairs—corduroy and denims
  Shorts: 3 pairs walking shorts in denim or cotton-polyester
  Shoes: 3 pairs—1 penny loafer, 1 either tie or loafer, 1 tennis
  Swim wear: 2 swim trunks teamed with blast jacket above

For informal wear:
  Suits: 2—three-button traditional, 1 with vest
  Sport jackets: 3—1 of heavy tweed, 1 of dacron-wool, 1 a blazer
  Dress shirts: 8—all button-down, 1 with glen collar, 3 white; others pastel, stripe, or tattersall
  Ties: 8—stripes, paisley, club reps
  Shoes: 2—1 wing tip, the other semidress
  Coats: 1—all-weather topcoat listed above will do, 1 dress topcoat (optional)

For formal wear:
  Tuxedo: 1 black (may be rented)
  Shoes: 1 black with plain toes
  Shirt: 1 with pleated front to go with tuxedo

Accessories:
  Hats: little worn on many campuses—1 with unblocked crown desirable, for sportswear or dress, shaped to suit the wearer's face
  Gloves: 2 pairs minimum
  Silk pocket squares: white for a formal suit, colored to go with business suits and sport jackets
  Belts: 3 to 5—coordinated with shoes by texture and color for both dress and casual wear
  Hosiery: some knee length with wide elasticized area at top, some ankle length, as desired
  Jewelry: cuff links and matching shirt studs for tuxedo; tie tacks as desired

Lounging wear, underwear: as desired

Figure 5–14. Double-breasted to this young traditionalist means a four-button jacket in navy worsted. His accessories are regimental stripes in a four-inch tie, a silk pocket square, and a broadcloth button-down shirt.

Figure 5–15. This navy blazer with charcoal gray pants, traditional vest, and club tie is a perennial on most campuses. So is the all-weather coat that the young man carries. Buttons are of spun silver.

Figure 5–16. This bold plaid jacket is popular, especially worn with the V-neck sweater.

Figure 5–17. Traditional three-piece suit in herringbone weave. Only new detail: the tab on the left side lapel.

Figure 5–18. A houndstooth patterned jacket, coordinated with spun hopsacking slacks and pullover sweater.

Figure 5–19. This jacket with a shirt look is in red and black checkerboard wool and is lined with fleece.

Figure 5–20. Stadium jacket, ski sweater, jean-style pants, and penny loafers are naturals for casual wear, and accordingly are found in most student wardrobes.

Figure 5–21. These nylon blast jackets and the rain hat are most useful for stormy days and water sports.

THE CAREER GIRL'S WARDROBE

Years ago, homemaking was practically the only career open to a woman. Today, attitudes have changed and nearly every business and profession has women in its ranks—women who may also be carrying responsibilities as homemakers.

As educational opportunities have expanded, women have earned college degrees enabling them to enter the legal and medical professions, scientific fields, nursing, specialized teaching, writing and editing in publishing houses, and businesses in which they eventually achieve executive positions. The wardrobe needs of women in such careers call for special consideration.

There is no need to hold forth on the importance of a good wardrobe for a young career girl. Even women who fancy themselves independent of public opinion cannot function physically or mentally at their best unless their clothing is appropriate and reasonably attractive. For the career girl, the wardrobe is almost sure to be an important factor in on-the-job success as well as off-the-job happiness.

Clothes on the Job

Clothes for the working hours of all career girls have some characteristics in common. Whether they involve a uniform or generally accepted daytime apparel, clothes must look business-like and be in top condition. Tight, figure-revealing garments, low necks, bare shoulders, naked backs (even in summer), and jingling jewelry are, of course, out of place.

According to one eminently successful career woman, the office or laboratory is not the place to indulge oneself in extremes in style—fads or frilly, feminine clothes. But mannish clothes are not acceptable either for women in the business world. The happy in-between, the conservative, understated dress or suit, is an ideal choice. Most career women in both business and the professions must operate in a man's world, where a certain amount of formality exists. The atmosphere is definitely impersonal. This calls for clothes that are discreet, tailored yet feminine, and in subdued colors. The general effect should be of quiet good taste.

Careers for women, as for men, occasionally require uniforms. Consider the dietitian, with her Master's degree in nutrition, whose spotless uniform helps to create her air of competence. Close examination of her uniform will reveal that it is of high-quality material, tailored to her own special body lines, and probably relatively expensive even though it can be laundered. And observation over several years' time will reveal that the design of her uniform tends to reflect current fashions.

The medical technician, the registered nurse, the scientist in her laboratory, all wear some kind of uniform—whether it be a lab coat or a washable dress designed for the feminine figure. They all slip into this uniform for the day's activities but wear street clothes on the way to and from work.

The career girl often must go directly from her place of business to an affair where dressier clothes are required. Yet she has no time to go home to redress. She needs considerable ingenuity to outfit herself appropriately for a day of such varied activities. A costume that can be "dressed up" or "dressed down" by the use of accessories usually meets her need.

One career woman recently solved such a clothes problem by wearing to the office a simple but lovely black wool dress with plain earrings and choker necklace. In the evening she went to a semiformal hotel dinner in the same dress after substituting as accessories a small, white feather hat, her best white kid gloves, baroque pearls with earrings to match, and black pumps with heels. The wife of the corporation president, who was giving the dinner, looked at her admiringly and commented: "You always wear the right things!"

For most career women, street wear rates as the most important category of garments. Semitailored suits and dresses in subdued colors prove the best choices. The teacher in the schoolroom, however, can wear somewhat more casual clothes and a wider range of colors. The career woman who must see the same group of people every day often feels the need for considerable variety in daytime dress.

High heels are a poor choice for most types of work, though there are business positions in which employees are expected to wear them. Nowadays, fortunately, low- and medium-heeled shoes come in many attractive designs. And if the career girl has been careful to get shoes of good construction and perfect fit, they will not put lines of weariness onto her face no matter how long she must be on her feet.

A Year's Budget for the Career Girl

Table 5–1 presents a proposed budget for a young career woman in the city, a woman in her mid-twenties, perhaps, whose position involves contact with the public. She has no debts and no dependents to complicate her life. She obviously enjoys a fairly high standard of living and spends more for clothes than would the average college student or homemaker—probably as much as an entire family would spend on the same income.

Yet analysis of one year's clothing expenditures for the career girl (Table 5–2), shows that the cost of each item is reasonable, even conservative, for a person of her social and professional interests. She operates in general on a three-year cycle for major clothing purchases, and this is her year for buying a general-purpose winter coat. She will continue to wear the winter coat purchased several years ago, of course, but not for the most important occasions. She may buy a dress coat next year and will add a new suit to her wardrobe each year, alternating one for spring with one for winter.

Table 5–1

Budget for the Young Career Woman with Income of $6,500

Item	Amount	Percentage
Total income	$6,500	100
Taxes: federal and state income, and property	$1,300	20
Shelter: half of $150 per month apartment shared with another career girl	910	14
Household operation: utilities, laundry, special cleaning, papers, magazines, small equipment	325	5
Food: 2 meals at home, lunches eaten out; some home entertaining	780	12
Clothing	780	12
Personal care: cosmetics, beauty parlor	195	3
Medical and dental care	195	3
Insurance: life, health, theft	325	5
Savings	455	7
Transportation	325	5
Recreation: including vacation trip	520	8
Miscellaneous: gifts, church, club dues, dry cleaning, shoe repair, etc.	390	6

Table 5–2

One Year's Clothing Expenditures for the Young·Career Woman
with Income of $6,500

Item	Estimated Cost
Winter coat, tweed	$80
Winter hats: 2	30
Winter suit	75
Wool dress	40
Winter crepe, dark	45
Knit suit	50
After-five dress, street length	50
Spring silk costume, dress and jacket	65
Spring hats: 2	25
Dark sheer dress, dressy, all season	40
Cotton suit	35
Dark linen dress	35
Pastel linen dress	35
Street shoes: 3 pairs	45
Dress shoes: 2 pairs	30
Hose: 15 to 18 pairs	18
Handbags: 2	22
Gloves: 4 pairs—2 leather, 2 cotton	15
Underwear: bras, girdles, slips, panties	30
Costume accessories	15
Total	$780

This career girl probably bought a spring coat and an all-weather coat last year—or perhaps the year before. Many of her dresses and suits purchased over the last two or three years are still wearable, especially those which are classics, and they add variety to her apparel. She has plenty of nightwear and lounging clothes, as well as sportswear, carried over from other years.

Figures 5–22 through 5–29 indicate the type of clothes that a career girl can wear with the assurance that she is appropriately and attractively dressed. Like the wardrobe for the college girl, some of the models were created by the nation's top designers and would be too expensive for young career women. They are shown here to suggest the lines and fabrics desirable. A smart shopper can find similar costumes in lower-priced lines.

THE TROUSSEAU

For the young woman the trousseau is often the most important collection of clothes she will assemble in her lifetime. Whether it is lavish or simple, each garment is planned to show

Figure 5–22. Coat dress of worsted in a classic design for street and office wear. With hood removed and costume jewelry changed, it could serve for varied occasions. (Courtesy of *Vogue.* Copyright © 1965 by Condé Nast Publications, Inc.)

Figure 5–23. For the occasional weekend in the country this easy-fitting blouson suit with hat to match would be perfect. Designed by Tiffeau & Busch. (Courtesy of *Harper's Bazaar.*)

Figure 5–24. This coat dress is beautifully adapted to city living. (Courtesy of American Wool Council.)

Figure 5–25. A Handmacher suit with side-wrapped skirt.

137

Figure 5–26. A well-tailored tweed suit and topcoat form the hub of a businesswoman's wardrobe. (Courtesy of Davidow Suits, Inc.)

Figure 5–28. The small yoke and short sleeves of this evening dress are jewel-embroidered; the jacket is semifitted.

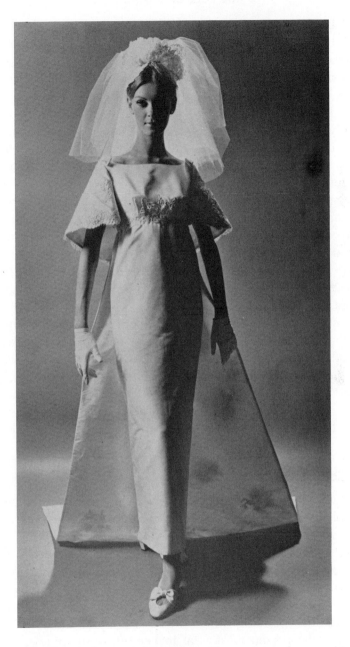

Figure 5–29. A demure bridal gown with capelet and removable embroidered train. Designed by Priscilla of Boston.

her at her loveliest. Into its assembling go iridescent daydreams of the life ahead. Planning the trousseau, then, is of utmost importance to the bride and warrants thoughtful consideration of her husband-to-be, of the two families involved, and of the community to which she will go.

Traditionally, the parents of the bride buy her trousseau, but actually the bride herself often does much of the financing. Seven of every ten brides in the United States have been employed before marriage and undoubtedly many have bought some of the items desired.

In many cultures throughout the world, in both sophisticated and underdeveloped countries, social pressures are such that the family of the bride typically spends all its accumulated savings for a daughter's dowry and wedding festivities. In many communities in our own nation, lavish expenditures beyond the means of the families are encouraged by persuasive advertising and by custom.

To strike a balance between sentiment and common sense in planning her wedding with her fiancé, and to gain the whole-hearted cooperation of the two families, the engaged girl sometimes needs to use all her skill in handling human relations. The sooner basic decisions are made about the type of wedding the better, as they will reduce immeasurably the tension that often seems to accompany such affairs, particularly large formal weddings.

First Considerations

Many things will influence the wedding plans and choice of apparel for the trousseau. Let us consider some of these.

What are the fiancé's preferences as to the wedding? Would he like a big formal affair? Or a families-only ceremony? Or an informal chapel wedding with only the closest of friends present in addition to members of the two families? What are his tastes as to women's clothes? The wise bride will inform her fiancé of plans for the wedding and the trousseau from the start. After all, he is the person most vital to her future happiness, and he will have to look at her clothes more than anyone else. His disapproval of a garment could not help but take away some of her own pleasure in wearing it.

What if their tastes clash? There is no time like the present to begin to learn the fine art of compromise. She can quiz him to discover his favorite colors, if she has not already found out, and his pet peeves in women's appearance such as splashy prints, stretch pants, or heavy eye makeup. If they disagree, she can decide if the moot point is trivial enough to concede gracefully, or important enough for her to launch an artful campaign to win him over to her taste.

What is the economic status of the bride's family and of her fiancé's? How much can her parents afford to spend on her trousseau? What type of wedding do they want her to have? Are his relatives more affluent than hers? Will she live in their community and be expected to share in their social activities?

What kind of life will she lead as a married woman? Will much of her leisure time be spent outdoors—in swimming, fishing, skiing, boating? Or will dining out at smart hotels and attending dancing parties figure importantly in her leisure life? Or will she be part of a young married set that enjoys entertaining in the home and on the patio? Will she be a full-time homemaker or will she have a job outside her home part or full time? Will she live in the city, the suburbs, or the country? Where it is bitter cold part of the year—or beastly hot? Or where temperatures are equable?

Is her higher education still incomplete and will she continue her studies after the wedding? Will there be no change in residence? Will her parents continue financing her education or will she and her husband share that responsibility? In one typical midwestern state university in 1965–1966, one of every seven women students was married.

Where do they plan to go for the honeymoon and for how long? Wherever they go, they should take only what they will really need, packables which will require little or no care. Attractive but rather inconspicuous clothes will be good choices. The couple will be spotted as newlyweds anyhow, and there is no need to attract more attention with a conspicuous wardrobe.

Planning the Trousseau

What should the trousseau contain beyond the bridal dress and apparel for other social occasions connected with the marriage? Some bridal consultants suggest a year's supply of outer-wear and accessories, two years' supply of underwear and negli-gées, and coats to take the bride through the next three years. This sounds like an extensive outlay—more than many families could afford—but not all these garments need to be new, of course. Much of what the bride already has will still be wear-able and pleasing. After all, if marriage entails a change of environment, as is usually the case, all her clothes will be new to her husband's friends and associates.

Planning the trousseau requires some work to gain an accu-rate picture of what she has on hand and what she wants to buy. Like the college girl, the bride should start her wardrobe planning with an inventory of what she has on hand. She needs to set down in writing a list of currently owned garments that will be useful in her future life. This is the time to discard the things that she has outgrown, both physically and mentally. These have no place in her inventory.

Then comes a list of the proposed honeymoon activities and probable activities after marriage. Finally, the bride can work up a list of items to buy for her trousseau. She will be guided by the same principles as those given for the college girl—the choice of basic color, color coordination of the various garments, em-phasis on quality rather than quantity, and the like. The items listed below give the bride something tangible to consider. In some categories she may need more, in others less; and some she may not need at all.

Suggested Trousseau

Coats: 4—1 light topcoat, 1 winter, 1 all-weather, 1 rain
Suits: 1 casual, 1 dressy
Daytime dresses: 3 for winter, 3 for summer
Party dresses for afternoon, informal evenings, and formals: 2 for win-ter, 2 for summer and spring
Hostess gown or at-home costume
Sweaters: 4
Skirts: 2
Pants: 1 pair slacks or bermuda shorts
Blouses and shirts: 2 for each suit, 2 for sports
Shoes: 6 pairs—2 pairs dress shoes, 2 pairs street shoes, 1 pair sandals, 1 pair evening pumps

Hosiery: 2 dozen stockings

Gloves: 6 pairs—1 short off-white, 1 beige cotton, 1 eight-button, 1 navy, brown, or black, etc.

Night robes: 1 bathrobe, 2 housecoats

Bras: 6—3 dark, 3 light

Girdles: 3—1 dark

Slips: 6—2 tailored, 2 dressy, 2 dark

Sleepwear: 6 pajamas or nighties, 3 for winter, 3 for summer

Housewear: 2 casual wash dresses (slacks or bermudas if pants are preferred for housework)

Luggage: 1 to 3 pieces of matching, inexpensive, canvas luggage of very light weight

Dress for the Ceremony

The time of day and the place selected for the wedding ceremony will determine requirements for the dress. A big formal wedding, whether in a church, at a hotel, or at home, dictates a floor-length white gown with a train and a veil. The veil can be either short or long. No matter what the setting of the ceremony, a low-cut wedding gown would be in bad taste; chest and back should be covered. If sleeves are full length, gloves are not worn. With three-quarter or short sleeves, gloves have traditionally covered most of the exposed area, but nowadays wrist-length gloves are the favorites of many young brides.

The bride will carry only a bouquet or a prayerbook and perhaps a handkerchief. Jewelry should be simple; pearls are traditional. Shoes should be of white silk and comfortable enough for the bride to stand in for several hours, if there is to be a reception.

For a ceremony held after six the husband-to-be will wear full-dress evening clothes—white tie and tails. For a ceremony earlier in the day he will wear morning dress—a cutaway coat, striped trousers, light-gray vest, wing collar, and a wide gray ascot tie. All-black shoes and socks are traditional for the bridegroom.

If the wedding is to be less formal, but still in a church or hotel or at home, the bride can suit herself as to the length of the gown and also the color: white or a pastel. The veil will be short. If the hour is after six the bridegroom will wear a tuxedo —or in some parts of the country a white dinner jacket for summer. If the hour is before six he can choose between a dark blue suit and an Oxford jacket with gray vest and striped trousers— or, for summer, a white suit.

For an informal wedding, in a chapel or hotel or at home, the bride's dress will be of street length, either in white or a pastel, and the bridegroom will wear a dark blue suit. At home the bride wears neither hat nor veil nor gloves.

For a civil wedding by a judge or justice of the peace, the bride can select either a suit or a daytime dress of any becoming color with street accessories. The only color not acceptable is black. The bridegroom wears a business suit.

The wedding dress chosen, whatever the type, determines what the bride's attendants will wear. It is her prerogative to select the colors and designs to be worn by these attendants.

Local customs as to wedding attire sometimes differ from those dictated by etiquette books. In such situations, the bride usually chooses to follow local custom rather than to have a wedding that will make her fiancé and one or both of the families feel uncomfortable.

Even if the bride has chosen a floor-length gown or ballerina- or waltz-length dress for her wedding, she needs to give some thought to selecting a design which can be used as a "dressy dress" later. Though the idea of laying it away never to be worn again, except perhaps by her own daughter, appeals to the sentimentalist, being able to wear the dress on special occasions thereafter has its own appeal—as on anniversary days, for an evening at the theater, or for a dinner party. The bridal gown in Figure 5–29 shows how one famous designer creates a frock that can be worn as a party dress after the wedding, by removing its train and perhaps also its cape.

The Going-away Ensemble

The going-away ensemble needs to be appropriate for the honeymoon trip and for arrival at the place where the couple will spend the first days of married life. If the wedding has been informal, the suit or dress worn for the ceremony might be appropriate. A suit, hat, gloves, handbag, and luggage have been the traditional going-away ensemble, but they are no longer a must. If the affair has been a summer wedding and the couple will be traveling by car during the honeymoon, a cool casual dress, without hat and gloves, is now considered perfectly correct.

One suggestion: The sensible couple will not plan a honeymoon requiring a wardrobe that will be useless afterward. For example, a honeymoon on a dude ranch would undoubtedly require riding clothes, a questionable investment if the couple will have no opportunity for weekend rides afterward.

NOTES

1. Virginia Britton, Talk at 44th Annual Agricultural Outlook Conference (Washington, D. C.: Consumer and Food Economic Research Division, U. S. Department of Agriculture, 1966).

2. Ruth Jackendoff, *Consumer Clothing Expenditures: an Analysis of Trends* (New York: The Wool Bureau, Inc., 1964).

3. Unpublished letter dated October 13, 1966, written to the authors by B. F. Thompson, Director of Publications, The Singer Company.

4. Clarence Newman, "Home Sewing Booms as Women Seek High Fashion at Low Cost," *Wall Street Journal,* August 6, 1963, p. 1.

5. Gaylon B. Booker, "Cotton in Retail Piece Goods" (Memphis, Tenn.: National Cotton Council of America, 1964), p. 9.

6. Edward K. Hobby, "Simplicity Itself: Casual Fashions Appeal to Home Sewers, Pattern Makers," *Barron's,* XLIV, No. 49 (December 7, 1964), p. 9.

7. Ralph Waldo Emerson, *Letters and Social Aims,* preface to "Parnassus."

FURTHER READING

DANVILLE, BEA. *Dress Well on $1 a Day.* New York: Funk and Wagnalls, 1956. Down-to-earth tips for achieving chic on a limited budget, written by an Englishwoman transplanted to the United States.

"What Every Man Should Know about Dressing Right!" New York: The American Institute of Men's and Boys' Wear, Inc., 1964. A 24-page booklet written for the young businessman, but helpful also to the college student.

STUDY SUGGESTIONS

1. Make an inventory of your current wardrobe and a critical analysis of it, using the outlines in Appendixes A and B. Then write a terse statement for the high school senior to guide her in her purchases during her final year and the summer preceding college entrance.

2. Interview a prominent campus senior as to the importance of clothing in her college career and her advice to high school seniors planning on entering college.
3. Select a basic suit or dress and demonstrate its versatility through accessories which would make it appropriate for a variety of occasions. Calculate the cost of all these accessories and compare that figure with the cost of the basic outfit.
4. Study *Seventeen*'s report on the average costs of wardrobe items. Do they seem to you high compared with prices you paid for similar items? Compared with prices typical of your area? Send for the report on the latest *Seventeen* survey to see if the spending pattern has changed significantly.
5. Discuss with some professional woman in your city the year's budget for the career girl given in this chapter.
6. Plan a wardrobe for a young woman who has been teaching for the last ten years in your hometown. Select someone who is active in community life. Relate her expenditures to her salary and her plans for professional advancement and for vacations and travel.
7. Plan a wardrobe for the manager of a business involving contact with the public. Evaluate her wardrobe in relation to her special interests and goals.
8. Interview a recently married student to learn what she did for her trousseau and what advice she would give another student contemplating marriage before obtaining her sheepskin.
9. Invite this newlywed to give a talk to the class on assembling a trousseau.
10. Consult several bridal magazines to see what they recommend for a trousseau. Does the list represent the mixture of sentiment and common sense urged in this chapter?
11. Interview the bridal consultants of several department stores to find out what services they offer and at what cost.
12. If a member of the class expects to be married soon, plan a trousseau for her, after discussing with her the proposed wedding and postwedding activities.

II

PRODUCING CLOTHES: ART AND INDUSTRY

6

France: Leader of the Fashion World

For centuries France has been the undisputed leader of the fashion world. The Crusades, which began in 1096 and ended in 1291, undoubtedly helped to lay the foundation for this leadership. They were essentially a French enterprise—launched by a pope of French descent who preached on French soil the sermon which aroused the religious fervor of Western Europe.

The Normans of the northern provinces of France supplied the most effective leadership during the Crusades. Their Norse heritage of love of adventure, religiosity, and desire for territory made them naturals for the role of wresting the Holy Land from the Moslems. Their warrior princes enjoyed to the fullest the Moorish life with which they came in contact between campaigns—the frescoed walls, mosaic floors, Persian rugs, embroidered silk hangings, and, no doubt, the glimpses of women dressed in Oriental gauzes covered with sequins.

When the Crusades waned in the late thirteenth century the French emerged with the most prestige as the greatest power in Europe. Their geographical location gave them a natural advantage: in Medieval days the most easily traversed route from the Middle East to the Atlantic crossed France, as well as the best route from the northern countries of Europe to the Mediterranean and from Italy to Great Britain. More than half the borders of these countries are on the sea.

DRESS AFTER THE CRUSADES

Clothes remained comparatively simple until the middle of the thirteenth century, when the luxuries introduced by travelers from the East became available. Formerly, there had been only a wealthy noble class and a poor peasant class, but now a middle or merchant class emerged. These traders in Eastern ports and the manufacturers of goods at home soon grew wealthy enough to afford luxuries. They strove to keep pace with those of noble birth and developed a lively interest in clothes.

By 1300 Europe had lost its religious fervor and had become secular, legalistic, and scholastic. Contacts with the culture .of

Figure 6–1. The hennin, a tall conical hat with veil attached at the tip, popular in the fifteenth century. "Portrait of a Lady with Pink" by Hans Memling. (Courtesy of the Metropolitan Museum of Art, The Jules S. Bache Collection, 1949.)

the Middle East and the Orient, with their scholars and their arts, prepared the way for a revival of learning in Europe.

Court life after the Crusades became an increasingly important factor in the spread of civilization. More sophisticated and luxurious than ever before, it provided fertile soil for the development of the arts and letters and for the flowering of fashion, which draws its inspiration from all the arts.

The style of dress for women changed greatly. Clothing reached such proportions of magnificence that fortunes were squandered on fabrics and jewels. The loosely belted medieval gowns of luxurious fabrics were replaced by close-fitting costumes, often with voluminous trains. Fantastic headdresses were worn with these gowns. The hennin, a tall conical hat with a sheer veil flowing from its peak, was one of these head coverings (Figure 6–1).

The parti-colored gown, with each half a different color, was a favorite with the women of the nobility. It often bore the coat of arms of the wearer's family as well as that of her husband.

In the early part of the sixteenth century a new silhouette was introduced: the floor-length, bell-shaped skirt. Elaborate trimmings, bared bosoms, and ornate jewelry were among the distinguishing marks of the costuming of this period, all reflecting Italian influence. The earliest form of the hoopskirt also belongs to this period. A petticoat extended by hoops of iron, wood, or whalebone was worn beneath an ornate underskirt, which was exposed in front by a waist-high slash in the overskirt.

FRENCH LEADERSHIP

French leadership in fashion was established early in the 1600's, during the reign of Louis XIII. This leadership evolved partly by default, for social and political conditions in Italy and in England at that time did not encourage the flourishing of the arts in general or of the costume arts in particular. The minor arts which contribute to the fashion picture—goldsmithing, jewelry, and lace making, enameling, pottery and porcelain production—though influenced by the Italians, took on a definite French character and came to rank with the best in Europe.

The preeminence of France as a producer of textiles and laces was established by Colbert, devoted minister of Louis XIV, in the late 1600's. Eager to make France a great manufacturing nation, Colbert encouraged foreign factories to move to France, brought in Venetian lace makers, forbade French factory workers to leave the country, and started lace centers at Alençon and various other cities which soon became famous throughout the world. Around 100 establishments were started under patronage of the crown. Colbert bought the already well-known Gobelin tapestry works in Paris and transformed it into a factory for general upholstery in which designs were executed under the direction of the royal painter, Charles Le Brun. Colbert set high standards of quality for production and prescribed severe punishment for failure to achieve them.

INFLUENCE OF WOMEN OF THE COURT

Among the leaders of fashion was Madame de Pompadour, who in 1744 became the official mistress of Louis XV. A woman of great beauty and intelligence, Madame de Pompadour was a patron of many of the gifted painters, writers, and craftsmen of the day. She encouraged the king to give generous subsidies to the silk mills of Lyon, which became the finest in Europe.

During her twenty years at the court Madame de Pompadour influenced not only fashion but the course of national events, through her knowledge of politics and her skill in diplomacy. The people of France resented her, however, because of her extravagances. Unwittingly, she played a part in bringing on the revolution, through such policies as protecting and subsidizing writers like Voltaire and Rousseau and abetting the expulsion of the Jesuits.

Madame de Pompadour has been described as the epitome of the Dresden china figurine. Typically, her billowing, floor-length skirt was open from hem to waistline in the front and worn over a petticoat of the same silk. Ruching, ruffles, and lace trimmed her gowns, which were mostly of flowered silks. Jewelry as well as clothes meant much to her. Quite naturally, she inspired

Figure 6–2. Madame de Pompadour inspired designers of textiles, furniture, and coiffures as well as of dress. Portrait by M. G. de la Tour in the Louvre. (Photo by Giraudon.)

designers of dress for both men and women, and of textiles, furniture, and furnishings. Her name was given to a special style of hairdressing and to specific designs of chairs, sofas, and mirrors. Figure 6–2 shows Madame de Pompadour at her loveliest. With her death from tuberculosis at the age of forty-two, much of the resentment toward this courageous and highly intelligent woman evaporated.

Madame du Barry was another fashion leader. A pretty and fun-loving girl, she was a milliner's apprentice when Madame de Pompadour died. She, too, became mistress of Louis XV and was at the court during his last five years—and for nineteen more. She was beheaded in 1793 by the revolutionaries, who were in-

Figure 6–3. Madame du Barry, who influenced fashion for more than two decades, spent great sums for jewelry. Portrait by Mme. Vigée LeBrun in the Louvre. (Photo by Giraudon.)

censed by her extravagances, especially by the sums she spent for jewelry. Figure 6–3 is a photograph of a well-known painting of Madame du Barry. Both she and Madame de Pompadour made lavish use of perfumes, which they carried in exquisite, jeweled cases and even in a tiny compartment of their rings. Paint and powder, which had become a court requirement in the reign of Louis XIV, were used with better taste than formerly, and black beauty patches of all shapes and sizes were worn. When Madame du Barry came to the court in 1769, hairstyling had become so important that there were said to be 1,200 hairdressers in Paris alone.

Even more influential in the apparel arts was Marie Antoinette (Figure 6–4), who was married to Louis XVI—then the crown prince—before she was fifteen years old. After becoming queen, she and her dressmaker, Rose Bertin, dominated the fashion world. Twice a week, Mademoiselle Bertin brought new designs for both dresses and hats to the court for the queen's

Figure 6–4. Marie Antoinette, who long dominated the fashion world. This portrait at Versailles is one of more than twenty of her painted by Mme. Vigée LeBrun. (Photo by Giraudon.)

approval. So extensive was the queen's wardrobe—of satins, velvets, and brocades—that three large rooms of the palace were needed to store it.

A COUNTRY GIRL'S INFLUENCE

A vivacious country girl, Rose Bertin went to Paris at the age of sixteen and was made court milliner nine years later, two years before the death of Louis XV. Later, she was given the title Secretary of Fashion. She was devoted to Marie Antoinette, who was eight years younger than she, and became her confidante as well as her dressmaker.

A gifted designer, Mademoiselle Bertin had sufficient business sense to found a fashion house. It soon became known throughout the world through the ambassadors to the French court, and was first to export luxury fashions. To publicize her designs she dressed life-sized dolls in the current fashion and sent them to London and to other European cities, where ladies of the court took orders for these designs. Later, smaller dolls, called "fashion babies," carried news of the fashion world even over to the American colonies. This was before the founding of fashion magazines. The etching in Figure 6–5 shows Mademoiselle Bertin at the height of her influence.

Figure 6–5. Rose Bertin, first French designer to found a couture house of worldwide fame. Etching by Ingres. (Photo by Giraudon.)

During Marie Antoinette's regime, exaggeration of line became ever more pronounced. Hoops and *panniers* (frames to extend the hipline) eventually brought skirts into fashion that enlarged the hip width to a full six feet. Figure 6–6, a Flemish painting, shows such a skirt. Cords were inserted into the framework of the skirt to enable the wearer to telescope and lift the two side wings and the back pouf for sitting or for stepping into a carriage. However, sitting in such a costume was still so diffi-

Figure 6–6. Wife of Charles IV of Spain, wearing a dress with *panniers,* which extend the hipline to around six feet. Detail of portrait by Laurent Pecheux. (Courtesy of the Metropolitan Museum of Art, bequest of Annie C. Kane, 1926.)

cult that a more practical dress, the *polonaise,* was designed. With its full-gathered skirt looped up into three puffed sections over an underskirt, it could be worn for walks and was the forerunner of the tailored suit.

Necklines of this period were cut extremely low; sleeves extended to the elbow and ended in fluttering ruffles. Headdresses, powdered and decorated with strings of pearls and flowers or fanciful ornaments, were so high that their wearers had to kneel in their carriages or extend their heads out of the carriage window.

Figure 6–7. Shepherdess dress, popularized by Marie Antoinette for country wear. Detail of "The Interrupted Sleep" by François Boucher. (Courtesy of the Metropolitan Museum of Art, the Jules S. Bache Collection.)

The portrait of Marie Antoinette (Figure 6–4) shows her before this extreme period. Later, in response to the "back to nature" movement inspired by Rousseau, she adopted what we think of as the shepherdess dress (Figure 6–7) for country wear. The sheer cottons used for these dresses marked the introduction of the lingerie frock in Europe. Children's clothes ceased to be miniatures of those of adults and, partly through English influence, became simpler and better adapted to childhood.

REVOLT AGAINST EXCESSES OF DRESS

The French Revolution in 1793 brought the beheading of Marie Antoinette and a temporary eclipse of fashion—based as it had been on the luxuries of court life. After the revolution, revulsion against excesses of dress, as against other excesses of the court, brought a return to simplicity of line like that of early Greek and Roman dress. Semitransparent cotton dresses became the vogue, often worn even in winter with few underclothes except for flesh-colored tights. Those tights were similar to the full-length body stocking made by some American manufacturers today—a sheer, knitted one-piece covering from the soles of the feet to low on the neck. Petticoats edged with lace frills, however, soon became popular, with pantalets of flesh-colored satin as an alternative. The wearing of drawers, first introduced by courtesans, did not become general until the 1830's.

The Empress Josephine greatly influenced the return to simplicity during her thirteen years as wife of Napoleon Bonaparte,

Figure 6–8. Empress Josephine, the belle of Paris society when she first caught the eye of Napoleon Bonaparte. She influenced the return to simplicity in fashion and popularized the empire gown. Portrait by Prudhon in the Louvre. (Photo by Giraudon.)

and even after their divorce. Not wanting to seem taller than her husband, she wore heelless or low-heeled shoes, often elaborately embroidered. She also wore and popularized the empire gown, still known today, with the waist raised to a line just below the bosom and a slender, graceful skirt.

Josephine loved beautiful clothes and wore them with grace, as is evident from the painting in Figure 6–8. White and light green were her favorite colors. Most of her court clothes were of white with embroidered tracery of green or of green and gold. For her wraps she was especially fond of bright red, with ermine for lining. She was the first to wear fine batiste underwear, which she was said to have changed three times a day.

Napoleon himself was much interested in clothes and is reported once to have remarked pointedly to one of the women of the court, "That's a beautiful dress you're wearing—the same one you wore two weeks ago!"

EMPRESS EUGÉNIE'S INFLUENCE

Empress Eugénie, beautiful blonde Spanish-born wife of Napoleon III, brought about a return to the hoopskirt, partly because she wanted to conceal her pregnancy. A "crinoline," actually a framework made of hoops of steel, and several starched petticoats were used to hold out floor-length skirts, which by 1860 measured ten yards around. Later, the skirt was shortened, and petticoats of colored taffeta became the vogue. Bodices were fitted and boned, high at the neck except for evening wear. Every lady had dressing gowns to wear when she sought relief from tight lacing.

In the 1860's the princess dress appeared, cut in gores from the neck to the hemline. Shawls, capes, and flaring coats accompanied the gored skirt. One color scheme introduced by the empress was a combination of shades of brown with black velvet. In this period the jacket and skirt costume appeared for the first time. It was a tailored, somewhat mannish costume with a jacket shorn of lace and frills.

Eugénie's interest in dress and patronage of the French fabric mills and the manufacturers of trimmings contributed much to

Figure 6–9. Empress Eugénie, whose beauty and excellent horsemanship aroused the interest of Napoleon III. She brought a return of the hoopskirt and later introduced the tailored jacket and skirt costume. Portrait by Winterhalter in the Louvre. (Photo by Giraudon.)

the prosperity of France in this period. The painting of her shown in Figure 6–9 makes it easy to believe the reports of her beauty, elegance, and charm, which contributed much to the brilliance of the imperial regime.

Around 1860 hats were fastened to the hair with hatpins. The little round Empress Eugénie hat with its flat crown, ostrich plumes, and two long "follow me" streamers in back has enjoyed periodic revivals, the latest one in 1931.

Empress Eugénie established Charles Frederick Worth as court dressmaker around 1860, thus helping to launch the haute couture as we now know it. Worth, an Englishman, was married to a Frenchwoman named Marie Vernet, who modeled the clothes he designed and thus became the first live mannequin. Worth was also the first to show fabrics made up into dresses. Before that time dressmakers worked with materials provided by their patrons. Under Worth's influence, dress designers began to develop their ideas in fabrics of their own choice, often working with a designer of textiles to get a desired effect.

Figure 6–10 shows the sequence of French fashion leaders from 1744 to the founding of the Paris haute couture.

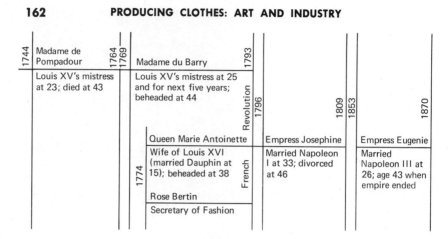

Figure 6–10.   Sequence of fashion leaders, 1744 to 1870.

THE CHAMBRE SYNDICALE DE LA COUTURE PARISIENNE˙

To represent the French dressmaking world in matters of law, taxes, and employment, the Chambre Syndicale de la Couture Parisienne was organized in 1868. Charles Frederick Worth was the first president. He recognized the need for protective measures for the growing industry and for a supply of workers capable of producing the beautiful handmade garments which customers had come to expect from Paris designers. By the mid-1960's the Chambre Syndicale had around 600 members, each of whom paid a membership fee in proportion to the number of employees in the firm.

The Chambre Syndicale sets the dates for the twice-yearly showings of new collections of models of the couture, issues admission cards to approved buyers and to members of the press, and enforces rules as to sketching and copying in an effort to prevent style piracy. The Chambre Syndicale also directs a school for the training of French youth for work in the couture houses. In the French dressmaking world, the artistry of the designer must be supported by the craftsmanship of skilled seamstresses if a garment is to be truly successful. Probably in no other country is there such emphasis on the teaching of the needle arts, on the exquisite hand finishing of garments.

Within the training school is a section for students from abroad. Figures 6–11 and 6–12 show some of these students in

Figure 6–11. Classroom at the Chambre Syndicale's school for the training of youth for work in the haute couture. The three students seated in the foreground are from the United States. (Photo courtesy of the Chambre Syndicale de la Couture Parisienne.)

Figure 6–12. Marjorie Dunton, press attachée for English-speaking countries, in her office at the Chambre Syndicale de la Couture Parisienne, surrounded by international students of the Chambre Syndicale's school. All but one of this group are from the United States. (Photo courtesy of the Chambre Syndicale de la Couture Parisienne.)

a classroom, and with one of the press attachées of the Chambre Syndicale. Graduates of the school, many of them in their own businesses, are now found around the world—in the United States, Canada, Australia, Japan, the Philippines, and several countries of Europe.

The president of the Chambre Syndicale since 1964 has been M. Daniel Gorin, whom John Fairchild in his book *The Fashionable Savages* calls "the granddaddy of the Paris couture." In 1937 M. Gorin became its general secretary, and during the four years of the German occupation of France (1940 to 1944) worked successfully with its president, the late Lucien LeLong, to prevent the forcible removal of the Paris couture to Germany. Among his many honors is the Chevalier of the Legion of Honor.

M. Gorin is also president of the National Federation of the Couture, official advisor of the French government on foreign trade, and founder and vice-president of the National Confederation of Industries of Art, Fashion, and Production. Figure 6–13 shows M. Gorin in his office.

Figure 6–13. Daniel Gorin, president of the Chambre Syndicale de la Couture Parisienne and a Chevalier of the Legion of Honor. (Photo courtesy of the Chambre Syndicale de la Couture Parisienne.)

TRAINING YOUTH FOR THE HAUTE COUTURE *

The couture industry of Paris is indisputably based on hand workmanship. *The Wall Street Journal* reported in 1964 that in the main workroom of the House of Dior, for example, three sewing machines were servicing forty workers.

In the public elementary schools of France every girl learns the rudiments of sewing. After she is graduated from this school, around the age of fourteen, she may take an examination on sewing techniques. If she passes it, she receives a work certificate. Armed with this she can become an apprentice in some couture house. During her three-year apprenticeship, she also must take courses in the school, set up by the Chambre Syndicale de la Couture Parisienne to supplement her training in the couture house. In these courses she not only learns to do the exquisite finishing of garments for which the French are famous, but also studies such subjects as design and the history of costume. These young seamstresses are known as *midinettes*.

After her three-year apprenticeship, when the girl is about seventeen years old, she takes an examination for the Certificat D'Aptitude Professionelle, or certificate of professional aptitude. Two more examinations, with perhaps a year or two of work in a couture house, then lie between her and the status of *première main qualifiée*, or fully qualified worker. After they finish the elementary school, some girls attend one of the other professional technical schools instead of the school established by the Chambre Syndicale; but most houses seem to prefer students from their own organization.

THE QUALIFIED WORKER

The pay of the qualified worker is $1 an hour, but her actual salary is closer to $1.50 an hour, according to officials of the Chambre Syndicale, because of the various fees paid for her by the employer: social security, family allowances, care for accidents or illnesses during working hours, vacations on pay, and the like.

* Terms often used in books and articles on the French couture are listed in Appendix D.

The morale of these women working for the couture or in an *atelier* of any member of the couture is high. They want to work only in "the sacred square" of the haute couture, the four "corners" of which are the Opéra, the Place de la Concorde, Alma, and St. Philippe du Roule. Each worker hopes that some day she may rise to the rank of *modelliste,* one of the designers of the house. The *modelliste* presents his or her designs to the staff of the house for criticism and perhaps suggestions for alterations, and then supervises the translation of the ideas into garments in the workroom. These garments are sold as models produced by the house; they do not bear the new designer's name. More than one *modelliste,* however, has become a big name in the haute couture—among them St. Laurent, who studied first in the school of the Chambre Syndicale, then worked in the House of Dior, and became head designer at Dior's death.

FROM INSPIRATION TO MODEL

Designers of women's apparel differ in their approach to their work. Some start with sketches, others with a trial fabric such as muslin or linen. The most skillful designers may work directly with the fabric selected for the model, gaining inspiration from its unique draping qualities. Whatever the approach, each designer has ideas to express. Many have had an extensive education in one or more of the arts, including architecture. Some have gained their understanding of basic design chiefly through working with a talented house designer.

After he makes the first sketches, the designer usually develops the design in a trial fabric or toile. The model is then criticized, altered, and perfected. Next, he selects fabrics and accessories—the belt, buttons, and trimmings. After the mannequin who will show the creation has been chosen, the trial garment is adjusted to her figure. Skilled workers then make the final garment. Thus is developed the high fashion for which France is famous.

Inspiration for new designs comes from a wide variety of sources. Art galleries are treasuries of creative ideas. Contemporary art may supply the inspiration for a design. For example,

Mondrian's canvases were reflected in Yves St. Laurent's 1965 collection, with straight lines and areas of bright color.

From a current movie may sprout a profusion of designs. In the United States the much-publicized filming of *Cleopatra* brought hundreds of designs on the Egyptian theme in clothes, hairdress, cosmetics, perfumes, and jewelry. In Paris *My Fair Lady* and *Tom Jones* had similar impacts.

A fabric may itself supply the inspiration for the cut of a beautiful dress. Dior is quoted as saying that he got the idea for his New Look in 1947 (Figure 6–14) from a glimpse of "the heaving hipline of a female Paris fishmonger." Travel is an unfailing source of design ideas; inspiration may be gained from native costumes, architecture, and sometimes even the landscape.

Figure 6–14. The New Look, 1947, with long skirts, rounded hips, and "liberated bosom." Christian Dior's New Look collection electrified the fashion world. (Photo by Maywald, courtesy of Christian Dior, Paris.)

THE PARIS HAUTE COUTURE

The haute couture of Paris, since its founding, has been made up of a relatively small group of leading designers from among the hundreds of custom dressmakers in France. Their houses are members of the "creative branch" of the Chambre Syndicale. In 1966 the twenty-seven members were: Balenciaga, Balmain, Capucci, Pierre Cardin, Carven, Castillo, Christian Dior, Courrèges, Georgette Renal, Givenchy, Grès, Guy Laroche, Hermès, Jacques Estérel, Jacques Griffe, Jacques Heim, Jacques Launay, Jean Patou, Jeanne Lanvin, Louis Feraud, Madeleine de Rauch, Maggy Rouff, Molyneux, Nina Ricci, Philippe Venet, Yves St. Laurent, and Ungaro. Only Chanel remained outside the fold, although her influence was still felt.

Some of these designers first gained recognition for their creative ability in countries other than France. In 1965 some American fashion writers singled out six of the haute couture designers as having the most influence at that time: Cristobal Balenciaga, Yves St. Laurent, Hubert de Givenchy, Gabrielle Chanel, Christian Dior, and André Courrèges.[1] Each had made and was still making a unique contribution.

Cristobal Balenciaga, the son of a seamstress in a Spanish fishing village, caters to the sophisticated woman and is considered by many to be the world's greatest designer, particularly of coats and suits. His models are characterized by perfect tailoring, restrained elegance, and chic. He is aloof, shuns publicity, and presents his collections only after other showings have been held.

Yves St. Laurent is known for his fresh and decidedly feminine designs. Following Dior's death in 1957, he was chosen to head the House of Dior—at the age of twenty-one. There were doubts as to his ability to assume such responsibility, but even his first showing was a success. Shortly after his third collection, St. Laurent was called up for military duty and the House of Dior replaced him with Marc Bohan. Now St. Laurent has a house of his own and is recognized as one of the foremost designers of France.

Hubert de Givenchy first gained recognition through his designs of separates. Endowed with great imagination and talent, and well educated in the arts, he designs for youth and particularly for the "young elegants."

Gabrielle Chanel has greatly influenced many other important designers both at home and abroad. In 1954, after years of retirement, she again opened her designing establishment. She

Figure 6–15. Gabrielle Chanel, one of the most influential of the world's designers. She is still a force in the fashion world in her eighties. (Photo courtesy of the House of Chanel.)

revived her famous soft cardigan suits, stressed beautiful textured woolens in lovely colors, and made gold buttons and dangling chains virtually her signature. Figure 6–15 is an excellent photograph of this famous designer.

Christian Dior showed his first collection, christened the New Look, in 1947, and it was a tremendous success. Aided financially by Marcel Boussac, a textile magnate, he undeniably held top place in the fashion world during the next decade; his death in 1957 was considered a tragedy. Figure 6–16 shows Dior as he looked at the height of his fame.

Marc Bohan, a realist as well as a great designer, took over the Dior firm after St. Laurent's brief tenure, and the establishment has flourished under his leadership. Figure 6–17 shows him selecting a fabric for one of this costumes. The fine craftsmanship that the house had stood for has been maintained. Creations of this house are sold as Dior originals.

The House of Dior does not design only for wealthy private customers; for the less affluent it has also turned out some ready-to-wear apparel—*prêt-à-porter* (ready to carry) as the French call it—and has sold it in a little store inside the house. Licensing agreements throughout the world have made highly profitable the sale of Dior-designed gloves, handbags, sweaters, lingerie, perfumes—and men's wear. By 1964 the Dior firm had become the largest fashion organization in the world, with a house in London and in New York as well as the original one in Paris (Figure 6–18). In that year it accounted for 50 per cent of all French fashion export business, according to *American Fabrics*.

André Courrèges studied engineering and worked for a time in that field before turning his attention to women's dress. He was associated with Balenciaga for ten years before opening his own salon. His straight, pared-down costumes, at first usually white, with short skirts and boots, had a strong influence on clothing design. Many of the inexpensive dress houses in the United States copied his models, since they so accurately reflected the mood of the times.

In 1965, however, Courrèges left the haute couture to design ready-to-wear clothes and turn out a thousand copies of a model instead of the couture's usual ten. By eliminating the haute couture's traditional three fittings, and by cutting and assembling the garments so as to reduce labor costs, he could sell each for $200, a fifth of his haute couture prices.

SHOWINGS OF FASHION COLLECTIONS

Showings of designs which reveal the new fashion trends usually take place in late January and July, after weeks of intense activity. Typically, a house presents between 100 and 200 models

Figure 6–16. Christian Dior, one of the world's greatest designers. He once declared, "Fashion is something of the marvelous, something to take us away from everyday life." (Photo courtesy of Christian Dior and *American Fabrics*.)

Figure 6–17. Marc Bohan, head of the Christian Dior empire, selecting a fabric for one of his models. He was a personal friend and disciple of Dior. (Photo by Studio Jean-Paul Cade, courtesy of Christian Dior.)

Figure 6–18. Paris headquarters of the Dior empire, the world's largest and most influential house of haute couture. It does a volume of business of considerably more than $10 million annually, yet is built on handicrafts. (Photo courtesy of Christian Dior.)

at an opening. Great secrecy surrounds the workrooms. When a mannequin goes from the workroom for a conference with the designer she is swathed in a sheet so that no outsider may see the model before the opening day.

Many of the designers' establishments are in beautiful old mansions, which provide elegant settings for the showing of creations. The *vendeuse* or saleswoman who attends to the individual customer is often a woman with social background, one who can deal successfully with wealthy clients.

People from all over the world attend the showings. Old friends of a given firm receive special invitations; others must apply for admission and are carefully screened by the Chambre Syndicale de la Couture Parisienne before they are sent an admission card, in an effort to protect designers from would-be fashion pirates, who come to copy not to buy. Members of the press are invited to showings at different hours from those for buyers. Most houses now show the press first.

Each house of the haute couture exacts a fee (called a *caution*) from every representative of a manufacturing firm or retail store attending its opening. This fee is deducted later from prices of purchases. In 1966, however, houses like that of Jacques Heim asked instead that the representative purchase one model or two paper patterns. St. Laurent also set no fee that year but required each store and each manufacturer to buy at least two models. The House of Dior charged the manufacturer $2,000 but permitted the firm to send two people to the opening; it charged the retail store only $500.

The lowest price asked of the individual customer for a dress at that spring's openings was $600. Minimum for suits and coats was $1,000, set by Balmain, Grès, Molyneux, and Venet. Elaborate design and costly materials can bring the price of an original up to $3,500 or more.

A firm buying a model for wholesale copying naturally pays a much higher price than does a private customer. Some firms buy a design outright in order to copy it exactly or to adapt it; others have a model shipped to them "in bond"—that is, on loan for six months to a year, during which time it may be displayed or copied, if that is in the contract. In the United States designs sent in bond are duty-free.

Each garment on arrival in the United States is inspected by customs officials before it is tagged. A long needle is used to pass a string through the hem of the garment, and the ends are secured firmly with a United States Customs seal. This seal may not be removed during the period of the loan.

A ST. LAURENT OPENING

Newsweek's report of the Paris showing of clothes for the fall and winter of 1963 gives the atmosphere of a typical opening.[2]

It begins with a description of the scene at the salon of Yves St. Laurent:

. . . The pale, gawky young man with the luminous eyes and slim hands . . . spoke, "Allons, mes enfants, il faut commencer. . . ."

The ritual began. Eight young women, each as cool as a votary in a Greek temple, stood ready to go on stage, almost motionless, while the young man ran his long, nervous fingers over a jacket here, smoothed out a skirt there, and gave a final caress to the folds of a chiffon evening dress. Then the first of the girls stepped out, carefully, precisely, moving before the intent, saurian gaze of the audience with short and measured strides, like flamingos in a rock garden.

The young man was Yves St. Laurent, 27, high priest of France's haute couture, and he was waiting for the audience's response—his nerves drawn tight as an E-string tuned a shade too high. At first the applause came in little bursts. Then, as model after model paraded before the audience, the bursts grew into a tumultuous storm of approval. St. Laurent relaxed . . . ventured a small, nervous smile.

The tight little smile was the big fashion news from Paris last week, and big fashion news from Paris is big news everywhere. . . . In the happy hysteria that followed his showing, St. Laurent was mobbed by a wildly emotional crowd of admirers. . . . Dancer Zizi Jeanmaire shot off her chair like a rocket and hurled herself into his frail arms. Susan Luling, the former director of the House of Dior, grabbed him in a happy hammer lock. . . . Diana Vreeland, editor-in-chief of *Vogue,* fired off a verbal salute . . . "It was simply, superbly, fabulously, du-vine," she said. Eugenia Sheppard, fashion editor of the *New York Herald Tribune,* delivered her verdict with crisp incisiveness. "St. Laurent," she said, "holds Paris in the palm of his hand today."

Inside this gossamer jungle, a sweltering, shoving army of dress buyers, press ladies, models, photographers, and dress designers spin around in a tight little world of their own. Out of their frenzied actions would come a new mode for the winter of 1963. In just a few weeks' time, women in Perth and Paducah will be critically eying themselves in store mirrors, checking the welt seams on a reproduction of one of the 2,875 dresses shown in Paris this summer. . . .

WHY FRANCE'S FASHION LEADERSHIP?

Why did France become the leader of the fashion world and why does it maintain that supremacy?

First, as has already been pointed out, France has an excellent geographical location. *Second,* as has also been shown, Paris early established itself as the center of culture and refinement, the leader in the arts, the chief source of inspiration both for scholars and for artists. France provided fertile soil for the growth of the apparel arts through its democratic spirit, which brought tolerance for individuality and even for eccentricity; its love of beauty in all aspects; its magnificent buildings, broad avenues, and lovely parks; its opera, theater, and museums. Moreover the French have long considered fashion designing to be as important as any of the other arts—painting, sculpture, music, or architecture.

Third, in no other nation has dress been such an absorbing interest. It is regarded not as a frivolity but as something with which to embellish life and make it more agreeable—"an inexhaustible stimulant," as Jacques Heim once commented in his magazine *La Gazette Matignon.* Nowhere else does so much painstaking, even loving, care go into the making of a design— in the fabric, in the dress, and in accessories. As John Fairchild points out:

Paris designers have working for them those little artisans and the great fabric creators who are thinking only of something "new." Special jewelry, buttons, zippers, and even clasps. Wide belts, skinny belts, half belts. Shoes with new shapes. Every fashion accessory, couture oriented.

The artisans run to their master, the couturier, and after seeing thousands of new things, he becomes inspired and chooses. In servicing the couturier, there is little money for the artisan, but he hopes that if Chanel says, "Yes," he will be launched.[3]

In the textile houses much handwork is done. Skilled craftsmen thereby achieve unusual textures and designs that cannot be produced by machine. Sometimes they hand dye the yarns to get the exact hue or tint desired. Often they get their artistic effects through hand processes, screen printing and block printing. Textile designers often produce a material for a particular dress designer in a limited amount to insure its exclusiveness. The high cost of apparel coming from the couturiers of France results partly from the high cost of these luxury fabrics. The textile mills of France have long been among the best in the world, in spite of the necessity for importing most raw materials.

Among the many long-established textile firms allied with French fashion are Lesur, Staron, and Ducharne, all of which now have branch offices in the United States. Ducharne brings out around 150 new silk print patterns a season, an impossible achievement for American mills, geared as they are to quantity production, with automatic looms, high-speed warpers, and, of necessity, a minimum number of constructions. American mills produce high-quality materials, sometimes of limited yardage in collaboration with designers and manufacturers of exclusive lines.

Fourth, the French government has long recognized fashion as a great source of national wealth and through the years has passed laws and regulations to foster "the needle trades" and dress design, thus helping them to expand into an industry of first importance.

Design in France is protected by the government quite as vigilantly as is the work of novelists and composers. After a costume is made from a design it is photographed—front, back, and sides—and is then registered. By contrast, the United States has done nothing to protect dress designs from unauthorized copying. A dress design in France is considered property, and an unauthorized copyist is severely punished, sometimes with a prison sentence in addition to a fine and damages. The style piracy law was passed in 1952, carrying penalties of up to $4,000 in fines and two years' imprisonment. In a typical case in 1955, the guilty party was fined 200,000 francs and the injured party was awarded damages of 4 million francs.

Fashion in France has a more basic role in the national economy than is true in any other country. Fashion is to France what the automobile industry is to the United States. Put together all the interlocking fashion industries—the haute couture, the fabric mills, the makers of lace, trimmings, shoes, gloves, and findings —and you have tremendous sums of money and large numbers of people involved. Two of every five women in France are employed in the garment and allied trades.

Fifth, leaders of the fashion world enjoy great prestige in France, prestige equal to that of bankers, industrialists, novelists, statesmen—indeed to that of any other professional or business group. Members of the haute couture have often been awarded the Cross of the Legion of Honor, created by Napoleon Bonaparte as the highest award of the French government, to be given to those who have performed distinguished service to the nation either in military or in civilian life.

Madame Jeanne Lanvin, one of the leading couturières from the late 1890's until her death in 1946, was awarded the Cross of the Legion of Honor in 1926 and in 1938 was made one of its officers. Lucien LeLong, president of the Chambre Syndicale from 1937 to 1945 and first important member of the Couture to sell ready-to-wear clothes, was made a chevalier of the Legion of Honor in 1937, when he was thirty-six years old. Madame Alix Grès, who started as a sculptor then shifted to dress designing, was one of the youngest women in the nation to win this coveted honor. Robert Ricci, son of the founder of the House of Ricci, and Pierre Balmain are among later members of the couture to be made chevaliers of the Legion of Honor. Eugène Rodier, late head of one of the famous textile houses, was given the scarlet rosette of Commander of the Legion. Madame Marie-Andrée Gastanié, director-general of the fashion magazine *Officiel de la Couture*, won the Cross of the Legion of Honor in 1962.

THE FRENCH FASHION INDUSTRY IN WORLD WAR II

The most serious threat to the supremacy of the French fashion industry came in World War II. During the four years of German occupation, 1940 to 1944, the German authorities wanted to move all the design houses and the textile factories to Berlin to establish the world's fashion center inside Hitler's Reich.

Fortunately, Lucien LeLong, then president of the Chambre Syndicale, and Daniel Gorin, at that time its secretary, had the combination of courage, diplomacy, and shrewdness needed to prevent this catastrophe. Accordingly, at the end of the war France was still in possession of all the essentials for revival of its biggest industry, fashion. The first peacetime collections of the haute couture, shown in 1947, clearly demonstrated the resilience and the creative genius of the French.

READY-TO-WEAR IN THE HAUTE COUTURE

Ready-to-wear was once almost a dirty word with the Paris haute couture. Economic pressure, however, gradually forced even the best houses into it. According to John Fairchild of *Women's Wear Daily*, the tragedy of most of these houses was

ıuld not make money from their custom-made ap-
world's stores and manufacturers were living off
h style piracy.[4]

essmaking in Paris has always been costly. As Fran-
executive editor of the French newspaper *L'Express*,
ıny house of the haute couture must be in a fashionable part of Paris, where rent and taxes are sky high.[5] Assembling a collection represents a big investment. Dior's spring
showing of 1965, for example, with its 174 models, represented
an outlay of $200,000 in labor and materials. The average cost
of each dress in labor alone was $470. Then there was perhaps
an $80 minimum for materials, and of course its share of the
overhead costs.

What saves the day for any house are its sidelines, such as
perfumes, lingerie, girdles, ties, shoes, bags, gloves, lipstick.
Chanel's No. 5 perfume made her wealthy. France's annual income from perfumes is around $350 million a year. Each house
also gets a varying sum from its international licenses, which are
issued for the use of the house name and sale of the products of
the house.

The result of these economic pressures was a big surge into
production of ready-to-wear during the 1960's. By December,
1965, twenty-one of the top twenty-eight Paris houses had been
drawn into it, and had become in reality couture manufacturers.
That year two of the fashion leaders, Yves St. Laurent and André
Courrèges, fell into line. Only Balenciaga and Chanel remained
aloof. Some were making their ready-to-wear apparel in their
own workrooms and selling it in boutiques inside the house.
Dior, Givenchy, Nina Ricci, and Molyneux were among these
designers.

Contract firms sprang up to handle the manufacturing and
selling for others. But in 1965 ready-to-wear represented only
about a tenth of the total revenue of the haute couture, perhaps
$35 million. The Paris manufacturers had still not solved all the
problems of sizing, fitting, and finishing for mass production.[6]
Yet *Women's Wear Daily* reported that the boutique, the little
specialty shop handling ready-to-wear, had become *the* place to
shop in Paris.

OTHER EUROPEAN FASHION CENTERS

Today, other European countries have gained recognition for their designing of beautiful clothing. England can boast a group of designers who have become internationally known, especially for men's and children's apparel and for beautiful textiles. Among the many associated with British fashion are Norman Hartnell, John Cavanaugh, Hardy Amies, and Digby Morton— and, for youth, Mary Quant.

Italy has held a place of importance in the fashion world since World War II. Her increasingly successful shoe business, her fabric and glove industries, her thriving sweater and knitwear businesses—all of which undersell those of Paris—promise well for the future of Italy's fashion industry. Italian sportswear, with Emilio Pucci as its most successful exponent, has had great impact on American fashion.

Italy has a rich heritage in the arts from which its designers can draw inspiration, and a climate that attracts many people of leisure for vacations and shopping. Its seasonal fashion shows are held in the rival centers of Rome and Florence, usually just before those in Paris. Famous palaces provide elegant settings for these openings. Among the most successful and influential designers of the 1960's are Pucci, Alberto Fabiani, Irene Galitzine, Patrick de Barentzen, and Nicol and Zoe Fontana.

Though designers in these European fashion centers have achieved marked success on their own, the Paris haute couture tends to look on them rather paternalistically—or to consider them clients rather than equals in the fashion world.

NOTES

1. John Fairchild, *The Fashionable Savages* (Garden City, N. Y.: Doubleday and Co., Inc., 1965), pp. 11 and 14.
2. "The Rites of New Fashion," *Newsweek*, LXII (August 12, 1963), pp. 43–51.
3. Fairchild, p. 11.
4. *Ibid.*, p. 12.
5. Françoise Giraud, "After Courrèges, What Future for the Haute Couture?" *New York Times Magazine*, September 12, 1965, pp. 50–51.

6. "Paris Puts Its Magic into Ready-to-Wear," *Business Week*, No. 1894 (December 18, 1965), pp. 78–82.

FURTHER READING

BEATON, CECIL. *The Glass of Fashion.* Garden City, N. Y.: Doubleday and Co., Inc., 1954. A book on women's dress, designers, and fashion leaders.

DAVENPORT, MILLIA. *The Book of Costume.* New York: Crown Publishers, 1948. Source book on costume of the Western world, profusely illustrated with reproductions of paintings and engravings by artists of the various centuries.

FAIRCHILD, JOHN. *The Fashionable Savages.* Garden City, N. Y.: Doubleday and Co., Inc., 1965. Part I, Over There, pp. 7–60. A gossipy discussion of the fashion world of Paris.

PAYNE, BLANCHE. *History of Costume.* New York: Harper & Row, 1965. Chapters on the sixteenth and nineteenth centuries. Product of years of study of historical costume.

PICKEN, MARY BROOKS, and MILLER, DORA LOUES. *Dressmakers of France.* New York: Harper & Row, 1956. Facts about the French couture, with biographical sketches about the designers who have made fashion history.

ROSCHO, BERNARD. *The Rag Race.* New York: Funk and Wagnalls, Inc., 1963. Chapter 6 on differences between the French and American garment business. The book is written by a man whose family was a part of the Seventh Avenue garment industry and who also knows the French couture.

WILCOX, R. TURNER. *The Mode of Costume.* New York: Charles Scribner's Sons, 1942. Chapters 26–28 and 30–33. Brief discussions of the costumes of various historical periods, with good drawings as illustrations.

STUDY SUGGESTIONS

1. Prepare a report for class on the French couture. Chapter 6 of *Rag Race* by Roshco is one good reference.
2. Present to the class biographical details on selected leaders of the French couture.
3. Examine the leading fashion magazines to find out how many designs are credited to foreign designers. Are French, Italian, and English houses all represented?
4. Do these magazines report on the twice-a-year collections of these foreign designers?
5. Study *The Book of Costume* by Davenport and *The Mode in Costume* by Wilcox, and trace the changes in fashion during the sixteenth, seventeenth, and eighteenth centuries.

7

Evolution of the Clothing Industry

The American way of producing clothes contrasts sharply with the French. In the United States practically all clothing is mass produced, machine-made, and often moderately low priced; in France it is almost entirely custom-made by hand, and expensive. In this country, clothing production is primarily a business; in France, it is primarily an art.

Three factors in large measure account for these differences. The settling of a new country, whose Constitution was based on the principles of democracy, encouraged uniformity and practicality in dress rather than the elegance and formality appropriate to the way of living of the French upper class. The rapid industrialization of the country and its growing wealth placed money in the hands of many people rather than of a favored few. Social restrictions were relaxed and women took part in public life. A study of the evolution of clothing production in the United States provides insight into social and economic forces which have influenced American industry.

GARMENT MAKING IN THE HOME

In early colonial times in America, every girl in the family was taught to sew, for the women of the household made all the family's clothes: the underwear, sleeping garments, and outerwear, even men's suits and coats. They made fabrics by hand, arns spun by hand then woven on a hand loom. It took all e women of a family at least a year to spin enough yarn for ach to have a new dress.

Usually, a grandmother or a maiden aunt or a trusted slave served as the chief seamstress. Local dressmakers and tailors supplemented the efforts of these home seamstresses. Some of them kept informed about European fashion through fashion dolls sent from London or Paris. Traveling dressmakers and, occasionally, tailors also found plenty to do. Each was usually hired months in advance and would live with the family until she had "sewed them up." Her arrival was eagerly anticipated, both for the news and gossip she could pass on and for her craftsmanship. Wealthy citizens, such as George Washington, had some of their clothes tailored in London.

START OF FACTORY PRODUCTION

First came the tailor's shop, which made clothes only for men. Craftsmen who had learned the tailoring trade before coming to the New World opened shops, and with the help of other tailors, some of them women, turned out what were virtually custom-made garments.

Growth in demand for men's clothes led to a shift in methods of production. Custom making gave way to processes that permitted a shop to turn out several garments in the time formerly required to make one. The tailor, or the merchant, as he was sometimes known, hired journeymen to work for him or sent the precut garments to contractors who distributed them to the farmers' wives or the villagers for sewing.

At first, such clothes were of poor quality and certainly of poor fit, as sizing was a hit-or-miss affair—mostly miss. The elite of the young nation continued having their clothes made by custom tailors. Quality gradually improved, however, so that by 1835 the men's suits offered in the shops were of medium grade.

Sailors in the seaport cities of New England were among the first patrons of these ready-to-wear shops. They were usually in port too short a time to have custom clothes made, and often were out of the country for several years on voyages. Accordingly, around 1830 merchant–tailors started making up clothes to outfit them. Their shops were called slop shops, chiefly because the garments, all made of coarse materials and cut in the same size, were to be stored in the sailors' "slop chests" while at sea.

In the 1840's these shops started manufacturing rough work clothes for the Negroes on Southern plantations. No samples of these garments exist today, for museums have not been interested in preserving work clothing. Many of the shops went bankrupt when the Civil War cut them off from this market; others were saved by orders for uniforms for the Union Army.[1]

Shops making the first ready-to-wear clothes were small and dark, with no display windows, and on fair days the clothes offered for sale were hung outside in the street. The fortunes of many a New England and New York family can be traced to these early shops; Brooks Brothers clothing store in New York is one of them.

Men's shirts were the next article of apparel to be ready-made. Charles F. Hathaway was the first to make these articles, which had ruffles and tucks and required much painstaking needlework. Figure 7–1 gives some idea of the elaborate dress shirts of that

Figure 7–1. Beruffled and tucked, Hathaway's shirts were high-fashion articles, attractively boxed. (Courtesy of Hathaway Shirts.)

period. They were often attractively boxed as a high-fashion garment. Hathaway started out in Plymouth early in the 1800's in his own home with workers from the community, making about two dozen shirts a week and distributing them himself to retailers by stagecoach. Later, he moved to Boston and opened a retail store which featured his shirts.

NEW INVENTIONS

By the end of the American Revolution new inventions were paving the way for less laborious production of clothing. Two Englishmen, James Hargreaves and Richard Arkwright, invented devices for spinning more than a single yard at a time, first by horse power, later by water power. Great Britain jealously guarded the secrets of these yarn mills, of course, and forbade the export of the spinning machines and even the emigration of mechanics and mill workers acquainted with their operation.

But with the migration of many peoples to the new and rapidly developing United States it was inevitable that knowledge of new inventions would also reach this country. A young apprentice in one of the Arkwright's mills, Samuel Slater, dreaming of a better life in the New World, disguised himself as a farmer, took passage for America, and presented himself to Moses Brown, a mill owner in Pawtucket, Rhode Island. From his six and a half years of work in the Arkwright mills, Slater was able to reconstruct a 72-spindle mill by 1790. Such mills soon made possible the production of enough American-made yarn to meet the need of the rapidly growing nation.

At that time, looms for weaving the yarn into cloth were still hand-operated in this country. Another Englishman, Edmund Cartwright, patented the first power loom in 1785. The loom was an imperfect contrivance at first and required around thirty years of experimenting to be made into a truly efficient power loom. The British, still jealously guarding their machinery specifications, were successful until 1812 in keeping Americans from discovering how power looms were constructed. In that year a New Englander, Francis Cabot Lowell, visited a factory in England which made cotton cloth and took mental notes on the loom construction so as to reproduce it when he returned to

America. Within two years he had built a cotton mill in Waltham, Massachusetts, the first mill in America to combine in one plant all the processes for manufacturing cloth.

FACTORS NEEDED FOR MASS PRODUCTION

Textile manufacturing got its start early in the nineteenth century. It grew rapidly, first in New England and later in the South, and supplied one of the most important elements for mass production of clothing, *an abundance of inexpensive cloth.* Other elements were necessary before clothing production could be anything but one of the handicrafts. So long as seams had to be sewn with a hand-operated needle and thread, little speed could be attained. *The invention of the sewing machine,* which could produce stitches many times faster than handwork, was an important step forward.

A supply of labor capable of performing the various tasks in a tailor shop or a garment factory was needed, as well as a *system of sizing garments* that would provide a reasonable fit for persons of different sizes and ages. Finally there had to be *a demand for mass-produced apparel* before people would be willing to depart from the customary way of acquiring clothing, that of home production or custom making. Each of these elements is discussed in detail below.

SEWING MACHINES SPUR PRODUCTION

The advent of the sewing machine was needed for garment making to become efficient. Inventors both in Europe and in this country tried to develop a machine to take the drudgery from the making of clothes. In 1832 Walter Hunt, a New York mechanic, hit on the idea of using an eyepointed needle, moved by an arm linked to a shuttle carrying a second thread, to produce an interlocked stitch, precisely as it does in today's machines. It sewed poorly, however, and after trying in vain to improve the machine, Hunt abandoned it.

A decade later Elias Howe, Jr., son of a Massachusetts farmer–miller, invented a similar but better machine and borrowed the money to get it patented in 1846. Though he demonstrated that it could sew 250 smooth and even stitches a minute, he could not interest any manufacturer in making it. Tailors fought the invention, believing that its adoption would make them beggars.

Accordingly, Howe borrowed money to send his brother to England to try to market it there. A London corset manufacturer paid 250 pounds for the machine and gave a verbal promise to take out a patent for it in England and then to pay Howe's brother three pounds for each machine sold—if the thing proved salable. The corset maker eventually made $1 million from the invention—Howe, not a cent. Howe himself then spent two years in London, working part of the time to adapt his sewing machine to corset-making needs. He returned to the United States with only a half-crown in his pocket.

While Howe was in England, other American inventors had been experimenting with sewing machines, including Isaac M. Singer, a one-time actor, theater manager, and adventurer. Singer invented his machine in 1850 and started energetically promoting it through advertising, exhibitions at fairs, and sending out agents. Howe at once charged Singer and the other inventors with infringement of patent and in 1854 a Massachusetts judge declared, "For all the benefit conferred upon the public by the introduction of a sewing machine, the public are indebted to Mr. Howe." [2] This was the turning point in Elias Howe's fortune. By the time of his death thirteen years later, he made around $2 million from his invention.

The sewing machine was operated at first by hand, then by foot, and finally by electricity. The speed of today's machine is many times that of early ones, of course, but it still requires an operator. Many varieties of sewing machines exist today, each made to perform a task that was once done by hand—some to sew on buttons, some to make buttonholes, others to do hemming and even to execute embroidery stitches.

CHEAP LABOR FOR THE FACTORIES

The third essential element for the mass production of clothing is a plentiful labor supply. When the first textile mills were started in New England, farm girls from good homes in near-by areas were hired as workers. The corporation launched by Lowell built dormitories for them, even hired housemothers, and started the girls in a social life centered around the church. Conditions elsewhere were not so wholesome, and living standards in general deteriorated. Even in Lowell's mills wages eventually dropped, and the farm girls no longer came in to work.

The middle 1880's, however, brought in another source of cheap labor, refugees from Europe, among them clothing workers eager to establish themselves in this land of opportunity. The biggest influx into the mill towns was of Italians, but there were also large numbers of Germans, Poles, Slovenians, Finns, Lithuanians, and Bohemians, all of whom tended to collect in cities.

Jewish immigrants began coming in after 1880 from Russia, Rumania, and Austria–Hungary. Tailors and shoemakers made up the largest group of these immigrants. They were among the poorest and least educated, and were looked down on by other Jewish groups, especially the business classes and the intellectuals.

SIZING OF GARMENTS

The invention of the sewing machine gave great impetus to the mass production of clothing. But before work could move ahead, it was necessary to settle on measurements for garments to fit people of various body proportions. Commercial patterns did not exist; each tailor or dressmaker had his own scheme for adding here or taking away there so as to provide his patron with a reasonably well-fitted garment.

The first attempt to develop a scale of sizing for garments was made at the start of the Civil War. Thousands of men were measured for height and chest girth, and these figures were turned over to manufacturers. Other important dimensions obviously were ignored, but these measurements were a starting point from which today's garment proportions have come. During World War I much more detailed studies of men's body measurements were made, again for the making of uniforms for the military services. Study of women's and children's body measurements came much later, in the 1930's.

Even today, the standardizing of garment sizes is incomplete and leaves much to be desired. Each producer of factory-made garments reserves the right to interpret the body measurements as he sees fit, though he uses a generally accepted designation for size. A misses' size 12 may fit a woman well in certain garments while in others, particularly those of a better grade, a size 10 often will fit better.

DEMAND FOR READY-TO-WEAR CLOTHING

Two historic events created a need for an immediate and large supply of apparel and thus hastened the shift away from the making of custom clothing: the Civil War, already discussed, with its need for uniforms for the army, and the Gold Rush of 1849. The Gold Rush created a demand for quantities of clothing for adventurers headed west to seek their fortunes. Levi Strauss was one of the New York fortune seekers who arrived by boat in San Francisco in 1850. With him he brought a peddler's pack of merchandise suitable for the pioneers, including canvas and duck for tents and Conestoga wagon coverings.

"You should have brought the heavy pants we need," a miner told him. Strauss promptly had his tailor make the miner some pants from this heavy material. Soon he had so many orders that he had to gather a group of tailors and seamstresses and build a factory for them to work in.

The metal reinforcements for the "levis," as these jeans were called, were first used by Jacob Davis, a tailor in Virginia City, Nevada. One of Davis' customers was a miner nicknamed Alkali, who liked to carry rock specimens in his pockets. Davis got tired of constantly repairing Alkali's torn pockets; so he took the pants over to a blacksmith who reinforced the pockets at the corners with copper rivets. Strauss and Davis patented the idea for the levis. Today, levis with their metal reinforcements at points of stress are sold not only throughout the United States but also in fifty-one foreign countries.

Within a few decades the quality of ready-to-wear clothing for men had so improved that it had achieved wide acceptance. Not only was heavy-duty clothing being produced, but also clothing for business and dress wear, through the adaptation of tailor's techniques to manufacturing.

WOMEN'S READY-TO-WEAR

Women's and children's clothes continued to be custom-made for some years after the first ready-made clothes for men had appeared. The first ready-made garments for women were mantles or cloaks, garments that required many of the same tailoring processes used for men's wear. Hoopskirts, the foundation for the bell-shaped skirt of the middle 1800's, had been factory made for some time because of the difficulty of working with wires and tapes. By 1880, however, 562 establishments were turning out women's coats and suits. Shirtwaists to wear with the then-fashionable blue serge suit followed inevitably. They became so popular that, by 1900, 400 shops were making them.

The prejudice against ready-made clothing gradually faded even though the garments could not measure up in quality to the carefully finished ones made at home. During the last decade of the nineteenth century, production of cotton dresses, muslin underwear, and children's clothing had its beginning. Ready-made dresses, however, are a product of the twentieth century. The first dresses were poor by present standards, but quality gradually improved. Women liked the convenience of ready-mades as they sought ways to save time. Today, good styling and workmanship in mass-produced clothing are taken for granted.

THE SWEATSHOP

The ever-growing demand for ready-made clothing and the appearance of the sewing machine, plus the steadily increasing flow of immigrants from Europe by the 1880's, created sweatshop conditions in the garment industry. Employers paid workers barely enough to sustain life and worked them long hours in wretched surroundings.

These immigrants arrived with little or no money and crowded into the slums of large cities, where others from their own country had already settled. Then they hired out for whatever wages they could get. Earlier and more skilled migrants contemptuously called many of them "Columbus tailors"—that is, men who had only recently discovered America and the art of tailoring. They were helpless to understand or cope with the contradictions of American life: political liberty degraded by corruption and economic freedom corroded by exploitation of labor.

The system of contracting work spread like a virus in the industry. The large manufacturer, with perhaps 100 workers in his factory, was ambitious to make still more money but was unable or unwilling to enlarge his factory. So he dickered with contractors to take garments cut in the factory to be sewed up elsewhere, at so much a garment. Manufacturers liked this contracting system, of course, since they did not have to provide workroom facilities, hire operators, or deal with a foreman.

The contractor, often someone who had himself been an immigrant not many years before, would line up workers at the lowest possible wage. Sometimes he would find a basement or an unheated loft over a shop or a room in a tenement building for a workshop, rent enough sewing machines for a team of "Columbus tailors," and set them to work.

Occasionally, a tailor would turn one or more rooms of his home into a workshop, buy some sewing machines on credit, and proceed to exploit his wife and children and as many others as he could crowd into the workshop to sew up the garments left by the contractor. Sometimes workers had to provide their own needles, thread, and even sewing machines, which they could rent from the boss. The manufacturer was indifferent to conditions under which his garments were made so long as he could sell them at a tidy profit. Neither federal nor state governments as yet felt any responsibility for citizen welfare. Unions were just beginning to be organized.

As late as 1886, little shops were set up with a team of workers, often nine of them, each responsible for a different operation. Figure 7–2 shows a typical dingy workroom, not one of the worst ones. Benjamin Stolberg in his book *Tailor's Progress* reports on conditions of that period:

The team had to turn out a certain amount of work every day. The contractor constantly added to the day's task. Originally it had been nine coats a day. It rose to 10 and 14, then to 18 and 20. Men often came to work at 4 A.M. Ten o'clock at night would usually see the

Figure 7–2. Immigrants working in a New York City sweatshop around 1900. This room, though dingy, at least had windows for ventilation. (Photo by Brown Brothers.)

day's task done. But if not, the team would work till midnight or until they were exhausted. Sometimes they would have to finish in the morning the previous day's work, which might take till noon. Thus a man who had worked six days of 15 to 18 hours might get at the end of the week three and a half to four days' pay.

Weekly wages for the best operators in the factory were $18. But working according to the task system, they would get only $12. Other members of a team who should have earned $8 or $10 were paid $5 at the end of the week. In 1886 weekly wages for men were supposed to be about $15 and for women $8, but after working 16 to 18 hours a day for a full week they could finish only about four days' tasks and they received pay for only four days.[3]

Stolberg further quotes from an 1890 report of the New York Bureau of Labor Statistics as follows:

Before new spools of silk were given out, the empty spools had to be returned; if they were lost, a fine of 50 cents had to be paid for each, the real value being nothing; . . . if an employee lost a trimming ticket before he had received the trimmings he had to pay the full value of the trimmings, which might be valued from $1 to $10. In some shops workers had to supply their own sewing machines or else rent them from the boss. Some shops forbade the workers to bring their lunches or to send out for a beer, a universal custom in those days. Workers might be fired for any reason, for arriving five minutes late or quitting five minutes early or going to the washroom.

Garment workers were notoriously subject to tuberculosis, rheumatism, and skin diseases caused by poisonous dyes in the clothes they handled. Disease and delinquency, crime and prostitution, were inevitable results of such wretched conditions. In the sweatshop period, it is estimated that one of every three people in the lower East Side of New York City slept in a room without any source of ventilation. Many of these rooms became garment workrooms at dawn, and the already foul air was made worse by the fumes of gasoline from the pressing irons, the sweat of the workers, and the odor of damp wool.

Labor strife was the inevitable result of sweatshop conditions. Workers banded together in unions to try to protect their interests. These unions, however, had their ups and downs, with rival organizations competing for members, and factions within each limiting their effectiveness.

THE RISE OF THE ILGWU

Finally, in 1900, an industrial union of all crafts in the women's garment trades was organized, the International Ladies' Garment Workers' Union (ILGWU). By that time the garment industry had become one of the major consumer goods industries in the nation, with 2,701 establishments, a capital investment of more than $48,000,000 and nearly 84,000 workers (almost a third of them women and girls), and an output valued at almost $160,000,000.

In its first three years the ILGWU grew rapidly, along with other branches of organized labor. It became interested in death and sickness benefits for members and in improving relations with employers. The depression of 1903–1904 hit the young organization hard; locals dwindled in number and unauthorized and unsuccessful strikes further weakened the union.

Two strikes in New York City in 1909 and 1910 dramatized the plight of women in the garment industry: the strike of shirt-waist makers, called the Uprising of the Twenty Thousand, which lasted almost three months, and the strike of the cloakmakers, which lasted nearly two months.

The girls making the popular shirtwaists, many of them teen-agers, were being ruthlessly exploited. Wages were $7 to $12 a week for fifty-five or more hours of work; one of every four of the workers was classed as a "learner" and was therefore paid only $3 or $4 a week. All had to pay for the needles used, for electric power, and in some shops for their chairs and lockers. Senseless fines cut their wages still further.

A mass meeting was called to consider striking. Most speak-ers at the meeting were urging "restraint." Then one of the workers, a girl in her teens, asked for the floor and launched an impassioned appeal. "I'm tired of speakers who talk in general terms," she declared. "I offer a resolution that a general strike be declared *now*." Instantly, all sprang to their feet shouting approval, according to one reporter. All raised their hands and took the vow: "If I turn traitor to the cause I now pledge, may this hand wither from the arm I now raise."

The strikers did a magnificent job of organizing: fighting the "gorillas" hired by the employers to harass them on and off the picket lines as well as the police, who sided with the employers; feeding the families of the strikers; and telling their story at meetings of interested clubwomen. Society women actively sup-ported the girls. Students at Wellesley College collected $1,000 for the strike fund. It ended with all strikers getting their jobs back, with a 52-hour week and higher wages. It was the first successful mass strike in the garment industry and it showed clearly that women workers, once considered impossible to or-ganize, were capable of working together for a common cause. It also brought a nebulous but important alliance between liberal-minded citizens and organized labor.

The summer after this strike of shirtwaist makers, the New York cloak makers went out on a carefully planned strike called the Great Revolt of 1910. More than 50,000 cloak makers, three-fourths of the members of the ILGWU, left their jobs. They demanded the "closed shop"—that is, jobs for union members only—and the end of various malpractices. Two months later they secured a "preferential union shop," practically the same as a closed shop; abolition of all work at home; weekly pay in cash; a maximum six-day, 54-hour week with ten paid holidays; the establishment of a board of sanitary control to clean up conditions in the plants; and machinery for arbitration of future grievances.

THE PROTOCOL OF PEACE

The settlement secured by the cloak makers, called the Protocol of Peace, was a landmark in employer–union relations. It was worked out by Louis Brandeis, then counsel for the Boston cloak makers, later a justice of the Supreme Court. The settlement advanced the concept that labor as well as management had social responsibility, and that labor had a stake in the prosperity and efficient management of industry. It acknowledged the right of workers to belong to a union and to be given preference in hiring (the preferential union shop), and set up permanent machinery for conciliation and arbitration of grievances and a joint board of sanitary control for voluntary factory inspection.

This settlement did not prove to be the magic formula for industrial peace that it was hailed as being, but it did bring real progress and established the dignity of workers in what had been America's most submerged industry. Using this formula the ILGWU got 1,796 of the 1,829 cloak and suit manufacturing firms to sign agreements. Ninety per cent of the cloak and suit trade in New York City became organized within the next two years. Manufacturers also strengthened their own organizations.

To employers, union practices at first seemed to be an invasion of their rights. The objective of the employer naturally was to maximize returns on his investment, and in so doing he paid wages that he believed were reasonable for the price competition he must meet. The employer often resented the wage level "dictated" by others and the limits on working hours imposed by an outside authority. He found that working with the union on setting rates of pay for each new garment was both time-consum-

ing and costly. Yet employers today accord the union great respect for the democracy and the decent working conditions that
exist.

FACTORY FIRE

The fact that much still remained to be done for the protection of workers in the needle trades was demonstrated just one
year later, in March of 1911, by the Triangle Waist Company
fire. This company operated a factory on the upper floor of a
condemned building in New York City. When fire broke out the
workers, most of them young girls, were trapped high above the
street, because all doors had been locked to keep them from wan-
dering out to the washroom too often! In fifteen minutes, 146
of these workers perished. The shock of this tragedy made the
state legislature set up a factory investigation commission, headed
by Frances Perkins, later to become Secretary of Labor under
President Franklin D. Roosevelt. The fire and the commission's
findings roused the nation to the need for factory inspection and
safety legislation.[4]

THE ILGWU's INFLUENCE

In the years since the Triangle fire, the International Ladies'
Garment Workers' Union has lived through many ups and downs
but has emerged as one of the strongest industrial unions in the
United States, with one of the most complete welfare programs
in American industry. It was the first union to support legislation for the government's right to investigate unions and to protect their growing welfare funds from misuse by their own officials. It was also the first to publish its financial reports in the
nation's press, the first to set up an engineering department to
help garment industries streamline their own production, and
the first to have a political department.

As Louis Levine commented in his book *The Women's Garment Workers:* [5]

The immigrant workers of the women's garment trades made their
distinct contribution to American life. They [the ILGWU] were the

first in the American labor movement to bring economics experts into the service of labor, to organize departments of research and investigation, to carry on special educational activities. They also helped to socialize America. For it was their spectacular struggle for a living wage and for constitutionalism in industry that from time to time stirred up deep sentiments of sympathy in the community at large and aroused a social consciousness where there were social indifference and misunderstanding before.

Seymour Freedgood in an article in *Fortune* declared that, "In an effort to keep the rapacious manufacturers from eating each other up, thus devouring thousands of jobs in the process, it [the ILGWU] has also become a major regulatory force concerned with keeping the frequently rickety firms it deals with, in, or out of, business." [6]

The history of the union from 1932 to 1966 was inseparable from the history of its dynamic president, David Dubinsky, often referred to as "the sharp-shooting sheriff of Seventh Avenue." Dubinsky was born in Poland, where at the age of fifteen he became a master baker and assistant secretary of the baker's union. The next year he was arrested for his union activity and sent off to Siberia. He escaped, however, and in 1911 arrived in New York City. Soon afterward he joined an ILGWU cutters' local and rose rapidly in the union.

Dubinsky became head of the ILGWU in 1932, when membership had dwindled—partly because of the depression—and the union was practically bankrupt. Under his leadership the union fought labor racketeering and Communist control, and eventually set up welfare and pension funds that enabled it even to make loans to philanthropic foundations for civic betterment projects in Puerto Rico.

The union's dealings with employers have passed from violent contests to the peaceful settlement of economic and social problems affecting the garment trades. Between 1933 and 1958 no general strike occurred in the ILGWU. In March of 1958, however, a strike of dressmakers was called, involving some 2,000 shops. This was settled the next month; none has occurred since.

Early in 1959 a campaign was launched to get manufacturers to use the ILGWU label, signifying that the items bearing it were produced under fair labor standards. The label is shown in Figure 7–3. Announcements of the drive appeared in many

UNION LABEL

Figure 7–3. Garments made in factories that are operated under a union contract may carry this label.

Figure 7–4. David Dubinsky, "the sharp-shooting sheriff of Seventh Avenue," was president of the ILGWU for thirty-four years. (Photo by Jerry Soalt for ILGWU's *Justice*.)

newspapers, in leading women's magazines, and in booklets and fashion films produced to acquaint people with the movement. These announcements stressed the importance of the label as a symbol of good working conditions and decent treatment of labor. Every item made by members of the ILGWU may carry such a label, but not all manufacturers have been willing to go this far in using a propaganda device.

The union's power has been waning in recent years, however. The union is tending to become a movement rather than a bargaining agent for workers. Because modern business methods are invading the garment industry, and because there has been a shift in garment manufacturing away from New York, the control held by the union is weakening.

In 1966, after thirty-four years as president of the ILGWU, David Dubinsky resigned. Figure 7–4 pictures him at that time.

His successor was Louis Stulberg, whom he had been grooming for the post. Stulberg, like Dubinsky, was born in Poland, and began his labor union career in a cutters' local. He had been general secretary–treasurer of the ILGWU for seven years when he took over the presidency. As a *New York Times* editorial commented, he is in some ways just the opposite of Dubinsky— retiring and meticulous, almost placid by comparison with the former head. He is not so outgoing or bubbling with enthusiasm and imagination.

THE POSTWAR SITUATION

After World War II the threat of a return to sweatshop conditions arose. The garment industry set up shops in depressed areas outside New York City, at first in New England towns that had been abandoned by the textile mills, and in deserted coal-mining areas of Pennsylvania. In both areas there were large numbers of unemployed women and girls. When union organizers came in to try to protect workers from exploitation, the industry moved to the South, where economic conditions were still more depressed.

Long-distance trucking became important, for taking cut goods from Seventh Avenue jobbers to distant contractors and for bringing the finished garments back to Seventh Avenue. As Bernard Roshco reported:

Although many transport companies are run by legitimate businessmen, the racket interests that never entirely left the garment industry are now found in trucking. In some cases the same shady interests control both the long-haul transport and out-of-town garment production. While fighting efforts to unionize their workers, they can ship their own cut rate products to New York jobbers eager for the chance to undersell their competitors by any means. The showrooms remain on Seventh Avenue, but whether a modernized version of sweatshop working conditions returns to the increasingly dispersed garment industry depends on whether a fair solution is found to the problem created by the migrant contractor.[7]

Apparel workers have a workweek four hours shorter than that of the average worker in manufacturing, and their hourly wage is considerably below the average. In 1950 their average weekly pay was $45, while the average for all manufacturing workers was $58. It took eleven years for the apparel workers to reach that $58 average, but by then the average for all manufacturing workers had risen to $92 a week. Also, the unemployment rate in this industry is significantly higher and labor turnover is faster than in industry as a whole, chiefly because of the way the industry operates.

NOTES

1. Paul Henry Nystrom, *Economics of Fashion* (New York: The Ronald Press Co., 1928), p. 408.

2. James Parton, "History of the Sewing Machine," *Atlantic Monthly* (May, 1867). Reprinted as a booklet by the International Ladies' Garment Workers' Union, New York, November, 1961 and 1965.

3. Benjamin Stolberg, *Tailor's Progress* (Garden City, N. Y.: Doubleday and Company, Inc., 1944), p. 10.

4. Leon Stein, *The Triangle Fire* (Philadelphia: J. B. Lippincott Co., 1962).

5. Louis Levine, *The Women's Garment Workers* (New York: B. W. Huebsch, Inc., 1924), preface, p. 9.

6. Seymour Freedgood, "One Hundred Million Dollars in Rags," *Fortune,* LXVII, No. 4 (May, 1963), p. 151 ff.

7. Bernard Roshco, *The Rag Race: How New York and Paris Run the Breakneck Business of Dressing American Women* (New York: Funk and Wagnalls, 1963), pp. 248–49.

FURTHER READING

DANISH, MAX D. *The World of David Dubinsky.* New York: Harcourt, Brace & World, Inc., 1957. An interesting biography of the man who was president of the ILGWU for thirty-four years, written by the editor of *Justice,* semimonthly publication of the International Ladies' Garment Workers' Union.

PARTON, JAMES. "History of the Sewing Machine," *Atlantic Monthly* (May, 1867). Reprinted by the International Ladies' Garment Workers' Union, New York, November, 1961 and 1965. An interesting account of the evolution of the sewing machine.

ROSHCO, BERNARD. *The Rag Race.* New York: Funk and Wagnalls, Inc., 1963. An absorbing book written by a Washington, D. C., reporter, who from his childhood on has had close connection with Seventh Avenue; the book gives intimate glimpses of what goes on behind the scenes in the garment industry.

Stein, Leon. *The Triangle Fire.* Philadelphia: J. B. Lippincott Co., 1962. A moving account of that disaster, reconstructed from interviews with survivors, and research on newspaper files and on court cases resulting from the fire.

STUDY SUGGESTIONS

1. Visit a garment factory near you and observe working conditions. What are the legal requirements today in factories as to heating, lighting, ventilation, crowding, toilet facilities, etc.?
2. Check some of the historical costumes in a museum for workmanship: those of colonial days, of pioneer days in your area, and of the middle 1800's, around 1900, and today. How much handwork do you find in the different periods?
3. Check the report of the latest annual convention of the ILGWU to see if unionization is losing or gaining ground in various areas, and in areas that have few unions.
4. How often do you find the ILGWU label in garments in your favorite shopping center? Do you find it more or less often in high-priced articles?

8

Clothing Production

Apparel making is one of the important industries in the United States. *In value of manufacturers' sales*, it ranks twelfth, being topped only by the following industries, listed in order of their importance: food, petroleum, electrical machinery, chemicals, motor vehicles, primary metals, non-electrical machinery, fabricated metals, aircraft, textile mill products, and paper.

When *the contribution of the apparel industry to the country's economy* is taken as a measure of importance, however, a less glowing picture is drawn. Although the industry added $7.8 billion to the national income in 1963, this sum was only 4.1 per cent of the value added by all manufacturing that year.[1] Low wages and low profits, results of the keen competition characteristic of the industry, brought low returns in national income.

The number of people employed in an industry provides another measure of its importance. In 1961, 1,066,800 production workers were employed in the apparel industry, whereas 793,200 made up the work force in textile mills. Because apparel production remains one of the semihandicraft industries, employment is higher than for textile production, an industry that is more thoroughly mechanized.

Around 100,000 workers were added in the apparel industry in the five-year period 1958–1963, although in that same period the number of clothing manufacturing plants dwindled by a thousand. In 1963 approximately 1,276,000 people were employed by producers of apparel; 427,000 in men's and boys' apparel; 600,000 in women's, misses', and children's apparel; and 249,000 in miscellaneous garments and textiles. These figures are given in the

1963 U. S. Census of Manufacturers as preliminary returns.[2] By 1966 production workers in the apparel industry had increased to 1,240,000, a figure somewhat below that reported in 1963 but 16 per cent higher than that of 1961; production workers in textiles rose to 846,000, a 6 per cent increase over 1961.[3] Growth in population had a bearing on the demand for these products, but the differential of 10 per cent in the growth of the two industries must be accounted for in some other way. Importation of foreign-made fabrics has increased and is probably one of the most important reasons for the slower pace in the growth of American textiles.

WAGE RATES

Employment and earnings in the textile and apparel industries are shown in Table 8–1. Workers in the apparel industry earn less per week than do those employed in textile mills, partly because they work fewer hours a week. Also, more men than women work in the textile mills, and men traditionally have higher earnings than do women. Yet the average hourly wage for both the textile mill employees and the apparel shop workers in 1966 was $1.92 an hour.

Table 8–1

Employment and Earnings in the Apparel Industry Compared with Those of the Textile Industry, 1966

	Textile Mills	*Apparel*
Number of production workers on payrolls unadjusted	848,000	1,240,000
Average weekly gross hours employed, unadjusted	41.9	36.4
Average weekly gross earnings	$82.12	$68.80
Average hourly gross earnings	$1.96	$1.89

SOURCE: Adapted from *Survey of Current Business* XLVII, No. 5 (May, 1967), pp. S–14, 15. U. S. Department of Commerce, Office of Business Economics.

The average hourly wage in garment manufacturing establishments increased approximately 44 per cent between 1950 and 1964, whereas the increase was approximately 76 per cent for all manufacturing during the same interval. In some firms producing apparel, especially outside New York, the rate has been little above the wage minimum of $1.40 set by federal law in 1967. The major reason for the low level of wages is competition among firms, which results in such low profits that revenue is not available for higher wages. The pay rate has been inching up, however. For example, the take-home pay for the typical worker with three dependents increased 4.2 per cent in 1965.

Wages for apparel workers vary, naturally, with the tasks. High-priced garments demand skill on the part of the workers, whereas low-priced garments are made by unskilled workers whose rate of pay is low. Some tasks, whether performed on high- or low-quality garments, are paid at the firm's highest rate. For example, cutters and pressers, mostly men, command top wages. Figure 8–1 shows a cutter at work, Figure 8–2 a cutting room, and Figure 8–3 a presser. Pattern drafters, like the one in Figure 8–4, are also paid well.

Geographical location also influences wage rates. Table 8–2 presents the wage picture in five cities in widely separated parts of the United States. You will note that in 1960 New York City had more than ten times the number of workers employed in Los Angeles and paid them at a higher rate, and that men everywhere were better paid than were women. Workers in Dallas, you will also note, received lower wages than those in the other centers no matter what type of work they did. Cutters in Dallas, for example, were paid $2.02 an hour, those in New York $3.21 an hour. New York workers of all categories were paid the most, largely because of the efforts of the unions to secure wages that were in keeping with New York's high cost of living. Throughout the New England states, as well as in New York, industrial workers have been pretty generally unionized; elsewhere in the nation the unions are less strong, and wages as a result are lower.

Another factor in the wage differential is that in New York most of the apparel produced is in the high-priced brackets, whereas in the other centers it is more often in the medium- to low-priced category. High-quality garments are made by skilled workers who can command high wages, and the range in hourly pay reflects the range in skills required.

Figure 8–1. The cutter, a highly responsible worker, may cut as many as 180 layers of cloth at one time. (Photo by Jerry Soalt for ILGWU's *Justice*.)

Figure 8–2. Section of the cutting room in a dress factory. The low platform on wheels on the table in the foreground carries the bolt of fabric as it unrolls. (Courtesy of Nelly Don, Inc.)

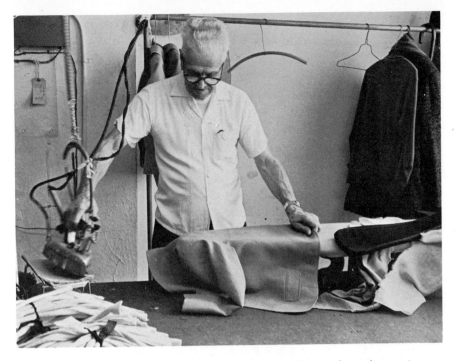

Figure 8–3. The presser is one of the most highly paid employees in a garment factory. (Photo by Jerry Soalt for ILGWU's *Justice*.)

Figure 8–4. The pattern drafter is another well-paid worker. (Photo by Jerry Soalt for ILGWU's *Justice*.)

Table 8–2

Number and Average Straight-Time * Hourly Earnings of Workers in Dress Manufacturing Establishments in Selected Areas, August, 1960[4]

	Boston		Chicago		Dallas		Los Angeles		New York	
	Number of Workers	Hourly Pay	Number of Workers	Hourly Pay	Number of Workers	Hourly Pay	Number of Workers	Hourly Pay	Number of Workers	Hourly Pay
All workers:	2,296	$1.98	3,111	$1.80	2,262	$1.39	5,511	$1.91	56,899	$2.48
Men	346	2.97	461	2.56	182	1.77	554	2.67	15,663	3.26
Women	1,950	1.80	2,650	1.68	2,080	1.36	4,957	1.83	41,236	2.19
Selected workers:										
Production operations										
Cutters	98	2.97	187	2.85	109	2.02	284	3.01	3,868	3.21
Pressers (hand)	110	3.10	233	2.29	149	1.25	384	2.20	4,122	4.26
Sewers (hand)	137	1.43	306	1.81	122	1.25	304	1.65	6,518	1.85
Machine operators										
Section system	401	1.79	862	1.58	983	1.35	423	1.71	1,424	1.98
Tailor system[a]	760	2.12	741	1.94	195	1.56	2,160	1.97	26,513	2.58
Thread trimmers[b]	69	1.30	57	1.35	44	1.12	290	1.17	2,287	1.36
Work distributors[b]	22	1.36	44	1.30	39	1.25	16	1.38	415	1.53

* Excludes premium pay for weekends and overtime.
[a] Virtually all men.
[b] Virtually all women.

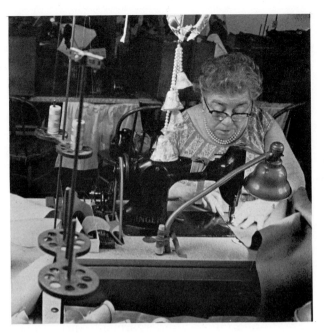

Figure 8–5. A sewing machine operator in a modern factory. Most operators have little personal interest in the current fashions. (Photo by Jerry Soalt for ILGWU's *Justice*.)

TODAY'S PRODUCTION METHODS *

The apparel industry employs hundreds of thousands of workers, some 600,000 in the women's garment industry and more than 500,000 in the men's and boys'. Electrically powered sewing machines and cutters are in general use: the traditional types for stitching seams plus those which blindstitch, sew on buttons, or tack on cuffs. Some machines even fold, stitch, and turn strips of bias to form a cording. Yet the industry is still semihandicraft. Figure 8–5 shows a woman working at an electrically driven sewing machine.

The *tailor* or *single-hand system* of production often prevails in shops where high-priced garments are made; the operator who cuts the cloth also completes the garment. In some shops, however, he turns over minor processes such as lining a coat or doing hand finishing to less skilled workers. This tailor system is much like that used in a custom operation: one person is responsible for the major work on a garment from cutting, to fitting, to completion.

---

* Terms commonly used in connection with the clothing industry in the United States are listed in Appendix D.

In many shops the *section method* is used; the work is broken up into smaller tasks, each to be carried out by a different operator—an efficient system which requires little skill on the part of the workers.

In the *bundle system,* a variant of this section method, the cut-out garment is moved from one worker to the next as a bundle, each operator performing one task then passing the garment on until it is completed. Figure 8–6 illustrates how partially made garments are transferred from one worker to another in one factory plan of operation.

Another variant, the *straight-line system,* brings finished parts of a garment, such as the completed collar or patch pocket, into the main assembly line for the worker to attach at the appropriate time—resulting eventually in a finished garment. This straight-line system represents the greatest efficiency and is adapted to making highly standardized garments such as shirts and tailored undergarments—articles of apparel that are made by the thousands.

Today, the women's outerwear industry consists of about 4,700 firms, two-thirds of which produce at least some of their garments in their own factories, according to a 1963 report. The rest are jobbers who farm out all their manufacturing, sometimes even the cutting, to one of the approximately 5,000 outside contractors, many of them equipped with antiquated sewing machinery and only a few of them using such elementary devices as time studies.[5] Figure 8–7 shows a factory employee studying the efficiency of a specific operation in the making of a garment. Some design features may be eliminated from the garment before it goes into final production, if too much time is needed to incorporate it. The cost of making the dress must be kept low so that it can compete with competitors' products.

Mass production houses are known in the trade as "cookie cutters." Those that turn out cheap apparel are called "Chinatowners," though no Chinese are employed in them.

Most of the workers in the garment industry are women, many of them middle-aged and little concerned personally with fashionable dress. They make up 80 per cent of the membership of the International Ladies' Garment Workers' Union. The little union label, with the needle and the thread encircling the letters

Figure 8–6. In this factory, as soon as the sewing machine operator finishes the work in her "tote box" nearby, she sends the box to its station by way of the conveyor belt for another supply of garments. (Courtesy of Louis Walter & Company, Inc.)

Figure 8–7. An efficiency expert studies the movements of an operator to see if he can find a way to reduce the time required to make a garment. (Photo by Jerry Soalt for ILGWU's *Justice.*)

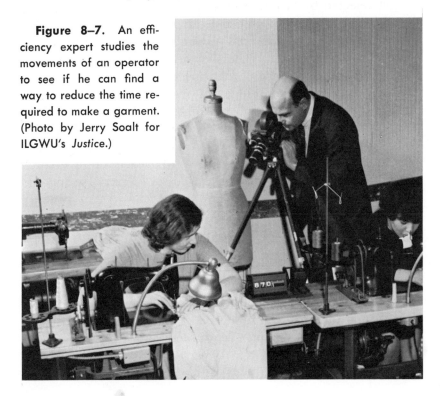

ILGWU, is sewed into most women's and children's garments made by the union, although its use is not obligatory (see Figure 7–3, page 197). The label symbolizes the advances toward good working conditions made through the cooperation of manufacturers, the government, and the union.

PEAK SEASONS OF PRODUCTION

Certain seasons of the year are especially important to the women's clothing industry: Easter, Christmas, the winter resort period, the fall opening of school. Three or four times a year the industry creates thousands of designs, makes up samples, and holds showings of them.

Many designs never go beyond the sample stage. The manufacturer eliminates those that require too skilled an operator for their construction and that cannot be made for the price-range desired. After the openings, the manufacturer also eliminates designs rejected by buyers from stores across the nation because they felt their clientele would not buy them. Often, fewer than half of the designs go into final production—only those for which orders have been placed. The showings are usually held three or four months in advance of the expected sale of the goods.

Manufacturers try to bridge the seasonal rush periods with production of staple items of apparel—those little influenced by fashion's whims—so as to provide continuous work for their most valued employees. The coat manufacturer, for example, may turn to the production of standard sport jackets or to tailored skirts to bridge the time between periods of full-scale spring and fall production.

THE RISING IMPORTANCE OF CASUAL WEAR

One striking fact about apparel production in the United States is the rising importance of casual wear and separates at the expense of more traditional (and more expensive!) garments such as suits and dresses. Table 8–3 shows the shift in purchases from 1939 to 1965. For men, coats and suits were less than a third as important in 1965 as in 1939. For girls and women, skirt volume increased nine times over that period, blouse volume six times, and sweater volume about three times. Dresses, coats, and suits were less than half as important in 1965 as before World War II.

Table 8–3

United States Apparel Production [6]

Category	1939 Total (million units)	1939 Per Capita (units)	1965 Total (million units)	1965 Per Capita (units)
Men's wear (men 18 years and over):				
Separate trousers	40.3	0.89	139.0	2.42
Suits	24.7	0.55	22.4	0.39
Sweaters	22.1	0.46	40.2	0.70
Overcoats and topcoats	5.6	0.13	4.4	0.08
Sports coats	1.0	0.02	12.5	0.22
Women's, misses', juniors' wear:				
Dresses	194.4	3.88	183.7	2.59
Blouses	34.6	0.69	202.4	2.85
Skirts	13.0	0.26	118.9	1.67
Sweaters	28.5	0.52	89.7	1.26
Coats	17.4	0.35	25.5	0.36
Suits	4.2	0.08	11.7	0.17

CONSOLIDATION OF FIRMS

Mergers of small apparel companies are increasing, and a growing number of firms are putting shares of their business on the stock market. By the spring of 1963 the general public owned shares in around ninety corporations of the garment industry.[7]

By the end of 1965 it was reported that some 135 companies had topped $10 million in annual sales, thirty-four had passed the $25 million mark, and four had exceeded $100 million. Jonathan Logan was the leader, expected to ring up some $160 million in sales for 1965, according to Univac estimates of daily market demand. Bobbie Brooks was not far behind with around $120 million for the year. Figure 8–8 offers a glimpse of a large, well-equipped garment factory.

In spite of the mergers, which reduced the number of firms to fewer than half its total twenty years before, there were still

Figure 8–8. A large, well-equipped factory in one of today's garment centers. (Photo by Jerry Soalt for ILGWU's *Justice*.)

more than 29,000 firms making apparel in 1965. The smaller ones must face brutal competition, and many do not survive. This is not surprising since the average margin of profits on sales hovers between 1.5 and 2 per cent.[8]

PRODUCTION CENTERS FOR WOMEN'S WEAR

The women's wear industry, or the "rag business" as it is called by the trade, has taken root in many parts of the United States. Every state in the union has some establishments producing apparel, but the mid-Atlantic area—New York, Pennsylvania, and New Jersey—exceeds all others both in number of plants and in the value added by manufacture. New areas have developed in California, Texas, and the Midwest.

The New York City area continues to be the leading production center for the industry. It turns out about eight times the amount sold by the next most important production center, California. It will probably continue to hold this position because buyers for retail establishments throughout the country look to New York as the center of fashion. Even the California producers have come to feel that, to reach buyers of the nation, their collections must be presented in New York City. Some have showrooms in New York for year-round promotion.

The leading production centers for women's wear, stated as a percentage of the total, are as follows: [9]

New York	59.7
California	7.4
Illinois	5.3
Pennsylvania	4.8
Massachusetts	3.6
New Jersey	3.1
Missouri	2.2
Texas	1.9
Ohio	1.8
Other States	10.2
Total	100.0

NEW YORK CITY'S GARMENT CENTER

Almost from the beginning, the women's clothing industry has been concentrated in New York City. The mile-square area centering around Seventh Avenue is the largest garment manufacturing center in the world. In this congested area of skyscrapers and littered streets, pushboys add color and sound as they trundle their racks of dresses and their carts of fabrics down the middle of the street shouting, "Watch it!" to pedestrians and car drivers alike.

The maintenance of an industry in the heart of a metropolis presents difficulties that can scarcely be imagined. Moving a shipment of dresses out of a stockroom on the top floor of a skyscraper and into a truck parked at the curb below is often more difficult than maneuvering a ship up to a dock. The truck may have to circle the block for an hour before a space is available for parking. Yet garment manufacturers choose to remain in New York so as to be as near their competitors as possible.

Two of every three women's garments sold in the United States are made in this area. Rents in New York are high. For this reason those who manufacture dresses to sell for less than $15 usually carry on production in nearby states and use their Seventh Avenue quarters only for designing and selling to the retailer.

Although women's wear makes up New York's biggest industry, no one firm in the trade equals in size those of other big American industries. Among the more than 5,000 firms in this area the average one employs fewer than twenty-five workers, with two or three partners and a $25,000 bankroll. Fifteen per cent of Seventh Avenue garment manufacturers go bankrupt each year.[10]

The industry that produces the clothes for the nation is a fiercely competitive business; a firm with as few as thirty to forty workers can and does vie with such big trade names as Jonathan Logan and Bobbie Brooks for the orders which can bring financial success. The garment industry is said to support, directly or indirectly, about one-third of the population of New York City.

The New York area has concentrated on unit-priced garments, or those that are sold individually rather than by the dozen. Unit-priced garments are almost without exception higher-priced than apparel sold by the dozen. Today, the New York market is best known for coats, suits, and dresses. The rapid growth of casual and sportswear has led to the development of important production areas away from the New York area.

The prestige held by New York City as a fashion center is due largely to the fact that many of America's best-known designers, as well as its couture manufacturers, maintain workrooms and showrooms on Seventh Avenue, clustered within a block or two of each other. Some apparel firms have formed the New York Couture Group to promote their common interests. In 1967 this group included sixteen dress houses and five coat and suit firms. Actually, they are couture *manufacturers* rather than couture *designers* in the French tradition (see Appendix D). The 1967 members in the dress category included Larry Aldrich, Branell, Pattulo-Jo Copeland, Ben Reig, Townley, Hannah Troy, and Vincent Monte-Sano and Max Pruzan. Coat and suit house members were Vincent Monte-Sano and Max Pruzan, Davidow, Arthur Jablow, Originala, and Jack Sarnoff (Molly).

The names of many well-known American designers do not appear on this list. Rather than adhere to the conditions set up by the group for seasonal showings of the collections, most prefer to operate independently. As a result, seasonal openings in New York City are held for several weeks each spring and fall. Buyers for retail establishments would find it much more convenient to have these showings consolidated within a week, for example around May 15 for the fall–winter collections and around October 15 for the spring–summer showings. There would be less need for repeated trips to market to see all the designers' collections—and less travel expense to add to the cost of doing business.

Other American designers have established their own firms and create ready-to-wear designs. Their models cannot be purchased for copying, but the trade keeps a sharp eye on them for ideas it can appropriate. Styles must be sufficiently popular to sell many copies or the firm cannot stay in business. Too much originality frightens off the buyers for the average dress department.

OTHER CITIES THAT PRODUCE CLOTHING

Since the mid-1920's, cities other than New York have assumed some importance in garment making, especially *Los Angeles*, with its emphasis on clothes for sports and casual living. This field of fashion, long neglected both by the French couture and by New York designers, has been successfully exploited by Californians, who are devotees of leisurely outdoor living. The casual clothes and the swimwear designed by California stylists have had great appeal for almost all Americans. The California climate attracted vacationers from the East, and indeed from all over the world, who found the vivid colors and easy simplicity of California-designed clothes most appealing.

Hollywood designers have influenced dress not only in the United States but also in other nations. Irene (Gibbons), Edith Head, and Howard Greer are among those who became well known, first for costumes they designed for movie actresses. Their names are still seen in the credit lines of American movies. The stage, of course, provides opportunities for creative expression and dramatic effects not possible in everyday living.

In 1965 the Los Angeles Fashion Guild had twenty members: Adele–California, Mike Anthony, Georgia Bullock, Cooper Couture, Charles Cooper, Wayne Fuller, Inc., Harrods–California, Helga Originals, Lee Herman, Peggy Hunt, Michaelson, Inc., Moe Nadler, Neal–McClintock, Michael Novarese, Oscar of Beverly Hills, Elis Porter, Helen Rose, Stanley–Nelson, Travilla, and Yvonne Originals.

San Francisco's Apparel City, built in the 1940's on thirty-two acres of land previously used in part for trailer camps, has helped to stimulate the growth of the California industry. It brings together in pleasant surroundings facilities for the designing, manufacturing, display, and sale of apparel for men, women, and children.

California today has designers whose names are well known, at least to buyers of retail establishments across the nation. Among those who started in California are Galanos, Gus Tassell, Rudi Gernreich, Helen Rose, Georgia Bullock, and Marusia. The first three have been among the winners of the coveted annual Coty American Fashion Critics' Award. Some have opened showrooms also in New York City.

Chicago's garment industry started in about 1860, producing cloaks, dresses, and women's underclothing. Today it is important for its garments in the middle-priced lines, especially in misses' sizes.

St. Louis has come to be best known for its clothing for the junior-sized figure. About thirty years ago manufacturers of that city set out to create a brand new demand so as to avoid competition with New York City. They studied the American girl, her measurements, tastes, and habits, and developed for her garments not available elsewhere. High school girls, college girls, and women with girlish proportions were delighted with their offerings, partly because the garments required few alterations. Today, St. Louis has a flourishing market for junior-sized garments.

Dallas, like Los Angeles, specializes in sportswear and play clothes, though it also makes dresses, coats, and suits, and has drawn national attention to its fresh and appealing designs. Factories have not been generally unionized and hence pay lower wages than do those in New York, a factor which has helped Dallas to hold prices down and to get established in the fashion field.

Kansas City has one of the largest manufacturers of moderately priced women's dresses among its garment factories—the Nelly Don Company, which employs more than 1,000 people under one roof. This company is atypical in an industry in which the average firm hires only thirty or forty workers. A section of the Nelly Don cutting room is shown in Figure 8–8.

PROSPECT FOR THE INDUSTRY

Though American production of apparel has increased steadily, healthy growth in the future will depend partly upon foreign markets. For the nation to maintain its economic well-being, the apparel industry must contribute significantly to the gross national product.

By 1960 some $86 million worth of American wearing apparel was sold abroad. Europe has been the fastest growing and most profitable of all the markets for American products. European women spend less and less time making their own clothes, as the tempo of their living increases. Europe's standard of living has been rising steadily. People want American-made wash-and-wear clothing, dungarees, casual wear, and lightweight apparel. American clothing manufacturers and textile mills hope to expand their markets also in Japan, Canada, and Australia, and in the underdeveloped areas of the world.

Competition

Competition from other nations has brought problems for the industry; shipments of apparel into the United States have increased markedly since 1947. Some of this apparel has come from nations which pay workers only a fraction of the wages paid in the United States, and which can sell products for considerably lower prices than those charged in America. These nations pose a threat to the industry.

Manufacturers in the United States quite understandably have urged setting higher tariffs to protect American workers from the competition of cheap labor. Economists, on the other hand, have pointed out that foreign nations must be able to sell their products somewhere if they are to have money with which to buy American products. Moreover, any nation whose industry is hurt by such tariffs is likely to retaliate by raising its own tariffs to shut out American goods. Sales abroad are essential to the expansion of American production.

Economists also point out that a nation will usually be more prosperous if it uses its time and money for specializing in production rather than producing everything itself. The United States breeds no silkworms and produces no silk today, though in pioneer days some immigrants did so. Instead it imports its silk and produces only cotton and synthetic fibers and fabrics.

An ever-increasing number of American manufacturers of fibers, fabrics, garments, and textile machinery are establishing branches in Europe to profit from lower labor and distribution costs and to escape tariffs. Some firms also let European businesses use their production processes and brand names, on payment of licensing fees and royalties. Nations occasionally sign agreements which lower customs duties on specific products. We can trade profitably with nations which want American goods but which can also sell us goods we cannot make so economically or so well.

The efficient way in which American apparel manufacturers schedule mass production of apparel has made possible tremendous growth in the industry, and continuous growth can be expected if free-trade policies prevail.

Foreign Trade in Apparel Products

As early as 1954 the United States became concerned about the increasing amounts of cotton fabrics being shipped in from Japan. An agreement was entered into with this nation in 1957 to regulate the amount of cotton textile products coming into the United States. In the meantime, several other nations had begun to export large amounts of cotton products into the United States.

This led the government to ask for a conference to find ways of regulating the flow of cotton products between exporting and importing nations. A *Long-Term Cotton Textile Arrangement* was adopted in 1962, covering a five-year period and providing for orderly growth in the exporting nation while protecting the importing nation from disruption of its own market. This agreement permitted any importing nation to enter into a bilateral agreement with another nation for mutual benefit.

The United States entered into such agreements with nineteen nations, subjecting more than 80 per cent of its imports of cotton products to specific ceilings. By the terms of the agreements, these ceilings were allowed to increase by 5 per cent each year.[11]

THE COMMON MARKET

Exports from the United States to Western Europe have been threatened, however, by the economic integration of six European nations: France, Italy, Western Germany, Belgium, the Netherlands, and Luxembourg. Shortly after World War II these six countries pooled their resources of coal, steel, iron ore, and scrap to form the European Coal and Steel Community. The arrangement worked so well that the six then set up the European Atomic Energy Community to create an atomic power program for the continent. Finally, they took another long step forward by creating the *European Economic Community,* usually referred to as the Common Market, which aimed at eventually wiping out all customs frontiers for the six nations, or creating a tariff-free internal market. Its promoters envisioned a political as well as an economic union, a superstate which would bind them together so closely that war among themselves would no longer be possible.

The Treaty of Rome, which all six member nations signed in 1957, provided ultimately for the free movement of goods, capital, labor, and services within these countries. The Common Market then comprised 170 million people, with a gross national product of some $175 billion. This market was expected to swell before long to $300,000 billion, which would make it the world's largest economic unit.[12]

The creation of this vast market is a challenge to United States industry. As mass production methods are introduced by European countries and the quality of goods improves, and major efforts are devoted to the marketing of these goods, American producers will need to develop new ways of doing business to sell their products in competition with those of Common Market nations. The United States will have to eliminate tariffs on those articles which it and the European Common Market together supply to most of the world.

Under the Common Market treaty, all six member nations agreed to a gradual revision of tariffs so that eventually all would have the same tariff against each type of product entering from outside. To reach this single-tariff level, some nations had to raise their tariffs, others had to lower them. As a result, most United States goods exported to such markets as West Germany and the Netherlands, which had low duties in the past, were subject to substantially increased rates, whereas goods shipped to France and Italy entered at lower rates. In 1965 Italian-made men's suits and women's dresses were subject to only a 9 per cent duty in West Germany, whereas American-made suits and dresses were taxed 16 per cent and were scheduled to rise even higher unless trade agreements more favorable to the United States were made.

Other nations as well as the United States were affected by the development of the Common Market. Great Britain hoped to escape the high tariffs which seemed to loom on the horizon by joining the organization. It was the first to apply for membership, followed quickly by the Republic of Ireland and Denmark. If these nations and the remaining Scandinavian countries become affiliated, some 90 per cent of the non-Communist world's industrial production will be concentrated in the Common Market and the United States. Should duties be eliminated among these European member nations, and should American products be subject to a high tariff to enter, the consequences for the United States could be serious.

Total United States imports of textile fibers and goods manufactured therefrom were $1,414 million in 1962, whereas the exports of such goods that year totaled $1,239 million.[13]

After working under their treaty agreement for five years, the six countries of the Common Market varied in their reaction to the economic union. *Women's Wear Daily* late in 1964 reported that Italy was enthusiastic and believed that the organization was the market of the future. Germany was somewhat less enthusiastic, though it had faith in the organization. In France, the retailers felt that they had benefited by the Common Market, but the political leaders were threatening withdrawal if France were not permitted to take over the leadership.[14] The European textile and apparel industries seem to have profited most from the Common Market, partly because it forced them to improve their products and to weed out firms producing inferior goods.

The six nations of the Common Market were having some of the same difficulties faced by the thirteen American colonies in the eight-year period between the end of the Revolutionary War and the setting up of the first federal government in 1789 under the United States Constitution. Few Americans today are aware of the suspicion and jealousy with which leaders of the original thirteen states viewed each other, how many were willing to sacrifice the general welfare to preserve any slight advantage of their own state, and how stubbornly many resisted the compromises that were essential for an effective union.

Europe, Canada, and the United States may someday be united with the Common Market in one economic system: an Atlantic Market, which for us would take the place of the European Common Market. *American Fabrics* magazine as early as 1962 was predicting this development by 1970. Most observers are skeptical about the speed with which such a union can be brought about, but feel that the idea of international cooperation has been generally accepted and that such a union probably is in "the wave of the future." [15]

Imports and Exports of Apparel

Imports of apparel in the United States for the period 1955–1965 showed a much greater increase than did exports. When measured in pounds of raw fiber equivalent, imports of cotton apparel increased more than fivefold and those of man-made fibers more than sixteenfold, as shown in Table 8–4; in contrast, exports of cotton apparel increased only 1.65 times and those of man-made fibers even less, only 1.04 times in that period.

Table 8—4

Imports and Exports of Apparel (in millions of pounds of fiber equivalents) [16]

	Total Apparel			
	Cotton		Man-made Fibers	
Calendar Years	Imports	Exports	Imports	Exports
1950	5.5	9.4	0.1	5.3
1955	21.3	10.6	1.3	6.9
1956	32.9	11.4	1.1	7.6
1957	35.5	11.0	1.7	7.8
1958	47.7	11.9	2.0	7.6
1959	74.7	11.8	4.9	7.4
1960	76.3	14.3	5.7	8.5
1961	60.3	14.9	5.0	7.6
1962	91.8	13.5	10.4	6.3
1963	94.2	14.4	12.8	6.6
1964	107.7	17.5	21.8	7.2
Change expressed as ratio between base year 1955 and other years (1955 = 100)				
1950	25.8	88.7	7.7	76.8
1955	100.0	100.0	100.0	100.0
1956	154.5	107.5	84.6	110.1
1957	166.7	103.8	130.8	113.0
1958	223.9	112.3	153.8	110.1
1959	350.7	111.3	376.9	107.2
1960	358.2	134.9	438.5	123.2
1961	283.1	140.6	384.6	110.1
1962	431.0	127.4	800.0	91.3
1963	442.3	135.8	984.6	95.7
1964	505.6	165.1	1,676.9	104.3

SOURCE: *Cotton Situation,* U. S. Department of Agriculture.

THE FUTURE

Garment making, as has been pointed out, is city located, fashion directed, seasonal, fiercely competitive, and fraught with financial risks. Though one of the principal industries of the United States, garment making is still an industry of small shops and semihandicraft conditions, whereas other industries reflect a high degree of technological advancement. The labor force, for the most part women, is largely unionized. Through mass production the clothing industry offers better products and more style to the consumer than the private dressmaker can.

Recent trends, however, point toward eventual changes in the industry. Decentralization of production has been taking place. Rather than remaining in the crowded city, some producers are moving into village or semirural areas and erecting modern buildings—taking advantage of the fresh labor supply and at the same time moving away from what they feel to be too close surveillance from the labor union. Some producers with offices in New York or in other fashion centers have factories in small towns hundreds of miles away from their showrooms, where orders are filled and from which the garments are shipped directly to retail stores. The trend toward the consolidation of firms has already been discussed. This merging of smaller establishments so as to benefit from improved professional management and more up-to-date business methods points to a shift away from an industry of small shops toward one that is dominated by a few large producers.

The greater productivity resulting from these business practices will inevitably remove some of the competitiveness from the clothing industry. Giant firms have diversified their products so as to capture the business of customers of all ages and body proportions. They have recognized the demand for junior styles, and now refer to particular figure types rather than to ages. Campus casuals, street wear, dressy dresses, sport clothes, and junior styles may all be produced by a single firm.

Will the lessening of competition among producers eventually lead to decreased interest in fashion? The American people probably will never be indifferent to fashion, though there is evidence that they are not overwhelmed by its every whim. The coexistence of different styles during any one season—some new, some that were marked for discard a year or more before—is evidence that American women and girls are taking an independent view of fashion. They accept it when it pleases them.

Without a doubt, commercial production of clothing will continue to grow. Few, if any, garments in a man's wardrobe are now made at home. More and more children's garments are purchased ready to wear. The index figure for the production of apparel rose from 82 in 1950 to 132 in the first quarter of 1964, with 1957 as the base year. This was an increase of 60 per cent over the fourteen-year period.

With the changes taking place in the status of women—the number working outside the home, the educational advancement which prepares them for executive and managerial positions, and their increased earning capacity—it is unreasonable to expect that they will be interested in pursuits that they followed in the handicraft stage of society. More than a third of all girls and women fourteen years old and over are working outside the home; in 1960 they made up 36.1 per cent of the total labor force, and by 1975 it is predicted that 38.2 per cent will be employed.[17] Half of the working women in 1950 were married and the percentage has been rising each year; for example, in March, 1963, 57 per cent of the working women were married and living with their husbands.[18]

Department of Commerce 1964 projections of population for women between the ages of fifteen and thirty-four, the junior bracket, indicated increases of 50 per cent between 1960 and 1980. Those who will be employed in this age group, and who will therefore be more affluent than the unemployed, are estimated to increase from 9.1 million to 16 million in those same twenty years. They will increase the demand for luxury goods. Such changes in the way of living for American families tend to strengthen the position held by the ready-made clothing industry.

NOTES

1. Priestland, Carl, *Focus: Economic Profile of the Apparel Industry* (Washington, D. C.: The American Apparel Manufacturers' Association, Inc., 1965), p. 8.

2. *Ibid.*, p. 11.

3. *Survey of Current Business*, XLVII, No. 5, p. S–11 (Washington, D. C.: Office of Business Economics, U. S. Department of Agriculture).

4. *Monthly Labor Review* (adaptation), LXXXIV (July, 1961), p. 747.

5. Seymour Freedgood, "One Hundred Million Dollars in Rags," *Fortune*, LXVII (May, 1963), p. 153.

6. "United States Consumer Apparel Expenditure, 1935–39 to 1965," *World Wool Digest*, XVII, No. 25 (December 8, 1966), p. 207.

7. Freedgood, p. 154.

8. David A. Hoddeson, "More Stylish than Ever: Apparel Makers Are Racking up Some Handsome Profits These Days," *Barron's*, XLV (December 20, 1965), p. 31.

9. *Leading Production Centers in Women's Wear* (Washington, D. C.: Apparel Manufacturing Industry, National Credit Office, 1964).

10. "A Rackful of Giants," *Time* (January 7, 1963), p. 9.

11. Priestland, pp. 56–58.

12. William H. Grant, "What the Common Market Can Learn from American Experience in Mass-marketing Man-made Fibers," *American Fabrics*, No. 57 (Summer, 1962), p. 85 ff.

13. Editors of *American Fabrics* with staff of Werner Management Consultants, "300 Million Consumers Create the Challenge and the Opportunity Posed by the Common Market," *American Fabrics*, No. 57 (Summer, 1962), p. 59 ff.

14. *Women's Wear Daily*, December 3, 1964, p. 8.

15. Editors of *American Fabrics*, p. 59.

16. Priestland, p. 57.

17. *Statistical Abstracts 1964*, LXXXV, p. 217.

18. *Ibid.*, p. 226.

FURTHER READING

ARNOLD, PAULINE, and WHITE, PERCIVAL. *Clothes and Cloth.* New York: Holiday House, 1961. Rather elementary but readable.

Editors of *Fortune*. *The Changing American Market.* Garden City, N. Y.: Hanover House, 1955. Chapter 9. A good presentation of the changes in the American way of life as they affect the clothing industry.

FREEDGOOD, SEYMOUR, "One Hundred Million Dollars in Rags," *Fortune*, LXVII, No. 5 (May, 1963), p. 151 ff. Well written and authoritative.

"How and Why of Foreign Licensing in the Common Market," *American Fabrics*, No. 58 (Fall, 1962), p. 44.

RICHARDS, FLORENCE S. *The Ready-to-Wear Industry, 1900–1950.* New York: Fairchild Publications, Inc., 1951. A good, dependable résumé of a half century of growth of the ready-to-wear industry.

ROSHCO, BERNARD. *The Rag Race.* New York: Funk and Wagnalls, Inc., 1963. Interesting to read and dependable.

STEWART, MAXWELL S. "The European Common Market and the United States," *Public Affairs Pamphlet No. 328.* A readable, concise, and authoritative treatment of an important trade problem.

"This Shrinking World," *American Fabrics*, No. 57 (Summer, 1962), pp. 57–59.

STUDY SUGGESTIONS

1. If there is a garment factory near you, visit it to observe the production methods used and the percentage of women employed. Try to learn the wages paid to both men and women. What type of work is best paid?

2. The leading department stores and ready-to-wear shops of your community probably buy garments from several manufacturing centers. Interview the buyer of one store to find out from which centers he orders, and ask him to show you representative articles from each. From which area do most garments come with the ILGWU label attached? Do garments carrying the same price tag appear to have the same relative quality regardless of origin? Does quality tend to be better, poorer, or similar in garments carrying a union label?

3. When you buy Italian-made shoes, how much of the price you pay represents the tariff the United States government charged in an effort to protect American shoe manufacturers?

4. What is the American tariff on Egyptian cotton? On French leather gloves?

5. Investigate stores in your community, including the chains, to find out how many nations are represented in the clothing or textile products they carry. Do you find any from Japan, Hong Kong, Taiwan, Mexico, West Germany—all of which are among the twenty-nine nations with which the United States set up long-term trade agreements limiting the importing of such products?

9

American Interpreters
of Fashion

Though most outerwear produced in the United States is in the ready-to-wear category, some designers do a flourishing custom business, designing solely for wealthy and socially prominent women. A custom designer is one who makes a garment for a particular client using either an original design or one that has been adapted to the client's figure problems.

Some of these designers, such as Chicago-born Mainbocher, are undoubtedly as gifted as anyone of the French couture. Before World War II Mainbocher had a couture house in Paris, but with the outbreak of the war he returned to the United States. Since then he has successfully operated an establishment in New York, selling only to private clients.

Such American couture designers, however, inevitably have less influence on the course of fashion than do French designers. They deal with only a small number of clients. Few sell models to the professional buyer, the key person in the wholesale trade. Because couture designs generally reflect elegance and sophistication rather than quick-changing fashion, they offer the copyist none of the intriguing innovations that are the heart of the fashion industry. Moreover, imported fashions, like other imports, have a prestige that helps to insure French designers first place in the American fashion world.

A few custom designers associate themselves with a retail store. Sophie of Saks Fifth Avenue is one. Their costumes are individualized so as to enhance the appearance of the wearer, and naturally are expensive.

RECIPIENTS OF FASHION AWARDS

Some American designers have been singled out for awards for "distinguished service in the field of fashion." Nieman–Marcus of Dallas has given annual awards since 1937; the Coty American Fashion Critics have presented citations since 1943. The seventy-five critics who comprise the jury for the Coty Award are among the nation's leading fashion writers and editors.

Geoffrey Beene (pronounced "bean") was given the Coty Award for 1964 after having had his own firm for only one year, and again for 1966. Among others who have received this cita-

Figure 9–1. Texas-born Sophie started her career in Philadelphia by designing for amateur theatricals. Later, she went to New York City as a stylist for Saks Fifth Avenue and was soon in charge of its custom-order salon, designing elegant and understated apparel. In private life she is Mrs. Adam Gimbel.

Figure 9–2. Geoffrey Beene was born into a family in which a career in medicine was traditional, but after leaving his Louisiana home he took a job with I. Magnin. Before long he was a student of fashion designing in Paris. He founded his own couture house in New York City in 1963.

tion are Norman Norell, James Galanos, Arnold Scaasi, Bud Kilpatrick, Nettie Rosenstein, Jane Derby, and Donald Brooks, all fashion greats who have helped to mold the taste of the American woman. Galanos, before he was out of his thirties, won the Coty Award three times in six years, and as a result was enrolled in the Fashion Hall of Fame.

Claire McCardell in 1955 became the first American fashion designer—and so far the only one—to be pictured on the cover of *Time* magazine. When she died in 1958 at the age of fifty-three, she was elected posthumously to the Fashion Hall of Fame, the first woman to win this distinction.

CREATIVE AMERICAN DESIGNERS

The three designers considered by most of the fashion-wise to be America's leading creators of design are:

Norman Norell, ranked as America's top creative designer, and one who can compete with the world's best. His clothes are inclined toward tailored lines and are "new" without being outlandish.

Mainbocher (Main Rousseau Bocher), one of the nation's few custom dressmakers. His creations are said to command the highest prices in the world's fashion market.

James Galanos, a designer of great originality and willingness to strike out for unusual effects. In his creativity, he often produces hard-to-wear clothes.

Listed below are seventeen other designers who are making a significant contribution in the fashion world, with a description of the type of apparel for which they are best known:

Ronald Amey, avant garde creations
Geoffrey Beene, lively clothes of excellent design
Bill Blass, quietly elegant clothes
Donald Brooks, clothes of simplicity and understated elegance
Bonnie Cashin, timeless favorites especially for the outdoor type
Oleg Cassini, dress that reveals the feminine figure
Luis Esteves, sexy clothes, usually with dramatic necklines
Seymour Fox, superb tailoring
Rudi Gernreich, who launched the topless bathing suit in the United States—outrageous designs, usually with a casual air
John Moore, erratic, original apparel
Mollie Parnis (Figure 9–6), softly feminine, flattering clothes
Ferdinando Sarmi, impeccable taste, beautiful evening clothes

Figure 9–3. Norman Norell was educated to be an artist but soon started designing costumes for films. He founded his own couture firm in 1960 and now makes some of the most beautiful clothes in the world.

Figure 9–4. Chicago-born Mainbocher had a couture house in Paris before World War II. Since his return to New York City he has done only custom designing. His prices are said to be the highest in the world.

Figure 9–5. James Galanos is a designer of rare originality, with unmatched ability to find new ways to put a dress together.

Adele Simpson (Figure 9–7), conservative costumes
Gustav Tassell, flawless tailoring much influenced by Balenciaga
Jacques Tiffeau, also influenced by Balenciaga, but with unques-
tionable originality
Pauline Trigère (Figure 9–8), faithful to the French couture tradition, concerned with brilliant cut and the qualities inherent in
whatever fabric is used
Ben Zuckerman, masterful tailoring of elegant garments in highly
individual styles

As mentioned in Chapter 8, California stylists also have made
a contribution in the design world, especially in sportswear and
casual wear. Among these are Georgia Bullock and Helga,
shown in Figures 9–9 and 9–10.

PIRACY OF FASHION IDEAS

Designing women's clothes is not always profitable. Creating
clothes for the few has not brought great financial returns to the
top designers, even though prices for their creations are much
beyond what any but the wealthy client can pay. Added to the
cost of producing a beautifully made garment of high-quality
materials is the need to provide a suitable showroom, attentive
salespeople, and a corps of mannequins who will display the various creations of the house to the best advantage. Only four or
five copies of a design may be sold during a season. Such a
design may actually result in financial loss to the house.

The firm that goes into mass production, however, may reap
big profits. Designers who adapt and simplify what is shown in
the expensive shops find employment here. Top designers will
not work for such a firm because they are not given free rein for
creativity. But no matter what the retail level, popular priced
or exclusive and high priced, the merchandise must sell. As one
young designer has written:

The manufacturer of a moderate or a low-priced line of apparel
can't afford to be original. His line is made up chiefly of old silhouettes that have had a good sales history. We do try to get a new
twist into our copies of designs that have caught on.
I must always keep an eye on the competition to keep on top of
the market. I have to know what the shops are selling, what the successful basic dress lines are, and how the dresses are trimmed. The
dress manufacturing business goes at a very fast pace, and few design-

Figure 9–6. Mollie Parnis is famous for her jeweled evening dresses. Her designs are never flashy and tend toward the softly feminine.

Figure 9–7. Adele Simpson at twenty-one was one of the youngest and highest-salaried designers in New York. Now she is president of the firm bearing her name. For her designs she makes no sketches but works directly with fabrics.

Figure 9–8. Paris-born Pauline Trigère has won every major American fashion award with her designs, which are always simple though intricate in cut and dramatic in effect.

Figure 9–10. European-born Helga (Mrs. Walter Oppenheimer) took her first lessons in haute couture in London. Expert cutting and fit teamed with unusual textiles and simplicity of design characterize her designs. She and her husband, an authority on textiles and merchandising, launched their firm, Helga, in California in 1947.

Figure 9–9. California born and bred, Georgia Bullock started designing as a child—for her paper dolls. While a student at the University of Southern California, she was a fashion model and did some designing for specialty shops. Today, she designs clothes of casual elegance for women on the go. Her husband is a merchandise executive with Bullock's Department Stores.

ers that I know have any feeling of security in their jobs. Even so, I love my work.

One big sportswear firm that I'm familiar with has twenty-four designers scattered among the various lines—junior miss, swimwear, etc. But the major role is played by the stylist, who coordinates color and fabric and who shops the market for sample goods. Then the designer has the job of making something of it. She needs ingenuity more than design ability.

The young woman who wrote this analysis of the role of the designer for low- and moderate-priced lines is a graduate of the College of Home Economics of a midwestern land-grant university. Though not yet thirty years old, she is in New York City working for one of the nation's largest ready-to-wear manufacturers.

Style piracy dominates the clothing industry in the United States. Manufacturers, intent on giving American women what is new, copy the creations of fashion artists and in a short time flood the market with imitations. Some are line-for-line copies; others are adaptations. The manufacturer who can copy the new idea a little bit sooner, at a slightly lower price than his competitor, is the one who makes the profit. And he continues to exploit his fast-selling number until someone else offers a knock-off, that is, a still lower priced copy of the garment. The executive director of the National Dress Manufacturers' Association has estimated that 90 per cent of the industry in one way or another engages in style piracy.[1]

One American manufacturer boasted to Madame Grès of the Paris haute couture that he had sold at wholesale more than $1 million worth of a coat she had designed the previous season. He had not bought her coat or even paid her the price of shipping it to him in bond so he could hold it a short time and copy it.[2]

The fate of an expensive creation is charted in an article in *Forbes* magazine:[3]

If a particular style goes well it will be adapted at different price levels. The dress selling for $185 will appear next in a less expensive store at $110, then it is adapted to sell at $79.50, then reproduced for $45; later at $29.50, and finally a dress dimly like it may sell in neighborhood stores for $10.

Obviously, the $29.50 and the $10 dress do not compare in quality and workmanship with the original, but the rudiments of the design still identify it.

BILLS TO PROTECT DESIGNERS

The first bill intended to protect designers in the United States against piracy was introduced into Congress in 1914; fifty-eight bills followed between that date and 1966, all successfully opposed by the ready-to-wear lobby, usually led by the National Retail Merchants' Association.

The bills of the mid-1960's were drawn to protect authors of designs for five or ten years, rather than the fifty-six years given to those who copyright literary works. These bills provided that if a retailer unwittingly bought a shipment of dresses of pirated design he could sell them but not reorder. Also, when the retailer was notified that he was selling articles which infringed someone's copyright, he had to report where he bought them.

"Congress has sufficient evidence to conclude that piracy is unfair competition," declared Jacques M. Dulin, patent research editor of *The George Washington Law Review*, in a résumé of design piracy bills. He concluded that Congress rather than the courts had the responsibility for protecting designers, and that design piracy laws such as those proposed in 1965 were neither unconstitutional nor likely to create a monopoly.[4] Style piracy will persist until Congress enacts laws to protect the creators of designs.

THE FASHION SPIRAL

The American fashion spiral starts with the Paris collections presented twice a year by Paris couturiers. In the elegant salons, mannequins parade in freshly minted frocks before buyers from the leading women's apparel stores of the United States, members of the American couture, designers and buyers from the big mail-order houses and from Seventh Avenue's ready-to-wear manufacturers, and the fashion editors—representatives of various magazines, newspapers, and trade publications.

Each representative is there for his or her own good reasons. The designers come for inspiration, new ideas, and a check on trends. The buyers look for models they can buy to copy outright or to adapt for American taste or display in their shops. The editors take notes fast and furiously as they gather fashion information to pass on to their readers. Those from fashion magazines such as *Vogue* and *Harper's Bazaar* will report on high fashion and trends to the most fashion-conscious women in the United States; those from magazines such as *Life* and *Look* and from the newspapers will report for general readers, most of whom have somewhat less intense personal interest; those from the trade publications such as *Women's Wear Daily* will provide the information needed by manufacturing, wholesale, and retail concerns. These scouts then rush back to the United States, eager to use the materials and the information they have gathered.

Next come the showings of Seventh Avenue's own collections: in June for the autumn fashions, in September for resort wear, in November for spring clothes, and in February for summer apparel. To these showings come buyers from all over the nation to put in their orders for the next season's clothes, hoping to hit the jackpot with orders of frocks and suits, hats and coats, that will strike the fancy of their clientele.

"There is none of the glamour of Paris about the American ready-to-wear shows," reported Bettina Ballard in her book *In My Fashion:*

We, the spectators, dodge the pushcarts in the street, we pack ourselves good-naturedly into over-crowded elevators, where everyone knows everyone else's face from years of such close proximity. We sit through a one-hour show at each manufacturer's, . . . a strictly working session, timed to the minute because the high-priced mannequins are hired for only an hour. Then we crowd out into claustrophobic halls along with the frantic mannequins who are always late for their next show, and there we wait for elevators that are too full to stop. . . .

There are no frills in the New York collections, other than the fresh flowers for the first day and hard candies passed around in big glass jars for energy, or a buffet or sandwiches and coffee for a few of the lunch-hour shows. But for the most part we pick up a hamburger between collections and see as many as we can in a day. Word goes through the Seventh Avenue grapevine with amazing rapidity as to the relative success of each collection, a cruel, but generally accurate, sort of censorship.[5]

A FASHION OPENING

The debut of designs created by an American couturier for a forthcoming season is similarly handled. As June Weir reported one of Geoffrey Beene's fashion openings in *Women's Wear Daily:* [6]

The showroom is packed. The models are excited. The dressers are zipping away like crazy. There stands Geoffrey—taking a sip of Diet-Rite-Cola—beside the little white tables loaded with dozens of gloves and boxes of jewelry. Everything is terribly well-organized and neat.

The big yellow sheets of paper pasted on the wall line up Yvonne, Cathy, Claire, Doreen, Ellen, and Pat. . . .

Now it starts. The tension mounts. The models flash by in their colorful coats: Yvonne in a tomato red smock back, Cathy in an endive, Ellen in a hot pink with matching dress. "Get Cathy's next one ready," directs Geoffrey. The ten dressers start getting the suits in order—some with long jackets, some with waistlength overcoats, all with softer skirts and worn with matching fabric snoods by Lily Daché.

How's the audience? "Very serious—not missing a single thing," says Claire as she rushes by. By now everyone is in black. And one of the best is Cathy's black wool with a deep neckline and pouffy taffeta flounce. "They love it!" she calls to Geoffrey. . . .

Back stage Joyce Christopher arrives to pin on her delightful little hair-pieces for the long dresses, which look so individual in slinky black or pale blue crepe. OUT THEY GO FOR THE FINALE—IT'S ALL OVER NOW—EXCEPT FOR THE BRAVOS FOR BEENE.

Some of these collections will be reminiscent of the Paris openings a few months before, but the designers will have modified and simplified the garments, especially those in the less expensive lines. Gone will be the tricky cut that requires painstaking handwork and fitting, and extra yardage. But the silhouette, the placement of the waistline (or its absence), the length of the skirt and the sleeve, and the handling of the neckline probably will be the same as those seen in some of the $500 and

$750 frocks displayed by the Paris couture. Colors and fabrics likely will be close to those of the French models; some of the $89.95 and the $129.95 brackets, made from imported fabrics, may be identical.

Some original designs will be offered, of course; Seventh Avenue designers are not slavish copyists. They give their own unique interpretation to whatever is "the new look" and sometimes bring in a fresh and even startlingly different treatment of a neckline or a skirt or a sleeve.

THE ROLE OF THE PRESS

The press has the leading role at the next turn in the fashion spiral. Fashion writers in the newspapers and magazines are eager to tell their readers the fashion story—by the printed word, by sketches, and by photographs of mannequins, designers, and society women wearing the new models. The avowed purpose of this publicity, naturally, is to make readers buy and to give them guidance for their purchases. Much space is devoted to photographs of international socialites, models, and actresses, posing in creations of the Paris and American designers in opulent settings.

Magazines which supply fashion news are eagerly read by fashion-conscious American women and girls: *Vogue, Harper's Bazaar,* and *The New Yorker* by almost all; *Mademoiselle, Glamour,* and *Seventeen* by youth. Readers do not always follow the lead of their favorite interpreters of the mode, of course. One example of readers' independence was their refusal during the 1950's to discard the bouffant skirt with its crinoline petticoat. The skirt was launched by Anne Fogarty around 1950. "It will be passé next fall," predicted most of the fashion world in the summer of 1953, but five years later it was still going strong. The crinoline petticoat disappeared soon thereafter but not the bouffant skirt; it was too comfortable and generally too flattering to be abandoned, even though it was no longer high fashion.

Until fairly recently, writers—at least in the women's magazines—could be counted on to give an honest evaluation of fashions, selecting designs that their editors felt were the best for

Figure 9–11. Queen Sirikit of Thailand was selected by fashion leaders of the United States as the best-dressed woman of 1964. (Photo by Kun Artistic, courtesy of News Photo Service.)

treatment, ignoring or deprecating the bad and the banal. The fierce competition of the magazine world for circulation and advertising has weakened this editorial independence. Advertising departments of periodicals today promise big advertisers more and more "services" through the editorial columns. A decade ago editors virtuously boasted of their freedom from the taint of promoting what appeared in their advertising pages, but the close tie between advertising and editorial sections is more and more apparent.[7]

The press also gives wide publicity to the lists of best-dressed women. The selection of these women, performed annually by an anonymous list of fashion-wise Americans, furnishes a dra-

Figure 9–12. Mrs. William Paley, New York socialite, for years was voted one of the world's ten best-dressed women, and finally was shifted out of competition by being elevated to the Fashion Hall of Fame. Her clothes bespeak elegance and quiet sophistication. (Courtesy of *Women's Wear Daily*.)

matic climax to the fashion year. The listing started in Paris in 1933, when a group of Paris designers led by Mainbocher got together to name their favorite clients. Their list proved a useful device for fashion promotion and was continued until World War II, when fashion activities temporarily stopped in Paris.

Eleanor Lambert, America's top fashion public relations director, picked up the project and got the New York couture to sponsor it. Each year a secret committee of fashion editors compiles a list of about 150 women with a reputation for being well dressed and mails it to about 2,000 fashion authorities, socialites, and celebrities, each of whom votes for the ten women he or she considers best dressed. With the help of the approximately 600 ballots that are returned, the committee selects the ten or twelve women to be recognized. The names are usually announced shortly after New Year's Day.

Queen Sirikit of Thailand (Figure 9–11) topped the 1965 list of the world's Ten Best-Dressed Women. In 1966 first place went to Mrs. Carter Burden, daughter of socialite Mrs. William Paley, an earlier prizewinner. Mrs. Paley is shown in Figure 9–12.

After a woman has been on the best-dressed list for five years, she is moved to the Fashion Hall of Fame and is no longer in competition. Mrs. Jacqueline Kennedy and Mrs. Paley are among the women enrolled there. To achieve a place among the best-dressed, a woman must be rich and in the public eye. According to one fashion writer, each spends between $20,000 and $100,000 a year on clothes (exclusive of jewelry)—not necessarily on a lot of clothes, but on clothes that have elegance and that are made especially for her.[8] In fact, elegance is the keynote of the best-dressed woman's wardrobe.

NOTES

1. James Poling, "Piracy on Seventh Avenue," *The Saturday Evening Post*, September 21, 1963, pp. 29–34.

2. John Fairchild, *The Fashionable Savages* (Garden City, N. Y.: Doubleday and Co., Inc., 1965), p. 13.

3. "Seventh Avenue Goes to Wall Street," *Forbes*, XCIV (July, 1964), pp. 24–29.

4. Jacques M. Dulin, "Statutory Design Rights—Solution to the Unfair Competition of Piracy," *The George Washington Law Review*, XXXIV, No. 1 (October, 1965), pp. 110–33.

5. Bettina Ballard, *In My Fashion* (New York: David McKay Co., Inc., 1960), pp. 277–78.

6. June Weir, "Back Stage with Beene," *Women's Wear Daily*, June 11, 1965, p. 8.

7. Ballard, pp. 303–04.

8. Eugenia Sheppard, "Making the Best Dressed List," *The Saturday Evening Post*, January 5, 1963, p. 60.

FURTHER READING

FAIRCHILD, JOHN. *The Fashionable Savages*. Garden City, N. Y.: Doubleday and Co., Inc., 1965. Chapters 10–18. Views of fashion leaders
through the eyes of an alert, gossipy writer, the man who is now pub-
lisher of *Women's Wear Daily*.
ROSHCO, BERNARD. *The Rag Race*. New York: Funk and Wagnalls, Inc.,
1963. Chapters 2, 3, 4, 5, and 11. Absorbing reading.

STUDY SUGGESTIONS

1. Study one week's issues of *Women's Wear Daily* and note the coats
   and dresses sketched or photographed. How many months will it
   be before the dresses illustrated can be expected to appear in local
   stores at the $29.50 price level?
2. Appraise *Vogue, Harper's Bazaar,* and *Mademoiselle* as guides to
   the selection of a wardrobe in your locality.
3. Look up the names of this year's best-dressed women. They are
   usually announced January 1 or soon thereafter in the *New York
   Times, Women's Wear Daily,* and the leading newsmagazines.
   Which ones have you read about over the last few years?
4. How many of the twenty big names in the design world of the
   United States do you find in *Who's Who in America?* What academic background does each have? Did any of them shift into the
   couture business from some other vocation, as is true of members
   of the French haute couture (from architecture, engineering, or
   sculpture, for example)? What honors have been conferred on
   each?
5. Examine dresses in a store which sells low-priced apparel. Since
   these undoubtedly will be "knock-offs," examine several and note
   the silhouette, sleeve, waistline, and neckline. Can you recall when
   those particular details became fashionable? Do the dresses have
   some faddish detail such as a bow or a big pin to distract attention from low-quality construction and from lack of fresh design?
6. Report on Jacques Dulin's article arguing for statutory design rights
   in *The George Washington Law Review* of October, 1965. Does he
   convince you as to the need for Congress to pass a style piracy law?
7. Interview the president or the manager of a department store or
   ready-to-wear shop to learn what he thinks of having a federal
   style piracy law.
8. Write your congressman or senator asking him to send you printed
   copies of the two or three most recent bills drawn up to combat
   style piracy. Compare the House and Senate bills. How many
   years does each bill propose to protect a design? What penalty
   would each exact for infringement of copyright? Where would the
   designer register his application for design copyright?

III

FROM RETAILER
TO CONSUMER

10

The Retailer

(one in the Area of retailing)

The retailer) is the link between the producer and the consumer. He is generally thought of as one who buys and sells, finds customers, and provides them with what they want, when they want it, and at prices they are willing to pay. Estimating what the consumer will want, planning a timely presentation of goods, and making an effective display of the goods so that their merits may be judged are among his most important functions. The retailer must take into account the cost of all the services involved in buying and selling, as well as the cost of the goods, and must set his prices so as to realize a net profit. Without a profit obviously he cannot long remain in business.

Although claims are often made that business molds the taste of the buying public, consumers have the final word as to what they will accept. Had consumers not been ready to spend part of their income for ready-to-wear clothing, that industry would not have grown to its present size.

Retailers of goods at all price levels must consider the ever-important social force of fashion. Consumers with their increased purchasing power need no longer adjust to the ideas of the producer or the retailer. Their refusal to buy forces business to provide what they want.

REFLECTION OF SOCIOECONOMIC LIFE

American retailing is a highly competitive and ever-changing reflection of social and economic conditions of the country. The general store and the dry goods store of half a century ago have been supplanted by newer forms of merchandising: the large department store, the chain store, the mail-order house, the supermarket, and, more recently, the neighborhood shopping center. Each in its way offers merchandise and services that people want. Some stores offer luxurious surroundings, high-quality merchandise, and many personal services to attract the more affluent and discriminating customer. Other stores sell lower-priced goods and provide limited services which satisfy the economy-minded shopper. In these stores, the principles of scientific management on which mass production is based have also been applied to retailing.

The disappearance of personal services common in the early days of retailing has been regretted by some consumers, but today's attractive displays and convenience and efficiency of doing business have contributed to the ever-increasing sales of merchandise. Protests have arisen with every new development in forms of retailing, but they have usually come from competitors, not from the buying public.

At one time the department store was looked upon with alarm by the small business owner, who thought it would monopolize retail trade and drive independent stores out of business. Mail-order houses were condemned by small town merchants, who severely criticized anyone buying from a catalog. Chain stores were said to drain off money from the community and to drive local merchants out of business. The truth is that such fears have been unwarranted and that the competition from these new forms of business has stimulated progress and contributed to our high standard of living.

STIMULUS TO PROGRESS

The retailing of clothing is a vital factor in the American economy. It contributes to the national prosperity by creating a market for the goods that our factories, with their ever-expanding productive capacity, can produce.

The clothing market today is highly complex. Apparel firms vary greatly in size, management, ownership, location of stores, and services rendered. Some stores, as our readers know, carry a single line of goods, such as hats; others offer multiple lines of related merchandise, as in a women's apparel shop; department stores sell clothing and home furnishings and many other lines of merchandise of concern to women; variety stores specialize in low-priced articles, including some clothing.

According to the 1963 report on retail trade of the U. S. Bureau of the Census, the sales of 44,412 women's clothing specialty shops totaled more than $5.5 billion; sales of 29,696 women's ready-to-wear stores reached nearly $4.5 billion; and sales in 18,139 family clothing stores amounted to more than $2.5 billion.

Wages paid sales personnel in such stores were not high. In March of 1967 the average for those working in department stores was $65.04 a week; in mail-order stores, $75.39 a week; in men's and boys' apparel stores, $71.66; in apparel and accessories stores, $59.71; in family stores, $59.39; in women's ready-to-wear shops, $55.21; and in the limited-price variety stores, $48.34.[1]

VARIATIONS IN OWNERSHIP

A retail establishment may be owned by an independent merchant or, as is the trend today, by a group of people. Manufacturers sometimes operate a retail outlet for their own products. Whether individually or collectively owned, the store can be either a single establishment or part of a chain. It may even be a branch of a large department store or of a specialty shop. All retailers, of course, try to find locations easily reached by their customers and close to parking facilities, such as a central shopping district in the heart of the city or in a neighborhood or suburban development.

SERVICES OFFERED

Services offered by retailers differ greatly. Self-service stores simply display the goods then wrap up articles selected by their patrons and accept payment. Other shops provide tempting arrays of merchandise in beautiful surroundings and employ well-informed salespeople to help customers make their selections; these shops extend credit and deliver the merchandise to the home of the customer. They often provide comfortable and attractive waiting rooms, parcel-checking counters, tearooms, general information centers, personal shopping services, and occasionally travel services. Some stores, among them Marshall Field's of Chicago, even provide wheelchair service for the handicapped. All these free services naturally increase the cost of store operation, but they attract customers and build good will for the store.

Author, in THE Wide World of Clothing, details five KINDS OF RETAIL MARKETS, they are listed as follows

KINDS OF RETAIL MARKETS

Retailing in the United States has followed a typically American pattern. Men who have made retailing history have shown a high degree of ingenuity and creative ability. Whether they operated in well-established centers along the East Coast or followed on the heels of the pioneers as they moved west, they were quick to see the needs and wants of the people and to try to satisfy them—and at the same time to prosper financially themselves.

1. The Department Store *define*

The department store is probably an outgrowth of the general merchandise store of the early years of this nation, although in certain cases it developed from a specialty shop or a dry goods store. Since the stores grew as towns grew, some plan of organization for buying and selling such diverse merchandise as dress fabrics and kitchen equipment was needed. Merchandising a single line of goods, such as hosiery, was made the responsibility of a special department. The whole retailing venture, with its various departments, soon resembled many shops under one roof.

Department stores were the first large-scale retailers to stress low prices. Many of these stores paid low wages and provided poor working conditions for salespeople, especially in the early years. Employees today still have lower wages than do those in a number of other occupations, but they often have more pleasant surroundings than the average. Many receive a commission on sales, which bolsters their base pay. In addition, employees are often allowed a discount on merchandise purchased in the store, a further boost to relatively low wages.

Policies that are accepted today as standard practice in retailing originated in the early department stores. The return of merchandise for refund or credit was at first considered radical, as was the guarantee that the quality of goods was honestly presented. Merchandise displays were introduced as a means of stimulating interest in the store's offerings, and extensive advertising became a part of doing business. Prices were marked clearly on merchandise and were used freely in advertising. Many innovations were introduced to try to make shopping a pleasure and to reassure the customer of the integrity of the merchant.

One early merchant, Marshall Field of Chicago, founded his department store on the idea that women needed to learn to appreciate high-quality merchandise. That he succeeded is evident from the reputation of Marshall Field and Company. At one time this establishment was probably selling the largest volume of merchandise of any department store in the world. It has maintained its reputation for high-quality goods for decades.

Another early merchant, R. H. Macy, is credited with originating the use of odd prices for merchandise, such as 49 cents and $1.97. He also introduced the idea of a uniform percentage markup over the wholesale price and popularized the slogan, "It's smart to be thrifty."

The average woman shopper likes the department store because it helps her to save time and energy. If she wishes, she can usually outfit the entire family from a single store. Moreover, the department store provides her with new and fresh merchandise because its large volume of business necessitates frequent renewal of stock.

One important advantage of shopping in a department store is that low-, medium-, and high-priced merchandise is offered under the same roof. Besides their standard lines of merchandise, many department stores have a "French room" or designer's shop for exclusive apparel, and a budget department or "bargain basement" to accommodate economy-minded shoppers. In the lower-priced departments surprisingly high-quality goods may be found: "distress merchandise" bought from an overstocked producer at a low price or from a retailer going out of business; apparel moved in from higher-priced departments because it was not selling well; or items bought in such volume that they can be sold for a special, low price. As shown in Table 10–1, the retail markup on garments in basement areas traditionally runs around 10 per cent below that on garments on the other floors of the typical department store.

Table 10–1

Retail Markup as a Percentage of Wholesale Cost, Department Stores [2]

Department	1954	1961	1962	1963	1964
Main store:					
Neckwear and accessories	64.2	68.4	68.1	69.5	69.8
Corsets and brassieres	73.6	74.5	75.1	75.4	76.1
Underwear and negligees	62.1	64.5	65.6	66.4	67.2
Coats and suits	65.0	68.4	68.9	70.1	70.6
Dresses	66.1	70.1	70.9	71.8	72.1
Blouses and sportswear	62.6	66.1	66.7	68.4	69.2
Infants', girls', and boys' wear	61.8	62.3	63.4	63.7	64.7
Aprons, housedresses, and uniforms	57.7	63.7	65.0	65.6	66.7
Basement store:					
Underwear, negligees, and robes	54.6	54.8	55.3	55.8	57.2
Corsets and brassieres	64.5	64.7	65.0	65.6	65.6
Women's, misses', and juniors' coats, suits, and furs	56.3	56.7	58.0	59.0	59.7
Women's, misses', and juniors' dresses	52.9	58.0	60.0	59.2	59.7
Women's, misses', and juniors' sportswear	53.1	55.0	55.3	57.0	58.5
Girls', infants', and children's wear	56.0	55.5	54.8	55.0	56.0
Aprons, housedresses, and uniforms	48.1	49.7	51.5	52.4	53.8

SOURCE: National Retail Merchants' Association.

Specialty shops such as the Country Shop of Marshall Field's (Figure 10–1) are found in many city department stores. The Bridal Salon in Nieman–Marcus of Dallas (Figure 10–2) is another example.

Speed and convenience are additional advantages of the department store if the shopper is in a hurry. She can easily inspect a large number of articles quickly without waiting for the services of a salesperson, as most departments have a big array of display counters and racks. If she finds shopping in the congested part of the city tiring she can often find branches of her favorite store in a suburban area with better parking facilities. One such shopping area is shown in Figure 10–3.

Many shoppers enjoy the department store because of its bargains. Practically every day is bargain day for some part of the store, at least for certain items. Advertising these items has become a potent device for stimulating the public to buy.

Figure 10–1. The Country Shop in Marshall Field's, Chicago, with its casual elegance, is typical of specialty shops found in metropolitan department stores. (Courtesy of Marshall Field and Company.)

2 The Specialty Store define

Specialty stores sell only one line of merchandise, but they vary widely in size, location, and ownership. The specialty store may be a small, single-counter shop selling hosiery or costume jewelry; or as large a firm as Bonwit Teller of New York, which sells a wide range of women's wear. Some shops stress economy, sell goods for cash, and provide no customer services. Others sell exclusive and high-priced merchandise to appeal to the fastidious shopper and employ a superior sales staff sufficient to give each shopper the individual attention she enjoys. Such a shop aims at creating a leisurely atmosphere and offering high-style articles or "something different." Accordingly, it serves as a launching pad for fads and new ideas.

Some specialty stores are patterned after the French boutiques and sell carefully selected high-style ready-to-wear clothing and accessories. Such a shop may be an independent unit, or it may be located within a larger store or even in a hotel.

Yard goods stores, relatively new additions to the retail field, are much appreciated by the shopper who likes to make some

Figure 10–2. The Bridal Salon in the Nieman—Marcus store in Dallas is a much-appreciated source of guidance for brides-to-be. (Courtesy of Nieman—Marcus.)

Figure 10–3. Ward Parkway Center of Kansas City. Its enclosed, air-conditioned arcade, 800 feet long, its shops for more than eighty firms, and its parking accommodations for 4,500 cars have helped to make it an attractive shopping center in a strongly competitive market area. (Courtesy of Meloney Associates.)

of her own or her children's wardrobe. Some of these stores offer only moderate- to low-priced merchandise, mostly cottons, blends of cotton with other fibers, and drip-dry fabrics. Others are widely known for their exclusive fabrics: imported materials, coordinated dress and coat materials, and suit and topcoat woolens for ensembles. They may offer designer fabrics produced in small amounts for an exacting producer of custom-made clothes. Fashion-minded shoppers eagerly buy up the remaining yardage of these fabrics at the end of a season, as the dress designer turns to other fabrics for her new collection. Patterns and findings are usually a part of such stores.

The Mail-Order House

The mail-order house had its beginning with Montgomery Ward and Company, founded in 1872. At that time, most of the population of the United States was rural and far removed from markets. Although such houses still transact a sizable portion of their business by mail, some object to the mail-order title. "Properly speaking, the mail-order business at Sears does not exist," declared Frank J. Schell, general mail-order merchandise manager of Sears Roebuck and Company. "Instead we have a catalog business—a kind of modern marriage of traditional retailing, ancient cataloging, and some new techniques that are specialized as well as prophetic." [3]

Some mail-order houses now operate retail stores. Sears and Ward's opened their first department stores in 1920 and 1925 respectively; today, they are scattered throughout the nation. One of the latest arrivals in the mail-order business was J. C. Penney Company, Inc., widely known for its chain of retail stores. By the mid-1960's Penney's had pushed ahead of Ward's in volume of catalog selling. However, Sears claimed half of the catalog market.

In order to widen their markets and strengthen operations, these catalog merchants have expanded their credit and telephone shopping services. Studies show that credit buyers purchase two and a half times more merchandise than do cash buyers. Other new developments in the business are selling insurance; planning "package tours," both within the United States and abroad; operating departments to service appliances; running a savings and loan business; and even dipping into the business of selling expensive paintings.

Ordering from a catalog has both advantages and disadvantages. The shopper can decide on purchases at leisure, free from aggressive sales personnel and at a considerable saving of time and energy. The catalog presents a wide range of merchandise and gives fuller and more accurate descriptions than does a label or the average salesperson. Also, the shopper can return the purchase if it fails to please her. The big mail-order firms which have retail stores even permit the customer to bring in the article she wishes to return and handle the wrapping and mailing back to the supply center for her.

The chief drawback of catalog buying is that the shopper cannot inspect merchandise before she orders. Color, fit, style, and quality of fabric may prove disappointing. Even a well-illustrated catalog cannot insure satisfaction in all these areas. Montgomery Ward's now supplies its retail stores with books of sample fabrics so that customers can come in to look at them and find out exactly what quality and color they are ordering.

Ward's also supplies its retail stores with color slides of coats, suits, and dresses for the potential buyer to examine. Like the color illustrations in the catalogs, however, these do not always accurately present the article, as color photography still has its limitations. Also, the purchaser sometimes encounters delays because the item ordered is no longer in stock. Then he may have to wait for his money to be refunded and to look elsewhere for the item.

Until recently, mail-order houses have made no effort to supply high-fashion apparel. In 1961, however, Sears Roebuck and Company added a Paris-label line of ready-to-wear fashions. Its buyers now attend the Paris openings and purchase designs which can be adapted to mass production techniques. Montgomery Ward and Company soon countered with Italian-designed coat and suit ensembles. Ward's also sends buyers to Paris and other European fashion centers. Mail-order catalogs now are virtually fashion magazines. Whereas once they were directed at rural and small town buyers, they now go to suburban and city families as well. Today, metropolitan areas account for more than half of the catalog merchant's sales.

The trend in at least some of the mail-order houses is to upgrade the quality of goods and to introduce a steady flow of new items in the catalogs, while continuing to serve the low- and medium-income family. The winter 1963 catalog for Sears, for example, listed shoes as high as $29, diamond rings priced up to $790, and mink stoles and jackets with $595 and $795 price tags. Ward's that year listed a $2,000 fur coat and a mink cape at $1,195. Offerings include those with appeal for the teen-ager and the young sophisticate, thereby swinging away somewhat from the taste of older and more conservative shoppers.

The Variety Store

The variety store, originally known as the "five and dime store," is a landmark in retail history. A typical American institution, it was launched in 1879 and soon created a place for itself by serving lower middle-income customers with products selling at 5, 10, and 15 cents. After World War I the ceiling price was raised somewhat, but economy merchandise continued to be stocked.

Customers found attractive the many small packages of both new and established products. The unit price was low, and the small size often afforded extra convenience for purse or travel case, as well as the opportunity to try out a product with a small investment. However, these small packages are often relatively expensive units.

In such chain stores as Woolworth, Ben Franklin, and Kresge, merchandise is displayed for self-selection, with virtually no service to the customer. Merchandise must sell itself or not be offered. Payment is in cash. The success of the variety store is evident from the thousands of establishments that have opened throughout the country. Each chain makes effective use of techniques of mass distribution and low markup.

Variety stores carry many articles of clothing, particularly underclothing, hosiery, and children's garments, but the quality is often low. Such items as television sets, refrigerators, and furniture are now being sold by some variety chains, particularly in cities. Thus, the variety store has entered into competition with the discount house. But the bulk of its business is still in items ranging from 10 cents to $5.

The Discount House

"Buying at wholesale" was once a practice of many economy-minded customers bent on escaping from what seemed to them excessively high prices of consumer goods. Shortly after World War II, however, such people turned to the discount house, a form of retailing in which goods are sold at prices lower than the publicized list prices.

The discount house developed as a result of high consumer prices encouraged by state resale (retail) price maintenance laws in the depression years of the 1930's. These laws permitted the manufacturer to set a minimum retail price for any product, thus prohibiting price competition among retailers. These so-called fair trade laws were enacted between 1931 and 1950 in all states but Missouri, Texas, Vermont, and Alaska (then a territory), and the District of Columbia "to protect the small businessman." The result was protection for the small merchant at the expense of the consumer.

The discounter came into the merchandising picture to meet consumer demand for low-priced goods. He usually operated in unpretentious quarters where operating expenses were low. A slogan common in the early 1950's was, "Walk up a flight and save $10." Typically, the discount merchant did not offer such services as free delivery. He sold for cash and permitted no return of goods. His aim was to realize profits through volume of goods sold. At first durable goods such as household appliances and furniture were the most important items, but even clothing came to be discounted. Such merchandise, which was widely known and identifiable because of national advertising and which normally carried a high list price, was offered in discount houses at a drastically reduced sale price. The designer's or the manufacturer's name was usually removed from the article but information that a skilled hand had turned it out was conveyed to customers. Dressing rooms were not provided. Customers tried on bargain dresses among the display racks without the help of a salesperson. Cashiers and supervisors were the only store personnel in sight. Customers acquainted with quality and design in clothes could make an excellent purchase, but others did not fare so well. Men's suits were also offered by discount stores, often at prices that were excitingly low.

Price cutting went on, even in the face of state laws prohibiting selling below list prices. These resale price maintenance laws proved essentially unenforceable, because the manufacturer had the burden of checking on retailer compliance with contracts and of prosecuting violators. Many states eventually abandoned such laws as price fixing and as an invasion of the rights of the dealer.

By the mid-1950's discount stores were being upgraded and were offering several consumer services. In 1962 a large discount department store was opened on Fifth Avenue, New York, one of the most important locations in the city. Goods were sold at prices below those asked by the conventional department store, resulting in a large volume of sales and a stock turnover of seven times a year, twice as fast as that of the typical department store. But naturally cost of operation in the upgraded store was higher than in surroundings which did not require carpets on the floor, attractive fixtures, and delivery of merchandise. Its original price advantage accordingly dwindled. Today, there are many examples of such upgraded discount stores.

In 1964–1965 a "quality stabilization" bill was considered by Congress in an attempt to revive price maintenance regulations and to deal with retail price cutting. The bill did not pass, but its promoters declared that they would try again to get such a measure enacted by the federal government.

So discounting continues. As Frank Meissner, a San Francisco marketing consultant, has said, "Thanks to the discount houses, we in the United States are coming close to matching mass distribution to mass manufacture for the first time." [4]

GROWTH IN RETAILING SINCE 1960

Significant growth since 1960 can be seen in the sales of certain groups of retailers, as presented in Table 10–2. The revolution that has been taking place in retailing leads one to wonder if any of the conventional ways of meeting consumers' demands will survive. In fact, there are some who believe that because

Table 10–2

Retail Stores—Sales, by Kind of Business (in millions of dollars) [5]

Type of Business	1960	1963	1965
General merchandise group	24,085	28,897	35,840
Department stores *	14,468	18,496	23,421
Mail-order houses (department store merchandise)	1,874	2,182	2,581
Variety stores	3,847	4,448	5,320

* Excluding mail-order sales.

of the rapid changes in retailing—the shift to chain stores, the rapid growth of discount houses, the introduction of self-service into all lines of business—merchandising of the future will consist of only two types, the specialty shop selling luxury goods to the affluent customer and the discount house.

STORE SERVICES

All stores perform certain customer services basic to their line of business. These services vary, depending on the clientele and the policies of the store. When economy prices are stressed, fewer services are offered; when the quality of merchandise is upgraded, more services usually follow—those that will satisfy established trade and attract new customers.

Any service performed by a retail establishment entails costs which are inevitably reflected in consumer prices. Whether the establishment provides a brown paper envelope for a yard of ribbon or a sturdy suit box imprinted with its name and filled with layers of tissue paper, the cost is borne by those who trade there. Stores are giving serious thought to eliminating some expensive services, or to charging customers for a few of them. Gift wrapping, for example, often carries an extra charge.

Extension of Credit

Credit is a convenience to many customers, a necessity for others. It is also a way of establishing a close relationship between the store and the customer. Credit accounts tend to build a regular clientele and to increase sales, for customers generally concentrate their purchases where they have accounts and buy more than they had planned.

A charge account makes it unnecessary for the customer to carry an appreciable sum of money when he shops. The credit customer likes the convenience of shopping by telephone—another advantage of such an account—and finds it easier to return merchandise when it has been charged rather than paid for in cash.

Charge accounts take various forms. The regular charge, sometimes known as the *open account*, permits the charging of purchases over a thirty-day period, with payment no later than ten days after the bill has been sent. A *revolving charge account* limits the credit extended to the customer by requiring him to make fixed monthly payments. However, as the customer pays off the debt he may make additional purchases up to the limit originally set for him. A service charge of $1\frac{1}{2}$ per cent a month on the unpaid balance is often attached to this type of account.

The *lay-away plan* is a means of obtaining credit without opening a charge account. For a small deposit the store will hold merchandise until the final payment is made. With this type of credit the store must provide storage space for the merchandise and must keep books on the payments made. The customer has to face the possibility of failure to complete payments, thereby losing all that he has invested. But for the person who has difficulty in establishing credit, the lay-away plan provides an opportunity to buy merchandise early in the season, when a much wider selection is available.

Installment credit, another form of buying without cash in hand, usually requires a downpayment, with additional payments on specified dates over a period of months. A charge is made for the credit extended. This form of credit is usually reserved for the purchase of expensive items, although some large mail-order houses extend such credit for the purchase of anything they sell, with no downpayment and with low charge terms and monthly payments.

Americans today accept the use of credit as the normal way of doing business. Debt no longer frightens them: the government certainly does not discourage it, business actively encourages it, and only a few voices warn against it. Outstanding installment indebtedness was more than $62 billion in mid-1965, more than $6 billion greater than the year before. In 1965, 49 per cent of all American families owed on installment credit plans. Merchants have found that credit customers buy more merchandise than do cash customers—sometimes three or more times as much. For this reason extension of credit is an important service, both for the customer and for the merchant.

Free Delivery

The delivery of purchases to one's door was once a service that customers took for granted. The shopper was relieved of carrying all bundles, whether large or small. Delivery service today has been modified, even by the large stores. Some provide free delivery two or three times a week but will not give this service on purchases of less than $2. At the other extreme, with no delivery, is the self-service or the "cash-and-carry" type of store.

The delivery of purchases is an expensive store service. The cost of trucks and their maintenance is only part of the expense; the well-trained representative of the store who delivers the purchase must be paid a wage in keeping with his responsibilities. He often accepts payment for telephone or C.O.D. orders, and must be courteous to the store's customers. In some cases an outside company handles the delivery service, working for several stores in the community. Parcel post and express services are used to deliver goods at some distance from the store, the cost being either borne by the store or charged to the customer. Taxis, Western Union messengers, and even schoolboys may make a delivery. The cost of delivering a package will depend not only on the distance from the store but on the price of the article. For example, if the purchase amounts to only $1, free delivery is obviously not profitable to the merchant. Campaigns to encourage customers to carry small parcels have been waged in many stores.

The Personal Shopper

Retail stores with customers from a wide trade area frequently develop a service to take care of orders sent in by mail. The person in charge of this service, called the personal shopper, is often given a name to be used in advertising and in correspondence. One specialty store calls her "Miss Julian." She takes charge of customers' requests, sending out specific goods ordered or making a choice when the customer has not specified an exact item. Customers unacquainted with a store often go to the personal shopper for assistance in locating desired items. On occasion, a patron will notify a store of her plans for shopping so that the personal shopper can assemble a selection of merchandise for her approval. The personal shopper can be of special help to patrons from abroad who are unacquainted with ways of doing business in this country.

Coordinated Shopping

Coordinated shopping services, much valued by the busy career woman or the girl assembling a trousseau, are offered in some stores in a special department or in a designated part of the women's ready-to-wear department. Consultants are available to help in the choice of a suitable wardrobe. The career woman who has little time for shopping and perhaps only mild interest in clothing finds an assembled array of wardrobe items and appropriate accessories really helpful on brief shopping expeditions. Once she is known to the consultant, she can expect to be notified of the arrival of merchandise that will fit her taste and her needs. For many stores, the good will gained through such assistance is an important means of building clientele.

The girl who is planning her wedding often uses the bridal planning service of a large store. This service is usually free if the wedding dress is bought in the store. The prospective bride values advice on wedding customs as well as on the choice of her dress and those of her attendants. Brides may also register their preferences for patterns of silverware or glassware in this store—a vast potential for business. As a final service a few city stores send an attendant to help dress the bride and to check the bride's and the bridesmaids' appearance before they start down the aisle.

Another form of coordinated shopping service is the shop for men only, often set up just for holiday seasons. A part of the store away from the heaviest traffic is cleared, and one or two knowledgeable saleswomen are put in charge of a wide array of gift items from departments throughout the store—such as lingerie, lounging robes, perfume, and costume accessories. In these shops men customers can make a leisurely choice without mingling with other customers. The saleswoman shrewdly plays on the male ego and often sells him items that are more luxurious than his common sense would approve.

Alteration of Apparel

An alteration department is found in most stores selling medium- to high-quality ready-to-wear clothing. This service facilitates the sale of goods. The various systems of measurement used by manufacturers of apparel are as much responsible for the need for alterations as are irregularities in body proportions. The customer rates good fit high among the qualities she expects. If a garment fits badly she will not buy it. Many alterations are as simple as changing a hem. Others, however, are time consuming and require skill on the part of the seamstress. This once free service is now available to the feminine customer at a charge. Alterations for men, however, are usually still free—and always free in the high-priced shops.

Repair and Maintenance

Repair service within the store is a great convenience to its patrons. Shoe repair, the refinishing of leather goods, the reweaving of damaged fabrics, repair of costume jewelry, and even watch repair are among the services rendered by some stores. The charges for work done are determined by the extent of the repair. Only for faulty goods inadvertently sold by the store is the repair work free.

Other Services

Customer services may extend far beyond those already mentioned. In some respects the fashion show is in this category, but its real function is to publicize fashion apparel. As one writer comments, it allows viewers "to windowshop while sitting down and to dream while wide awake." It is undoubtedly an effective way of presenting fashion's newest developments to the largest number of women in the shortest possible time.

Comfortable waiting rooms, a nursery where children may be left while parents shop, a tearoom and a snack bar, an information desk, a travel service—all are of special value to patrons and all inevitably must be paid for, in one way or another, by them. Such services help the store to meet competition.

INTERRELATIONSHIP OF MANUFACTURER, RETAILER, AND CONSUMER

Today's marketing practices are based on a recognition of the consumer as the prime force in the economy, according to the authors of *Principles of Advertising.* "The consumer-oriented business executive does not manufacture or buy what he thinks the consumer *should* want, but rather what he knows the consumer *does* want." [6] American business management constantly seeks to improve its products, to lower prices, and to widen its markets; the first two aims, of course, are means for achieving the third and primary objective.

Manufacturers offer the consumer a wide range of quality. Some goods measure up to the highest standards; others are inferior, sometimes because of the demand for low-priced articles, sometimes because of the producer's desire to increase profits through lower-quality workmanship, skimping on materials, or adulteration. Often, the manufacturer brings to the attention of the consumer articles she had never thought of buying, generally because she had been unaware of their availability. Thus, she learns about new things on the market—and may be led into impulse buying.

Clothing at all price levels can reflect current fashion features. Thus, the manufacturer of moderate- to low-priced goods is actually offering a service to the shopper who cannot afford to pay for original designs or even for copies of high-quality garments, yet who wants to keep abreast of fashion changes.

Some retailers feature line-for-line copies of garments purchased from couture houses abroad. Ohrbach's of New York is one such store, where economy-minded women flock to view high-fashion originals and to buy the copies at prices less than half those normally demanded by the couturier. The lower price is possible because several copies of the design are sold, less handwork is done on them, and sometimes cheaper fabrics are used.

Figure 10–4 shows a Lancetti original with its $85 copy made of the same material, linen with a striped silk blouse. A $60 version was also offered in a textured rayon with a printed jersey blouse.

As the shopper looks at the price tag on a garment she seldom considers what goes into its production. Cost of raw materials, cost of factory operation and management, and wages paid to the workers all enter into the price of that garment. Figure 10–5 shows the relative cost of each of these factors.

As long as low price rather than suitable quality for a specific use is emphasized, substandard goods will be produced under substandard conditions. Obviously, there is a limit beyond which the manufacturer cannot go in reducing his prices if he is to provide reasonable quality.

Price as Measure of Quality

Price, of course, is not an infallible measure of quality. A $79.50 suit may be worth no more than one priced at $59.50, in terms of either fashion or the quality of the fabric and the workmanship. Similarly, a $14.95 frock may prove a better buy than one carrying a $24.95 price tag. The lower price in each case may result from a shrewd purchase on the part of the merchant, from the distress sale of another retailer, or from a manufacturer's desire to introduce his line into a new area. Also, the high-priced garment may be a trademarked item that is sold nation-wide, carrying the manufacturer's "suggested price"; the retailer may be unwilling to sell it at a lower price.

Using price as the primary measure of value may result in highly unsatisfactory purchases. Some people rate the lowest-priced garment as invariably the best; others consider no garment worth buying unless it carries a high price tag. In the clothing field, however, price is not always a measure of worth, because of the many subjective values involved. For this reason

Figure 10–4. *Left,* couturier original, an exclusive model by the Lancetti couture. Much handwork went into the original, the price of which was not given. *Right,* the Ohrbach copy made from the same fabrics, linen and striped silk, priced at "only $85." Copied in rayon, with printed jersey for the blouse, the model was $60. (Courtesy of Ohrbach's, Inc.)

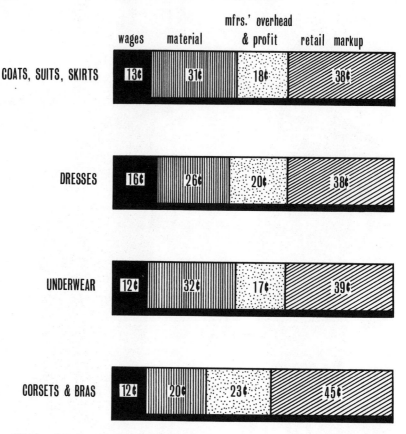

Figure 10–5. The percentage of each garment dollar used for wages, for material, and for the manufacturer's overhead cost and profit, showing the traditional markup in each category of garments. (Courtesy of International Ladies' Garment Workers' Union.)

a person must have a sounder basis for choice; the article should possess the qualities that meet his needs.

Estimating Consumer Desires

The retail merchant performs an important service as the intermediary between the manufacturer and the consumer. He brings together from far and wide products that he believes his clientele will buy. The variety of the goods he offers determines to a great extent the shopper's satisfaction. Her best thought-out plan for a well-coordinated costume fails if the hat or the shoes, or some other accessory, is not available.

The extent to which the merchant is able to interpret consumer desires is one measure of his success. He must make accurate estimates of goods wanted and prices his patrons will pay, and must have the goods available at the time desired. He must promote these goods through displays and advertising so as to increase demand. To the extent that such displays and advertising inform the prospective buyer of items on the market, the distributor has performed a service. If the promotions stimulate the customer to overspend, they are a disservice. Many shoppers, unfortunately, have no sales resistance when it comes to clothing.

The Informed Shopper

The whole system of producing and distributing clothing has matured considerably in the last fifty years. All manufacturers are concerned about the acceptance of their products. Most of them work zealously to create and maintain a good public image. The same can be said for most retailers. Chiefly through government regulations, the consumer can to an increasing degree place confidence in his purchases. Yet he still has the responsibility for becoming an informed shopper.

With incomes as high as they are today, some people have questioned the need for stressing good buying procedures. Does it matter whether consumers get their money's worth? If wealthy families do not, assuredly no serious results will follow. But for the millions of families whose incomes must be handled carefully to provide even a few luxuries beyond their basic needs, good buying procedures are of first importance. And for the large middle class, "good buymanship" increases the amount of luxury goods that can be acquired.

If the objectives of the manufacturer and the retailer were solely to advance consumer welfare, it would be relatively simple for a person to select the best article his money could buy. But they are not. The manufacturer and the retailer are in business to sell the most goods possible at prices that will assure a comfortable profit. They tempt the customer to buy new articles, even though he may already have a well-stocked wardrobe. Too often they withhold information which would enable the customer to make choices based on quality. Perhaps they feel that customers have sufficiently good judgment to make selections to fit their needs.

For most women today, acquiring a wardrobe involves shopping for ready-to-wear rather than for fabrics by the yard. Women use whatever ability they have to select apparel that is fashion-right, comfortable, suitable, and as individualistic as possible. The pocketbook, of course, sets limits on range of choices.

Too many women, unfortunately, go shopping without any preliminary planning. Because following past patterns of shopping is easy, they may buy garments similar to those purchased in the past—or they may take the advice of a friend who is less able to judge values—instead of doing the comparative pricing needed for wise use of money. Some women will pay unnecessarily high prices for clothing because high price has become a status symbol for them. These shoppers may have no feeling of pride when they do make a good buy. Such attitudes toward shopping are likely to further the interests of the merchant rather than those of the shopper.

Effect of Shopping Habits on Cost

The public's shopping habits have a tremendous effect on clothing cost. Some contribute to an efficient business transaction that leaves the retailer and the customer with a feeling of complete satisfaction. Other shopping habits are wasteful of time, energy, and money—some are even unethical.

No single factor influences clothing selection as greatly as does fashion. Comfort, beauty, economy, individuality—all these rate far below fashion as motivating forces. Faithful adherence to the dictates of fashion undoubtedly brings pleasure to many women, but it is essentially wasteful. Some women discard an entire wardrobe whenever there is a drastic change in the mode. Dior's New Look, launched in 1947, with its modified wasp waist and upthrust bosom, is the most striking example in the last quarter-century (see Figure 6–14, page 167).

The rejection of the old results in considerable loss both to the consumer and to the merchant, who is left with unsalable goods on his hands. Only through the raising of prices on the new fashions can the merchant hope to recoup his losses. The risk taken by the manufacturer in producing fashion goods, and by the retailer in stocking them, inevitably results in high retail prices.

Buying garments that cannot be related to the rest of the wardrobe is sure to result in dissatisfaction for the buyer. Yet how many people buy a sweater just because the color is irresistible, or a dress because it seems "such a bargain." The beautiful sweater that calls for a new skirt to harmonize with it, however, is not a good buy for the girl who already possesses many skirts and sweaters. Nor is the dress offered at a low-low price a good buy if it cannot be coordinated with a coat and accessories on hand. Impulse buying can easily become a habit, because clothing has become such a potent means of satisfying emotional and social, as well as physical, needs.

Far too many women and girls shop not to buy but purely for diversion, out of idle interest in what is on the market. They amuse themselves by having the salesman bring out box after box of shoes for them to try on, or by asking the saleswoman to pull down bolt after bolt of fabric with no intention of buying anything. They seem not to realize that such thoughtless shopping raises the price of merchandise. A third of the retailer's expense is for wages, according to studies of merchandising costs; and if one of every ten shoppers takes the time of the sales force purely for amusement, the retailer has to hire 10 per cent more staff to take care of them. Scouting the shops for the best buy is a perfectly legitimate practice, of course. One has no moral obligation to buy from every salesperson whose time he has taken, if he is honestly in search of some article.

Shopping during slack periods in the day is one way in which a person can help to hold down the prices he and his fellow shoppers will have to pay for goods. The merchant must employ a staff that can handle rush periods, usually around midday. If they wished, many midday shoppers could use the less crowded hours for their purchases. Then they would have the full and unhurried attention of salespeople, and the retailer could serve his customers with a smaller sales force.

The same reasoning applies for busy shopping seasons such as Christmas, Easter, and the late summer back-to-school days. Insofar as patrons avoid shopping at the peak of a rush season they are contributing to lowered costs of doing business and to lowered retail prices. "Do your Christmas shopping early" is sound advice for anyone who wants to get the most for his money.

Unethical Practices

The privilege of taking garments out on approval is one of the most frequently abused efforts of the retailer to build good will. Some women, particularly those who have established credit, often have several garments sent out—at considerable cost to the retailer—and sometimes return all of them. Such a shopper may be simply unwilling to take the time to make a decision at the store. She often returns a garment because she has belatedly decided that she cannot afford it, or because her true objective has been to copy the design.

Some customers are so unethical as to take a dress or a coat out on approval to wear for a special occasion. Coats have been returned after a football game with personal articles left in the pockets and the scent of the wearer's perfume on them. Millinery departments find telltale clues that point to a patron's having worn a hat before its return. After-Christmas returns are a great problem, especially for large stores. Some customers even attempt to obtain refunds on gifts never purchased in that store.

The retailer is always ready to exchange a faulty article for one in perfect condition, of course. In fact, it is the duty of the customer to return imperfect merchandise, thereby making her contribution toward improvement of the marketing system. The customer and the retailer share equally the responsibility for fair dealing and for the establishment of sound retail services.

NOTES

1. *Employment and Earnings and Monthly Report on the Labor Force,* XIII, No. 12 (June, 1967) (New York: U. S. Department of Labor, Bureau of Labor Statistics), p. 76.

2. Report of the General Executive Board to the 32nd Convention, Miami Beach, Florida, May 12, 1965 (New York: International Ladies' Garment Workers' Union), p. 101.

3. "Catalogs of Cheer," *Barron's,* XLII, No. 25 (June 18, 1962), p. 5.

4. "Retailing: Everybody Loves a Bargain," *Time,* LXXX, No. 1 (July 6, 1962), p. 58.

5. *Statistical Abstract of the United States: 1966* (Washington, D. C.: U. S. Bureau of the Census), p. 811.

6. Wirsig, Woodrow (ed.), *Principles of Advertising* (New York: Pitman Publishing Corp., 1963), p. 475.

FURTHER READING

KELLEY, PEARCE C., and BRISCO, NORRIS B. *Retailing.* 3d ed. Englewood Cliffs, N. J.: Prentice-Hall, Inc., 1957. A discussion of the position held by retailing, past and present. The many facets of the subject are presented in a manner easily grasped by lay readers.

LERNER, MAX. *America as a Civilization.* New York: Simon and Schuster, Inc., 1957. Part 5: Chapter 4, "The Wilderness of Commodities"; Chapter 5, "Business and Its Satellites." A comprehensive treatment of the civilization of the United States. Fascinating reading.

MUND, VERNON A. *Government and Business.* 4th ed. New York: John Wiley & Sons, Inc., 1965. A discussion of the legal aspects of business.

STUDY SUGGESTIONS

1. What services are offered by the leading department store of your community? Are these services free? If they carry a charge, how much is it?
2. What types of credit plans are offered in your local stores? What is the annual interest rate for each?
3. What shopping habits have you observed that raise the price of merchandise?
4. What unethical customer practices have you observed?
5. Invite the personal shopper of a store to talk to the class about her service. What type of person is most likely to solicit her help? The housebound or elderly? Busy mothers with small children? The young or the middle-aged? Men or women?

6. What type of yard goods stores are you acquainted with? Do they seem to meet a real need in the community?

7. What influence has the mail-order house had on prices?

8. Discuss the following statement: "Credit users buy two-and-a-half times more merchandise than do those in similar circumstances who pay cash."

9. Try to find in the variety store examples of articles that are displayed in small packages so as to be priced low, when actually the cost per item is higher than it is in regular-sized packages sold in department stores.

10. Examine the quality of clothing in a variety store. How does it compare with that of articles in the conventional department store? How do the prices compare?

11. Look up the history of resale price maintenance laws in your state. Are such laws still being enforced?

12. Check with your congressman as to whether there is a bill pending in this session of Congress for resale price maintenance.

11

Aids to Buying

What values are you looking for when you buy clothing? Utility? Protection? Or social and aesthetic values—the approval of others, for example, or the enhancement of your own good points of hair or coloring or figure? These questions might well be asked of everyone who goes shopping for apparel. Anyone asked to list those qualities most desired in clothing will probably include durability and may even name it first. Though present-day patterns of living indicate little concern for economy, Americans still show the influence of their thrifty forefathers. For some, of course, durability must come first. The man or woman engaged in manual labor, the boy outfitted for a hiking trip, and the child dressed for outdoor play all need durable clothes. Moreover, the college girl who wears her gray flannel skirt all four years of her undergraduate life has undeniably found great satisfaction in this durable garment.

Shoppers, however, often consider values other than durability as most important: color, fit, fashion, and good construction—all of which contribute to the esthetic value. Serviceability is a better word than durability to describe the quality they most desire. A cream-colored wool dress bought for special occasions, even though it requires frequent cleaning, may well have this characteristic of serviceability, particularly in seasons when pale colors are fashionable. It may satisfy an emotional as well as a social need if it is becoming and expresses the wearer's feelings.

An individual often finds it difficult to identify values that are important to him, even though they determine his choice of

273

clothes. He needs to recognize what his unique set of values is, and then how to buy so as to be satisfied with his purchases.

Spending money wisely is not a simple matter today. Intelligent buying of clothing presents a great challenge, in part because of the multiplicity of fashion's offerings and in part because of the bewildering flood of new developments in fabrics. Even a textiles specialist can scarcely keep informed on the rapidly changing fabric market. The many new man-made fibers, the blending of fibers, and the new finishes given to the familiar natural fibers—linen, cotton, silk, and wool—have all increased the importance of being informed about the performance of fabrics. In dealing with today's materials, past experience offers little help. How many people ten years ago had any experience with bonded or stretch fabrics? As fabrics change, the shopper must learn new ways of caring for them if he is to find them satisfactory.

The college girl naturally hopes for good performance in the new dress she has added to her wardrobe, but sometimes she is disappointed. She may find that the smart new color she thought so lovely fades after a few wearings. No doubt, the dress was produced and marketed so quickly that the manufacturer had no time for evaluating its quality. The rapid changes of fashion allow little or no time for testing. Besides, aesthetic qualities do not lend themselves to objective testing.

To buy wisely any article made largely of textiles, a person must know what kind of service he wants from it and what fiber will give him that service. No one textile fiber or fabric is best for all purposes. Cotton cannot be improved upon for some uses. It washes easily and is comfortable to wear next to the skin; it is therefore ideal for undergarments and children's clothing. Cotton is also prized for other uses, of course. Wool is often the best choice for a winter coat. A wool tweed, for example, is sturdy, does not wrinkle, and can be tailored to hold its shape through years of service. Some of the synthetic fibers have properties needed for special purposes. Spandex, the elastic type of fiber, is one of these. Certainly, knowledge of textiles provides important clues to a fabric's performance.

Clothing manufacturers are concerned primarily with fashion, and only incidentally with performance. The consumer, then, cannot expect to find in fashion goods the same standards of performance as the householder can in staple merchandise such as sheets. The selection of fashion goods admittedly is complex, yet even here there are reliable sources of information which the college student can utilize.

LABELS

Practically every garment bought today carries one or two labels, sometimes several of them. What girl has not found so many hang-tags on a dress that she has a hard time trying it on! Why so many? Each label carries a different bit of information that the producers think important: brand name, descriptive matter, directions for care, or fiber content. The labels for care, such as laundering or dry cleaning, are often sewn onto the garment as a permanent reminder.

Almost without exception brand names are found on labels. They help the shopper to identify quickly clothes that in the past have given satisfactory—or poor—service. If the brand name is the only information provided, however, one can only guess at the quality of the garment.

A truly informative label for a textile product tells the following facts: *ask yourself these questions*

1. What the product is made of
2. How it is made
3. How it will perform
4. How it should be cared for
5. Who the manufacturer was
6. Where the firm is situated

Analyze the hang-tags in Figures 11–1 through 11–5 to see how many carry all six facts about the garment concerned.

The identification of the fiber is of first importance because a garment's usefulness depends so much on the proper choice of fiber. It is hard today to identify fibers. Materials made of synthetic fibers often feel and look like fabrics made of natural fibers, but they perform very differently. Both the owner of a garment and the cleaner need to know what a given fabric is made of so as to assure reasonable service from it.

How the fabric is made is important both to the shopper unacquainted with recent developments in textiles and to the experienced buyer. Labels are needed, for example, to tell a potential buyer that a warp-knit fabric will not stretch out of

Figure 11–1. Hang-tags that vary widely in the amount of information given.

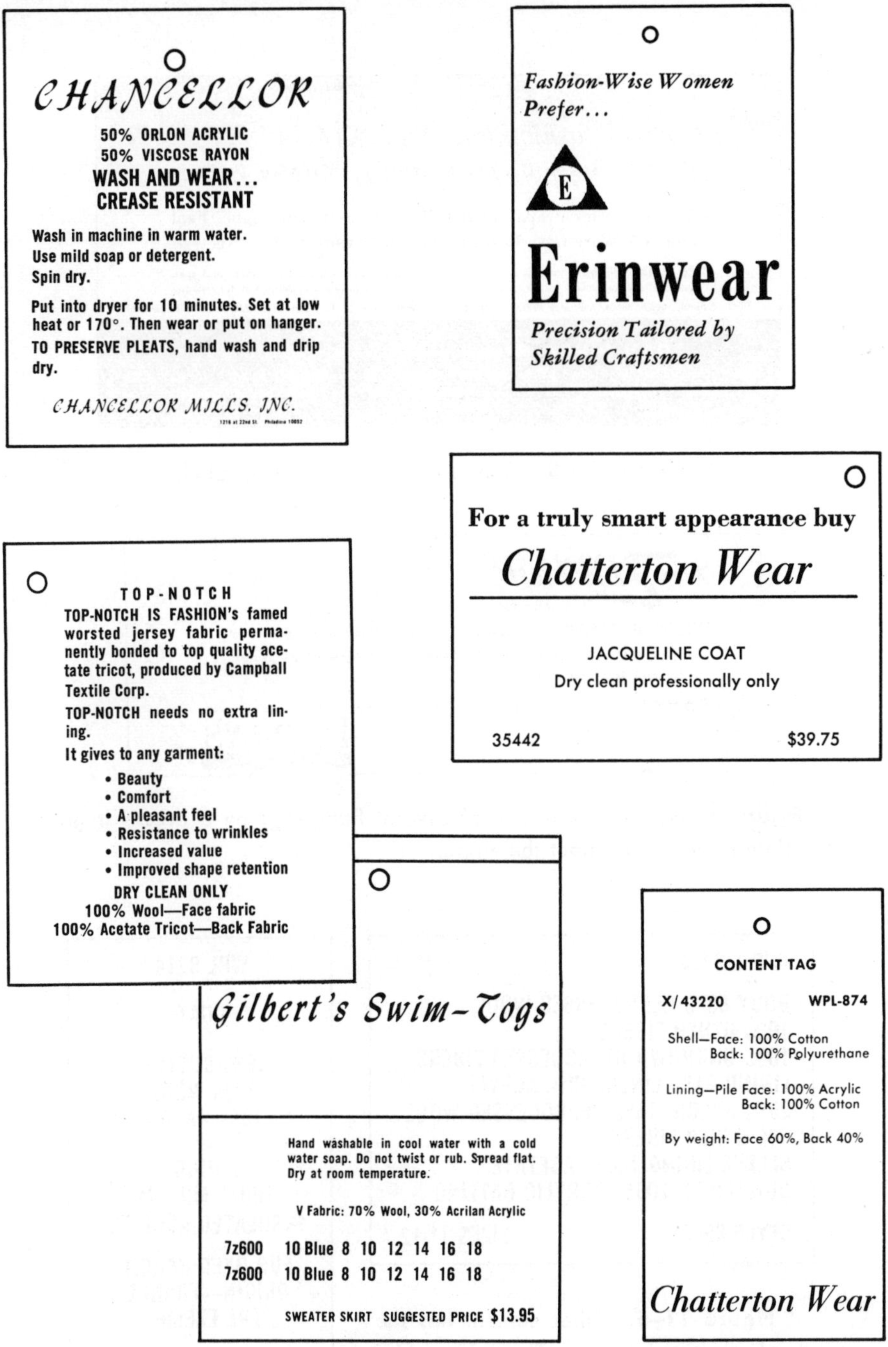

CHANCELLOR

50% ORLON ACRYLIC
50% VISCOSE RAYON
WASH AND WEAR...
CREASE RESISTANT

Wash in machine in warm water.
Use mild soap or detergent.
Spin dry.

Put into dryer for 10 minutes. Set at low
heat or 170°. Then wear or put on hanger.
TO PRESERVE PLEATS, hand wash and drip
dry.

CHANCELLOR MILLS, INC.

1216 at 22nd St.   Philadelphia 19852

Fashion-Wise Women
Prefer...

E

Erinwear

Precision Tailored by
Skilled Craftsmen

TOP-NOTCH
TOP-NOTCH IS FASHION's famed
worsted jersey fabric perma-
nently bonded to top quality acetate tricot, produced by Campball
Textile Corp.
TOP-NOTCH needs no extra lining.
It gives to any garment:

- Beauty
- Comfort
- A pleasant feel
- Resistance to wrinkles
- Increased value
- Improved shape retention

DRY CLEAN ONLY
100% Wool—Face fabric
100% Acetate Tricot—Back Fabric

For a truly smart appearance buy

Chatterton Wear

JACQUELINE COAT
Dry clean professionally only

35442 $39.75

Gilbert's Swim-Togs

Hand washable in cool water with a cold
water soap. Do not twist or rub. Spread flat.
Dry at room temperature.

V Fabric: 70% Wool, 30% Acrilan Acrylic

7z600   10 Blue 8 10 12 14 16 18
7z600   10 Blue 8 10 12 14 16 18

SWEATER SKIRT   SUGGESTED PRICE $13.95

CONTENT TAG

X/43220   WPL-874

Shell—Face: 100% Cotton
        Back: 100% Polyurethane

Lining—Pile Face: 100% Acrylic
             Back: 100% Cotton

By weight: Face 60%, Back 40%

Chatterton Wear

Figure 11–2. Not one of these hang-tags carries all the information
needed by the consumer.

Figure 11–3. This is a truly informative label.

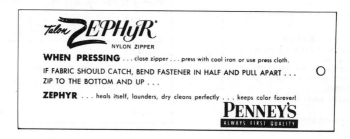

Figure 11–4. This was one of several hang-tags on a dress. It gives complete information about the zipper.

W P L 9714

BODY 80% REPROCESSED WOOL
10% OTHER FIBERS
10% UNKNOWN REPROCESSED FIBERS
LINING 31% LINEN, 30% ACRYLIC
20% NYLON, 16% REPROCESSED WOOL
3% OTHER FIBERS
SLEEVE LINING 100% ACETATE
QUILTED TO 100% ACRYLIC BATTING

STYLE 6541   SIZES 11-12

WPL 9714

COAT

49% COTTON
32% WOOL
19% RAYON

LINING
100% MILIUM
INSULATED ACETATE

FUR DYED RABBIT
ORIGIN—FRANCE
FPL EXEMP

STYLE   9494jp

SIZE   9

Figure 11–5. Fiber content has the emphasis in these tags. They give no information as to performance, care, or manufacturer.

shape, and that a stretch fabric will "give" crosswise but not lengthwise or, for some other use, lengthwise but not crosswise. Only a label can reveal hidden qualities, as the interlining of hidden parts to give body to a garment or the taping of seams to prevent stretching. The intelligent shopper will be glad to learn such facts from a label.

Evidences of poor performance of fabrics in dresses and suits are on every hand. Loss of shape, excessive wrinkling, pulling out at the seams, shrinking, crocking of the dye, fading—all are ways in which fabrics prove disappointing. A good label gives definite facts about performance: how much shrinkage to expect when the garment is laundered or dry cleaned; how the color will withstand exposure to sun, laundering, and perspiration; how well the fabric will resist soiling; how permanent the pleats are. Some producers use a finish called Scotch-guard to make fabrics resist soiling, or another finish combined with the heat-setting of pleats to insure their permanence. With information on performance, the potential buyer has the guidance needed for making a satisfactory purchase.

INDIRECT CONSUMER AID

At first, government agencies gave only indirect help to the individual shopper. They established specifications for fabrics and items of clothing bought for such groups as the armed services and such institutions as government hospitals. From these, government standards for certain textile products were developed. Consumers became interested in them as a way of improving their own buying, though their needs differed somewhat from the needs of government agencies. Their desire for accurate information about textile products led to the introduction of a truth-in-fabrics bill into Congress in the 1930's. This bill did not pass, but it became the basis for future legislation.

The Federal Trade Commission supplied another indirect aid to the buyer of fabrics. Charged as it was with preventing deceptive trade practices, it set up trade practice rules for the silk industry in 1938; [1] for the linen industry in 1941; [2] and for the rayon and acetate industry in 1952.[3] These rules attempted to promote fair competition among manufacturers, and incidentally to protect consumers from misrepresentation of fiber content. The rules worked no miracles, because they did not have the force of an act of Congress, but they did reduce fraudulent practices and misleading statements about fabrics.

CONSUMER LEGISLATION

By the mid-1960's four pieces of legislation dealing with the labeling of products used in clothing had been passed, three of them dealing directly with textiles and one with furs. Two are truth-in-fabrics legislation: the Wool Products Labeling Act and the Textile Fiber Products Identification Act.

The Wool Products Labeling Act [4] was the first piece of legislation enacted by Congress to make mandatory the labeling of a textile fiber. The act was passed in 1939, to become effective in 1941, and required the truthful labeling of all manufactured apparel and of all fabrics containing 5 per cent or more of wool, exclusive of ornamentation. Three types of wool must be labeled: (1) *new or virgin wool*—fiber that has been through the manufacturing process only once; (2) *reprocessed wool*—fiber reclaimed from woven or felted products which have never been used by a consumer; and (3) *reused wool*—fiber reclaimed from products which have already been used by a consumer, mostly that salvaged from the rag market.

The Textile Fiber Products Identification Act,[5] which became effective March, 1960, is the most far-reaching legislation governing the labeling of textile fibers. It concerns all apparel textiles not included in the Wool Products Labeling Act. The misbranding and deceptive advertising of any textile fiber product are thereby made unlawful. The act further requires that the label list every fiber in a given fabric if it amounts to 5 per cent or more of the total weight, that the listing be in descending order of the amount present, that the generic name of each fiber be given, and that the name of the country of origin be given for imported fibers.

The Flammable Fabrics Act prohibits the marketing of dangerously flammable textiles and wearing apparel.[6] It requires that highly napped material made of cotton or rayon, and fabrics used in stage settings and costumes, be treated with chemicals to make them resistant to fire.

The Fur Products Labeling Act, which took effect in 1952 and was amended in 1961, was enacted to protect consumers against misbranding and false advertising of furs and fur products.[7] It was drafted to stop the practice of giving fictitious and misleading names to furs—for example, calling muskrat fur "Hudson seal" or naming rabbit some kind of "mink." Now fur labels must tell what animal a pelt was taken from, the country of its origin, and whether the pelt was dyed, colored, or bleached. The act further requires that the use of paws, tails, or bellies of an animal, or of reused fur in an article be stated on the label.

Because the average shopper knows little about furs, the information on the label is of great importance. She may consider a stole lustrous, soft, and beautiful; but a practiced eye may detect the use of bleach or dye or the presence of irregularities in the skins. She may not notice that tiny pieces have been sewn together. Even with the fur labeling law, the shopper today would be wise to seek out a dealer on whose integrity she can rely for a fur purchase. The label gives no clue as to whether a given fur is of prime, medium, or poor quality. "If you don't know furs, know your furrier," is excellent advice.

The profusion of man-made fibers and the many new finishes used today make labeling laws particularly helpful. Finishes used on fabrics made of natural fibers often so transform them that even an experienced shopper needs a statement of fiber content. Cotton, for example, does not always look like cotton, and a fabric that looks like silk may not have a trace of silk fiber. The requirements of fiber identification have curbed the practice of some manufacturers of substituting inferior, low-cost fibers for those with better quality and higher price. However, the shopper still needs to learn the generic names of manufactured fibers so as not to be misled by the many glamorized trade names given to the same fiber.

Sixteen classes have been established for these man-made fibers, each with its characteristic chemical composition. Table 11–1 lists the generic names of the classes with their representa-

Table 11-1

Generic Classification of Fibers by Trademark [8]

Classes of Manufactured Fibers and Their Generic Names *	Representative Fiber Trademarks in Each Generic Group
Acetate	Acele Arnel (triacetate) Avisco Celaperm Chromspun Estron
Acrylic	Acrilan Creslan Orlon Zebran Zefkrome (solution dyed)
Glass	Beta Fiberglas Fiberglas Pittsburgh PPG
Metallic	Lurex Metlon
Modacrylic	Dynel Verel
Nylon	Antron Blue C Cadon Cantrece
Olefin	Herculon Reevon Vectra
Polyester	Dacron Fortrel Kodel Vycron
Rayon	Avril Lirelle } high wet modulus rayon Zantrel Avisco Bemberg Coloray Cupioni Fortisan Jetspun
Rubber	Lastex
Saran	Rovana Velon
Spandex	Glospan Lycra Spandelle Vyrene

* The generic groups Azlon, Nytril, and Vinal are omitted because they are not produced in the United States; Vinyon, because it is used only industrially.

SOURCE: Adaptation from Burlington Industries, Inc., 1965: *Textile Fibers and Their Properties.*

tive trade names in the column to the right. Four of the classes have been omitted from this table, either because they are not produced in the United States or because they are used for industrial purposes only.

FEDERAL TRADE COMMISSION

Trade practice rules formulated by the Federal Trade Commission have helped to regulate the sale of hosiery and shoes. Those set up in 1941 [9] made less confusing the shopping for hosiery. They covered truthful labeling and advertising and required that important facts about hosiery be disclosed: the fiber content; the size, which must conform with Consumer Standard C-S, 46–40; and any substandard quality, such as being irregulars, seconds, or thirds. The last fact must be plainly marked on the hosiery so as to carry through to the customer.

The Federal Trade Commission also drew up rules for the labeling of shoes.[10] These rules, adopted in 1962, require the disclosure of information as to all materials used in making shoes, both for labeling and for advertising. The use of imitation leather in any part of the shoes must be revealed. If the leather is embossed or otherwise processed to look like another leather— for instance, like alligator hide—the label must state the leather actually used. Moreover, labels must be fixed to each shoe so as to remain there until it is in the hands of the customer.

Guides Against Deceptive Pricing is a useful six-page pamphlet published by the Federal Trade Commission (1963).[11] It is not a statement of the commission's *rules* for retailers, or even of its own enforcement policies, but an aid to honest businessmen. The types of advertising which the commission warns against as being essentially dishonest are as follows:

1. "Formerly sold at $9.95; now priced at $6.95." The store may have normally sold the article at the $6.95 price, having raised it to $9.95 for only a short time so as to give the "reduced" price an air of honesty.

2. "Now reduced to $9.95." The original price may have been only a few cents higher, perhaps $9.97. The retailer knows that the average consumer will infer that the reduction is considerable, not trivial.

3. "Retail value $10; my price $7.95." Only a few small suburban outlets in the area may be charging $10 and the larger stores charging $7.95 or less for articles of similar quality.

4. "Manufacturer's suggested retail price $9.97; our price $7.49." The "suggested price" may actually be used by only a few small suburban stores, accounting for only a small volume of sales in the area. Using the "list" or "suggested" price is honest advertising only if most stores in the area are selling at the "list" price.

5. "Seconds (or irregular) hosiery at 89 cents a pair; regular price $1.95." The retailer fails to make clear that the $1.95 price is for perfect hose.

6. "Two pairs of gloves for the price of one; you pay $5.96 for the first pair and get a second pair for only 1 cent more." The normal retail price of the gloves may actually be around $2.97.

Other federal agencies also provide much information valuable to the consumer. The U. S. Department of Agriculture, through its Cooperative Agricultural Extension Service in the various states and agricultural experiment stations in state colleges and universities, and the Bureau of Standards publish pamphlets and bulletins on fabric use and care and on buying guides. These are available at a nominal price through the Superintendent of Documents, Washington, D. C. The *1965 Yearbook of Agriculture,* "Consumers All," is one such publication that gives helpful suggestions on buying and using clothing, as well as information on other aspects of everyday living.

THE CONSUMERS' ADVISORY COUNCIL

The Consumers' Advisory Council, the newest organization concerned with the consumer's protection and interest, was appointed in 1962 by President Kennedy. The council, composed of six men and six women with thorough backgrounds in consumer problems, was instructed "to advise the executive branch of the government on issues of broad economic policy." It was further charged with the responsibility of advising on governmental programs to protect the consumer and on the flow of consumer research material from the government to the public.

Although few additional helps for the consumer of textiles

and clothing are apparent at present, the consumer now has direct representation in the government and can more easily register his need for action against deceptive trade practices and false advertising.

PERFORMANCE STANDARDS FOR FABRICS

In 1960, the same year that mandatory labeling of fiber content of fabrics became effective, an American Standard was set up to establish minimum performance of textiles for apparel and home furnishings, regardless of fiber type. It is known as ASL–22–1960 (American Standards Association), and is a revision of the L22 minimum standard for rayon and acetate fabrics approved on December 31, 1952.[12]

Minimum performance qualities for fabrics in seventy-five items have been established. Of this number, thirty-eight are for women's and children's wear. Washability, dry-cleanability, and resistance to perspiration, mildew, and chlorinated water have been evaluated. Garments that meet the requirements of the standard may carry tags bearing an American Standards color code and an identification letter code. Five special classifications have been set up:

Letter Code for Care of Article	Color Code to Supplement Care Instructions
B—Washable at 160° F., with bleach	Purple
W—Washable at 160° F., without bleach	Green
C—Washable at 120° F., without bleach	Blue
H—Washable at 105° F., without bleach	Yellow
D—Dry-cleanable only	Red

The fabric that carries the purple label and the letter code B is the only one that will stand a bleach and hot water in washing. The green label and the letter W indicate that it is safe to use hot water but no bleach. The blue label and letter C call for warm water and no bleach; the yellow label and letter H (for hand washable), for lukewarm water and no bleach; and the red label with letter D, for dry-cleanable only.

Because these standards for performance are voluntary, not all fabrics carry the L22 label. Only producers interested in providing information for consumers are using them. Nevertheless, it is probably too much to expect their use on any fashion merchandise. The shopper who asks to see these labels is furthering the cause of good labeling.

SURE CARE LABELS FOR TEXTILE PRODUCTS

As a service to the American consumer, the National Retail Merchants' Association has sponsored the use of a group of symbols to facilitate the proper care of a textile product. These symbols, called Sure Care labels, can be stamped, printed, sewn, or cemented onto the article so that the consumer will know, for the life of the product, whether it is washable, dry-cleanable, or ironable—and how to handle it (Figure 11–6).

If the article can be washed by hand, a symbol of a hand is attached. For a garment that cannot be washed, a hand with an X through it is used. The symbol of a dry-cleaning drum is used if the garment is to be dry cleaned; if dry cleaning is to be avoided, the same symbol is marked with an X. B used as a symbol indicates safe use of bleach; an iron used as a symbol indicates that it is safe to use an iron.

Those who developed the symbols believed that such devices would be the greatest advance in informative labeling that the textile industry has seen. Unfortunately, compliance with their use is voluntary.

A Voluntary Industry Guide for Improved and Permanent Care Labeling of Consumer Textile Products has been developed by the Industry Committee on Textile Information in cooperation with the President's Special Assistant on Consumer Affairs. Adopted in March 1967, the guide is available through the National Retail Merchants' Association. This is an extension of ideas conveyed by the Sure Care labels.

PRODUCER–DISTRIBUTOR AIDS

The manufacturer knows many facts about his products, facts that can be a real help to prospective buyers if he makes them

SURE CARE SYMBOLS

Follow these symbols to WASH or DRY-CLEAN and IRON your clothes or home furnishings with satisfactory results. Look for the labels with these simple guides to happier washdays.

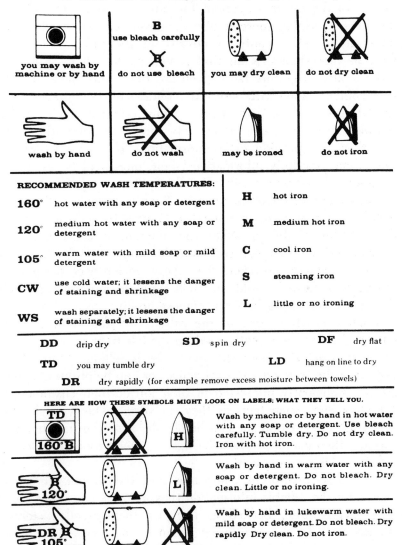

you may wash by machine or by hand	**B** use bleach carefully — do not use bleach	you may dry clean	do not dry clean
wash by hand	do not wash	may be ironed	do not iron

RECOMMENDED WASH TEMPERATURES:

160°   hot water with any soap or detergent

120°   medium hot water with any soap or detergent

105°   warm water with mild soap or mild detergent

CW   use cold water; it lessens the danger of staining and shrinkage

WS   wash separately; it lessens the danger of staining and shrinkage

H   hot iron

M   medium hot iron

C   cool iron

S   steaming iron

L   little or no ironing

DD   drip dry   **SD**   spin dry   **DF**   dry flat

TD   you may tumble dry   **LD**   hang on line to dry

DR   dry rapidly (for example remove excess moisture between towels)

HERE ARE HOW THESE SYMBOLS MIGHT LOOK ON LABELS; WHAT THEY TELL YOU.

Wash by machine or by hand in hot water with any soap or detergent. Use bleach carefully. Tumble dry. Do not dry clean. Iron with hot iron.

Wash by hand in warm water with any soap or detergent. Do not bleach. Dry clean. Little or no ironing.

Wash by hand in lukewarm water with mild soap or detergent. Do not bleach. Dry rapidly Dry clean. Do not iron.

NATIONAL RETAIL MERCHANTS ASSOCIATION
100 West 31st Street   •   New York 1, N. Y.

Figure 11-6. Sure Care symbols. If shoppers used their influence to get these symbols widely adopted for garment labels, they would save themselves thousands, perhaps millions, of dollars a year—and retailers and manufacturers would get fewer criticisms of merchandise. (Courtesy of Committee on Public Relations, National Retail Merchants' Association.)

known. On their informative labels some manufacturers give not only the required statement of fiber content, but also specifications of the fabric, directions for care, and guarantees of performance. Fashion merchandise, however, seldom carries such information. The beauty or novelty of the product, together with its modishness, is all that is needed to sell it. For such articles, often the only facts given are the brand name and the fiber content, along with descriptive phrases of such limited value as "latest mode" or "soft hand." Many producers believe that shoppers are not interested in facts about the goods they buy, and therefore provide little information. If shoppers indicate their desire for fully informative labels, more will be used.

Often, the shopper will rely chiefly on a reputable dealer when making an important choice. Such a dealer usually stocks well-known brands of merchandise to give the customer confidence in his reliability. When the community has several such dealers, the shopper has considerable range for selection. She should be aware, however, that every dealer necessarily is in business to make a profit and will promote most energetically the goods that bring him the highest profits.

Customers often turn to the salesperson for help. A well-informed salesperson, with good on-the-job training, can supply sound information about the goods she is selling. Many, however, lack the training and experience for real helpfulness. Some are not sufficiently interested in their job or their customers to volunteer even such facts as they do know. The wise shopper gets what information she can before she starts on her shopping trip and then compares the offerings of several reputable dealers before making a purchase.

The large mail-order companies and their retail stores are known for the reliable information they give the consumer about their merchandise, backed as it is by their excellent testing laboratories. In the mail-order business, of course, customers must rely on a printed description of the article being considered and therefore need complete and accurate statements about it. In the stores, the label on an article carries the same description used in the catalog. These mail-order houses pioneered in truth-in-advertising programs and provided labels with accurate, detailed information for consumers as a selling device.

Testing laboratories are maintained by some large merchandising organizations to evaluate their goods. Among these are Kauffman's of Pittsburgh, J. C. Penney Company, Inc., R. H. Macy, T. Eaton in Canada, and the two largest mail-order houses, Montgomery Ward and Sears. Their laboratories determine the service life of fabrics and garments and handle complaints about the firm's merchandise. Macy's maintains a bureau of standards to test the quality of some of the merchandise it offers for sale. A plain, white, tailored broadcloth blouse, stocked in a Macy store, may well bear the Macy Bureau of Standards label.

ADVERTISING

Advertising is an important factor in our competitive economy, but it is not always a reliable aid to the intelligent choice of clothing. When it offers truthful information about the qualities of goods, or stimulates the shopper to accept new developments that lead to an improved standard of living, advertising performs a valuable service. When it leads shoppers to accept a false scale of values, to let emotional motives override rational ones in buying, it becomes a handicap rather than an aid. Advertising undoubtedly can be credited with reducing prices on mass-produced ready-to-wear, for it has markedly increased sales.

Trademarks and brand names are inseparable from advertising and a boon to the shopper. Without them, the advertiser would be limited to general statements about a class of goods and could not identify one manufacturer's product. For the shopper, they provide names to ask for and thus make buying easier.

The advertiser provides detailed factual statements about staple merchandise more often than about fashion goods. He informs prospective buyers that such staple goods are available, perhaps at reduced prices, and emphasizes the qualities that make these goods superior to a competitor's offerings.

Fashion advertising appeals to emotional rather than rational motives for buying. It suggests how alluring the costume could make the wearer rather than how serviceable it would be or how it would help the buyer stay within her budget. Fashion advertising has developed a vocabulary all its own to describe colors, textures, and the current styles, and uses this vocabulary to persuade many otherwise rational people to discard a large part of a useful wardrobe for fashion's newest whims. It may describe a dress as "understated," "fetchingly frilled," "darkly intriguing," or "uninhibited," giving no factual information whatever; but it will make the fashion-minded woman feel it is highly desirable.

Max Lerner remarks: "If the American woman were in danger of forgetting a moment about clothes and cosmetics, lingerie and nylons and 'foundation garments,' deodorants and perfumes, the advertisers make sure the lapse is brief. 'It is our job,' said the head of a trade association of women's retail stores, 'to make women unhappy with what they have in the way of apparel and to make them think it is obsolete.'" [13]

Though advertising has its shortcomings and is sometimes used unethically, it has become an essential of modern marketing. If goods were marketed without advertising, the cost of selling in most cases would be much increased. As historian David Potter points out in his book *People of Plenty:* "Advertising now compares with such long-standing institutions as the school and the church in the magnitude of its social influence. It dominates the media, it has vast power in the shaping of popular standards, and it is really one of the very limited group of institutions which exercise social control." [14]

PROFESSIONAL CONSUMER ORGANIZATIONS

Some consumers in their search for the "one best buy" turn for advice to professional consumer organizations such as Consumers' Union of the U. S., Inc., and Consumers' Research. These organizations make comparative tests of brands of goods on the market and publish ratings based on their findings. Sometimes they disapprove of a brand, either because it does not perform well or because it is priced too high. Clothing and fabrics are reported on less often than are other consumer items; those tested are staple products such as children's jeans, women's orlon sweaters, and wash-and-wear blouses.

Some people question the reliability of the findings of these organizations, charging that the tests are inadequate, that the sample used is not large enough, or that the laboratory personnel is biased. Studies of the activities of these organizations, however, have allayed most suspicions.[15] The discussion provided in these publications, which precedes the list of brands and their ratings, gives excellent guidance for shopping. For example, a discussion of blouses advises the shopper to check seven different points and tells her specifically what to look for and what the marks of a good garment are. Too many people who consult these publications look only at the ratings.

CURRENT PUBLICATIONS

Some periodicals publish helpful information not only on new developments in textiles and clothing but also on selection and care. They include women's magazines, publications of general interest, newspapers, and trade papers.

Magazine articles on new products are often checked with the manufacturer, particularly when he is an advertiser in the publication. It is to his interest as well as that of the prospective buyer to have the information accurate. Such articles provide no comparisons with competitive products, however, and do not relieve the consumer of the responsibility for further checking.

Some magazines laboratory-test advertisers' products before giving them publicity. They do not rate competitive products, but they give the consumer information on the performance of those products. Obviously, the magazine may be tempted to give as favorable a report as possible on its own advertisers' products. Many newspaper articles are based solely on information supplied by the producer and thus are not objective.

NOTES

1. United States Federal Trade Commission Trade Practice Rules, *Trade Practice Rules for the Silk Industry.* Promulgated November 4, 1938. Pp. 151–62, 1946.

2. United States Federal Trade Commission Trade Practice Rules, *Trade Practice Rules for the Linen Industry.* Promulgated February 1, 1941. Pp. 293–318, 1946.

3. United States Federal Trade Commission Trade Practice Rules, *Trade Practice Rules for the Rayon Industry.* Promulgated October 26, 1937. Pp. 79–84, 1946; revised 1952.

4. Rules and Regulations Under the Wool Products Labeling Act of 1939, Federal Trade Commission. Effective date October 14, 1940. Public Law 76–850.

5. Rules and Regulations Under the Textile Fiber Products Identification Act, Federal Trade Commission. Approved September 1958; effective date 1960. Public Law 85–897.

6. Rules and Regulations Under the Flammable Fabrics Act. Approved June 30, 1953; effective date 1954. Public Law 83–88.

7. Rules and Regulations Under the Fur Products Labeling Act. Approved August 8, 1951; amended May 15, 1961. Public Law 82–110.

8. *Textile Fibers and Their Properties* (Greensboro, N. C.: Burlington Industries, Inc., 1965).

9. United States Federal Trade Commission Trade Practice Rules, *Trade Practice Rules for the Hosiery Industry.* Promulgated May 5, 1941. Pp. 319–39, 1946.

10. United States Federal Trade Commission Trade Practice Rules, *Guides for Shoe Content Labeling and Advertising;* adopted October 2, 1962. Federal Register, October 12, 1962.

11. United States Federal Trade Commission, *Guides Against Deceptive Pricing.* Effective January 8, 1964.

12. American Standards Association, *American Standard Performance Requirements for Textile Fabrics,* ASL–22–1960. Approved February 11, 1960.

13. Max Lerner, *America as a Civilization* (New York: Simon and Schuster, Inc., 1957), p. 602.

14. David Potter, *People of Plenty* (Chicago: The University of Chicago Press, 1954), p. 167.

15. Philip Seikman, "U. S. Business' Most Skeptical Customer," *Fortune,* LXII (September, 1960), p. 157 ff.

FURTHER READING

COLES, JESSIE V. *Consumers Look at Labels.* Greeley: Council on Consumer Information, Colorado State College, 1964. A concise and up-to-date booklet on labeling as an aid to wise choice of consumer goods.

ERWIN, MABEL D., and KINCHEN, LILA A. *Clothing for Moderns.* 3d ed. New York: The Macmillan Co., 1964. Chapter 9. An interesting college textbook covering clothing choice and construction.

LABARTHE, JULES. *Textiles: Origins to Usage.* New York: The Macmillan Co., 1964. An authoritative college textbook on textiles, stressing the performance of fabrics and of ready-to-wear garments.

Stout, Evelyn E. *Introduction to Textiles*. 2d ed. New York: John
Wiley & Sons, Inc., 1965. A competent presentation of new developments in fibers and fabrics for college students.

Tate, Mildred Thurow, and Glisson, Oris. *Family Clothing*. New York:
John Wiley & Sons, Inc., 1961. Chapter 16. A college textbook that
treats the changing needs of family members at different periods in their
life.

STUDY SUGGESTIONS

1. Analyze your own shopping pattern by studying the way you bought
   five garments in your wardrobe. Which did you purchase primarily
   because of the brand name? Which because of fashion's dictates?
   Which chiefly because of the recommendation of the salesperson? Which as a result of careful comparison with quality of other
   similar garments? Which primarily because of the price tag—a high
   price for a status symbol or a low one for a bargain?
2. Analyze the clothing advertisements of three stores. What appeals
   does each emphasize most often in its bid for business?
3. In several stores investigate the use of the Sure Care label on wom-
   en's dresses, children's clothing, and household fabrics such as cur-
   tains, bedspreads, and bath mats. Does the label appear to be used
   on high-, medium-, or low-quality merchandise—or on all three? On
   staple or on fashion items?
4. Look for a tag which bears an American Standards color code and
   its accompanying letter code signifying care of the garment. Compare this label with the Sure Care label. Which do you consider
   more helpful to the purchaser?
5. Analyze the information on garment labels: directions for care, performance to be expected, any special features of the garment.
6. Visit a furrier to find out the clues to fur quality. Ask him how a
   fur garment is made.
7. Check to see if the recent issues of professional consumer magazines rated any textile product. How helpful are the discussions?
8. Study the consumer guidance articles in a women's magazine. Do
   you find any advertisements for the products discussed—either in
   the issue containing the article or in the preceding or following
   issue? How objective does each article seem to be? How helpful?

APPENDIXES

APPENDIXES

A

Wardrobe Inventory*

Item	No.	Brief Description Color, Fabric, or Design	Condition			Year Pur- chased	Original Cost or Estimate	Cost of Items Purchased This Year (relist)
			Ex	G	P			
OUTERWEAR								
Hats and other headwear								
Coats								
Jackets								
Raincoats								
OUTERWEAR TOTALS								
INNERWEAR								
Formals and other Evening dresses "After-five" Dresses								

* Courtesy of Department of Clothing and Textiles, Kansas State University.

Item	No.	Brief Description Color, Fabric, or Design	Condition			Year Pur- chased	Original Cost or Estimate	Cost of Items Purchased This Year (relist)
			Ex	G	P			
Dressy dresses								
Casual dresses								
Uniforms								
Blouses								
Sweaters								
Skirts								

Item	No.	Brief Description Color, Fabric, or Design	Condition			Year Pur- chased	Original Cost or Estimate	Cost of Items Purchased This Year (relist)
			Ex	G	P			
Suits								
Shorts								
Slacks								
Levis								
Sweatshirts								
Bathing suits								
Special sportswear								
INNERWEAR TOTALS..								

Item	No.	Brief Description Color, Fabric, or Design	Condition			Year Pur-chased	Original Cost or Estimate	Cost of Items Purchased This Year (relist)
			Ex	G	P			
UNDERWEAR								
Slips								
Bras								
Pants								
Girdles								
Pajamas and gowns								
Robes								
UNDERWEAR TOTALS								
FOOTWEAR								
School shoes								
Dress shoes								
House slippers								
Other shoes and footwear								
Hosiery								
Anklets								
FOOTWEAR TOTALS								

Item	No.	Brief Description Color, Fabric, or Design	Condition			Year Pur- chased	Original Cost or Estimate	Cost of Items Purchased This Year (relist)
			Ex	G	P			
ACCESSORIES								
Gloves								
Bags								
Scarves and belts								
Costume jewelry								
Miscellaneous								
ACCESSORY TOTALS..								
TOTAL OF INVENTORY								

B

Wardrobe Analysis

1. Do you have a basic color in your winter clothes? ____Yes ____No

2. Do you have a basic color in your summer clothes? ____Yes ____No

3. How would you describe the quantity of clothes in your wardrobe for these different needs?

	Not Adequate	Adequate	Very Ample
School wear	____	____	____
Active sportswear	____	____	____
Church and datewear	____	____	____
Formal and semiformal wear	____	____	____

4. If you were to replace your entire wardrobe and could spend approximately the same amount of money would you:
   _____Have fewer clothes that were more expensive.
   _____Have more clothes that were less expensive.
   _____Have about the same number of clothes at a similar price.
   _____Other (explain)_____
   _____

5. If you were to replace your wardrobe and could spend twice as much money would you:
   _____Have twice as many clothes.
   _____Pay twice as much for a similar number of clothes.
   _____Have a few more clothes all of which were slightly more expensive.
   _____Other (explain)_____
   _____

6. If you were to replace your wardrobe but could spend only half as much money would you:

_____Have half as many clothes.

_____Pay half the original price so you could have the same number of clothes.

_____Pay slightly less for everything and have slightly fewer clothes.

_____Other (explain)_____

7. Do you have items of clothing that you are no longer wearing?   ____Yes ____No

8. If so, why don't you wear them?

_____Tired of them.

_____Skirts the wrong length.

_____Style not being worn here.

_____Unpopular color.

_____No occasion for wearing.

_____No longer fits.

_____Separates which don't match anything else.

_____Too worn to wear.

_____Needs repair or mending, or stain removal.

_____Poor selection.

_____Other (explain)_____

9. Do you purchase on sale:

	Often	Seldom	Never
Outerwear	_____	_____	_____
Suits and tailored dresses	_____	_____	_____
Dressy dresses	_____	_____	_____
Skirts	_____	_____	_____
Blouses	_____	_____	_____
Sweaters	_____	_____	_____
Lingerie	_____	_____	_____
Shorts, slacks, and bathing suits	_____	_____	_____
Footwear	_____	_____	_____

10. Do you make at home:

	Often	Seldom	Never
Outerwear	_____	_____	_____
Suits and tailored dresses	_____	_____	_____
Dressy dresses	_____	_____	_____
Skirts	_____	_____	_____
Blouses	_____	_____	_____
Sweaters	_____	_____	_____

Lingerie _____ _____ _____

Shorts, slacks, and bathing suits _____ _____ _____

Footwear _____ _____ _____

11. Do you believe that your past spending was well balanced?   ____Yes ____No

12. If not, what items were out of proportion? (Leave blank if well balanced.)

	Too many	Too few
Coats	_____	_____
Suits and tailored dresses	_____	_____
Dressy dresses	_____	_____
Skirts	_____	_____
Blouses	_____	_____
Sweaters	_____	_____
Lingerie	_____	_____
Shorts, slacks, and bathing suits	_____	_____
Footwear	_____	_____

13. My general opinion of my present wardrobe is:

C

List and Analysis
of Purchases Planned

Item	Article	Description	Estimated Cost
Outerwear			
Innerwear			
Underwear			
Footwear			
Accessories			
TOTAL . . . . TOTAL FOR COST OF ITEMS PURCHASED SO FAR THIS YEAR . . . . GRAND TOTAL			

1. Why did you choose to add these garments to your wardrobe?
   _____To replace a worn-out item.
   _____To fill a need revealed by the inventory.
   _____To add a current fashion note.
   _____To improve overall quality.

————To increase quantity.
————To improve color harmony.
————Other.

2. My general opinion of my wardrobe after including planned purchases is:

3. If you family spends 10% of its income for clothing, how much should the income be based upon the amount of money you spend for clothing *this year?*

Figure:

$$\frac{\text{amount spent} \times \text{number in family}}{\text{\% of family income spent on clothing}} = \text{family income}$$

4. Do you think the above figure is approximately the same, less, or more, than your family income?

D

Glossary of Terms

atelier—workshop or studio where fashion designers are developed.

boutique—shop where accessories, ready-to-wear, and apparel that requires one or two fittings are sold. In the United States, a shop where distinctive accessories and ready-to-wear are sold.

caution—admission fee for a showing of a designer's collection.

chic—the impression achieved through originality, style, and taste in clothes. The total effect achieved by wearing current styles treated with individuality and good taste.

Chinatowners—trade slang for the establishments producing cheap apparel. Chinese are not among the employees.

collection—group of designs shown by one designer.

cookie-cutters—trade slang for the mass production firms.

copy—a reproduction of a design, made outside the house that created the original.

couture—the custom dressmaking industry.

couture manufacturers—makers of wholesale high-priced clothes.

couturier—man designer.

couturière—woman designer.

fad—a short-lived fashion, quickly accepted and as suddenly dropped.

fashion—the prevailing mode, adopted by a large number of people at any one time.

fashion industry—the whole machinery of production, making everything people put on and creating the publicity that induces them to wear it.

fashion trend—movement toward a future mode; the line or direction along which fashion moves.

haute couture—prestige custom dressmaking.

high fashion—a new, usually costly, fashion that has been accepted by fashion leaders but not yet by the general public.

house—abbreviation for a dressmaking house or firm.

knock-off—trade jargon for a copy of a competitor's garment produced to sell at a price lower than the original. Such designs are said to be "adapted" or "translated," but never "stolen."

line-for-line copy—an exact copy of an expensive couture model, usually from Paris.

mannequin—person who wears a model to show potential customers how it looks.

midinette—seamstress.

model—one design in a collection.

modelliste—man or woman who designs anonymously in some house of couture.

modiste—woman milliner.

opening—the first showing of a new collection for the coming season.

original—design created to be shown in a collection.

prêt-à-porter—ready-to-wear. Literally "ready to carry."

rag business—trade slang for the women's garment industry.

salon—showroom in which a collection is presented.

section method—the method in which the work of producing a garment is broken up into small tasks, each to be carried out by a different operator. It requires little skill of workers.

Seventh Avenue (or S. A.)—the heart of the nation's garment business, contained in some 20 blocks of skyscrapers on New York City's Seventh Avenue and on Broadway between 34th and 40th Streets.

silhouette—shadow profile or outline. Named after Etienne Silhouette, French author and politician.

single-hand system—the method used for the production of high-priced apparel, wherein the operator who cuts the cloth also completes the garment.

straight-line system—a highly efficient method for manufacturing standardized apparel in which finished parts are brought into the assembly line at appropriate times to produce a finished garment.

style—the characteristic or distinctive expression of a mode. The distinguishing features are silhouette, cut, design, and type of article. No style can become fashionable unless it is widely imitated.

style piracy—unauthorized copying of a dress design, whether it be a couturier's original or a competitor's fast-selling interpretation of a current fashion.

tailleur—tailor attached to a designer's house.

toile—muslin in which a new design is tried out before it is developed in an expensive fabric. A toile has little detail but shows the cut and line of the model.

vendeuse—saleswoman.

Index

Italicized numbers indicate pages on which illustrations appear.

Scissors

358/55